The Broken Icon

THE
BROKEN
ICON

INTUITIVE EXISTENTIALISM
IN CLASSICAL RUSSIAN FICTION

Geoffrey Clive

THE MACMILLAN COMPANY · NEW YORK, NEW YORK

COLLIER-MACMILLAN LIMITED · LONDON

Grateful acknowledgment is made for permission to quote from the following:

T. S. Eliot, "The Love Song of J. Alfred Prufrock," from *Collected Poems, 1909–1962*, Harcourt Brace Jovanovich, Inc.

"Politics," reprinted with permission of The Macmillan Company from *Collected Poems* by William Butler Yeats. Copyright 1940 by Georgie Yeats, renewed 1968 by Bertha Georgie Yeats, Michael Butler Yeats and Anne Yeats, and by permission of Mr. M. B. Yeats, Macmillan & Co. Ltd., and the Macmillan Co. of Canada Ltd.

Farrar, Straus & Giroux, Inc. for Alexander Solzhenitsyn, *Cancer Ward*, 1968, and *The Love-Girl and the Innocent*, 1970.

Harper & Row for Aleksandr I. Solzhenitsyn, *The First Circle*. Copyright © 1968 by Harper & Row, Publishers, Inc. English translation copyright © 1968 by Harper & Row, Publishers, Inc.

The Macmillan Company
866 Third Avenue, New York, N.Y. 10022
Collier-Macmillan Canada Ltd., Toronto, Ontario

Library of Congress Catalog Card Number: 70-182019

First Printing

Printed in the United States of America

For Sy Hayden

All our shrewd and far-sighted policies were for nothing. If, instead of trying to make history, we had simply tried to consider ourselves responsible for the separate events that make up history, then perhaps this wouldn't have turned out so ludicrously.

A man should worry less about history and more about his own biography.

VICTOR SHKLOVSKY
A Sentimental Journey

It is possible to be more daring and to go more to the root of the matter, above all in those feelings which I would call *double* or contradictory, which meet more often than one thinks. One can only describe well what one has felt oneself . . . and I have had, I still have, these double feelings, which almost shriek, as one says, to meet, and to meet so well that they merge. Perhaps you will understand better when I've written what I have in mind—if I ever write it.

TURGENEV
Letter to Claudie Viardot

Acknowledgments

FIRST AND FOREMOST, I would like to thank my research assistant Henryk Baran, without whom this book could never have become a reality. His steadfastness, devotion, and good counsel were placed most generously at my disposal. Second, I am especially grateful to Steven Grant of the Russian Research Center at Harvard University for giving so freely and unstintingly of his help and advice. Third, I would like to thank the "Mensheviks of Morningside Heights"—Professors Michael Cherniavsky, Leopold Haimson, and Marc Raeff at the Russian Research Center of Columbia University—for the many conversations I have had with them over the years concerning the main paths of modern Russian history, as well as the detours of Gogol's troika. Marc Raeff and George L. Kline have been especially kind in giving my manuscript a critical reading. In the same connection, I am grateful to my brother John Clive of the Harvard history department for going over my manuscript with his customary scrupulosity. I owe further thanks to Alison Hanham for her kindness in proofreading the galleys. Last but not least, I am grateful to Charles Thomas Cole for sharing with me his insights into Russian life and literature.

The idea for this study was first broached to me by Zeph Stewart, master of Lowell House and professor of classics at Harvard University. Subsequently it was reinforced by Professor Martin Malia of the University of California at Berkeley. I wish to thank both these men for performing an invaluable catalytic function. Furthermore, I owe a debt of gratitude to Professor

Walther Kirchner for his consistent encouragement and support, and to my colleague Howard Cohen for help in formulating the footnote on the "theory of types" and for valuable suggestions on appendix 3, "Alienation."

In addition, I wish to thank numerous readers for making it possible for me to pursue this project in spite of the fact that I was losing my sight. Though these readers cannot all be named here, one seems to me to deserve special recognition: Kay Green, who devoted nearly a year of her Mormon service to rereading with me the classics of Russian literature.

Finally, I want to acknowledge the support I received from the following organizations: first, the George Santayana Fellowship in Philosophy of the philosophy department of Harvard University, 1968–69; second, the Penrose Fund of the American Philosophical Society in Philadelphia, for the summer of 1969; third, the Research Council of the University of Florida, for the summer of 1967; fourth, the University of Massachusetts at Boston, for the academic year 1969–70.

GEOFFREY CLIVE

Cambridge, Massachusetts
1972

Contents

INTRODUCTION   xiii

CHAPTER

1.   *Gogol and the Absurd*   1

2.   *Dostoevsky and the Intellectuals*   30

3.   *Goncharov and the Spectrum of Boredom*   63

4.   *Tolstoy and the Varieties of the Inauthentic*   86

5.   *Solzhenitsyn and the Inconsequence of Politics*   128

6.   *The Broken Icon*   157

APPENDICES
1. Descartes and Pascal   171

2. Hegel and the First Generation of
the Russian Intelligentsia   177

3. Alienation   181

4. On the Existential Import of Two
Philosophical Distinctions   187

NOTES   193

SUGGESTIONS FOR FURTHER READING   219

INDEX   225

Introduction

EXISTENTIALISM HAS BEEN variously defined as a school of philosophy, a literary movement, a life view, and an expression of contemporary anguish. While some critics emphasize its timelessness as a perennial commentary on "the tragic sense of life," others stress its distinctive roots in the predicament of modern man. So vague remain the boundaries of the term "existential," that even figures as widely separated in time as Socrates and Baudelaire have been interpreted in the light of such existential notions as commitment, nothingness, and authenticity.

The disagreement about existentialism is not confined to issues of classification but embraces as well contradictory views of its very essence. Those who link existential reflection with "Irrational Man" must somehow account for the rational justification which Kierkegaard offered for his destruction of traditional philosophical distinctions. On the other hand, those who identify existentialism with the realism of Aristotle and Aquinas are hard put to explain its emergence from post-Kantian thought and its overall revolutionary import.

Amid all the bewildering descriptions and conceptions of existentialism, one distinction stands out as crucial and unambiguous: it is that between the world of the existential philosophers proper and the world of intuitive existentialism as embodied in many works of classical Russian fiction. Whereas the philosophers of *Existenz* use highly technical language in formulating their systematic treatises, the Russian writers created a gallery of characters who embody existential themes and insights not only by virtue of the way they think but also through their actions. Much like Kierkegaard's pseudonymous authors, these fictional heroes exhibit life styles and states of consciousness of a vividness far more persuasive than any discursive argumentation. Without the benefit of the vocabulary of phenomenology, the Russian writers created a body of work in which the doubts and torments of superfluous men, madmen, and nihilists of every description prophetically bear witness to the spiritual crisis of our time.

No existential phenomenologist has surpassed Dostoevsky's Underground Man in representing the agonies of dread, Tolstoy's Ivan Ilyich in showing the failure of becoming subjective in the face of death, Turgenev's Bazarov in depicting what Bakunin called "the creative urge to destroy," or Goncharov's Oblomov in asking, "Why should I do something rather than nothing?" Beyond these striking examples, the landscape of nineteenth-century Russian fiction is populated with exceptional individuals, whose alienation from common sense or venerable authorities serves to underscore with inimitable intensity the extremes of human passion and introspection. While Western European fiction offers us isolated instances of divided consciousness, which on occasion even inspired Russian writers, the Russian tradition is unique in its collective concentration on the enigmas of modernity.

The subject matter of intuitive existentialism constitutes the themes permeating and crisscrossing this study. On the one hand, each theme is linked to a particular writer; on the other, the recurrence of such themes in these authors reinforces the position advanced here, which is that, to a greater degree and more imaginatively than other men of letters, down to and including our own time, they grasped the ambiguities of Reason and *Existenz* that continue to puzzle and haunt contemporary man.

This book is not intended as yet another survey of the great period in Russian prose or, most decidedly, as a formal study of particular works. My interest in this body of writing is ideological and philosophical rather than literary. While such critics as Shestov, Berdyaev, and Aldonov have approached major figures of Russian fiction from an existential point of view, the originality of this study lies in its comprehensive approach to the tradition of Russian fiction as a sustained expression of intuitive existentialism. If it be an oversimplification to look upon the classical Russian novel as a mere vehicle of ideas, it is equally fallacious to ignore a sustained underlying concern for existential reflection, which sets off the Russian achievement no less from the German *Bildungsroman* than from the English novel of morals and manners, or from the French school of realistic fiction. Though they skirt the pitfalls of metaphysical speculation beyond the Kantian critique of Reason, the Russians never lose sight of urgent questions which transcend all political allegiances and social norms.

In Gogol's *Dead Souls* the tedium of life under the tsarist autocracy permeates Chichikov's whole field of vision and action. No other writer has caught so well the choking atmosphere of corrupt officialdom, suspicious landowners, sullen serfs, and silly women reenacting time and again the same old routines—all prisoners of their leaden souls. The final magnificent image of the book, a troika dashing along an open road to Russia's indefinite future greatness, is set against all the drudgery and drabness prevailing *de facto*. Chichikov himself is an odd mixture of expedient utilitarian, weighted down by his own excessive finitude, and Romantic dreamer bewitched by illusions of happiness. His indefatigable, methodical quest for the "souls" of dead serfs, which he plans to mortgage to the state, is juxtaposed with his daring and dash. But the overriding impression left by Gogol's book is that of a bureaucratic landscape in which the dehumanization of man, save for the blessings of daemonic turns of events in unexpected directions, has reduced life to an exercise in desolation. A striking paradox of Gogol's tale is the liveliness of the dead souls, whom Chichikov regards with affection and concern, in marked contrast to the deadness of their surviving masters, oddly pointed up by the latter's unrestrained animality, petty boorishness, and paralyzing inactivity. Chichikov's bizarre journey comes to symbolize a desperate flight from Russian actuality which, according to Hegel's philosophy, was necessarily rational.

Internalized, self-tormenting boredom receives its archetypal expression in the character of Stavrogin. His twisted unconcern for the lives of others, coupled with his strenuous pursuit of malevolence, constitutes a kind of synthesis of the passionate indifference of Lermontov's Pechorin and the macabre ambition of Gogol's Chichikov. In Stavrogin's "Confession," Dostoevsky repeatedly ascribes the rape of a young girl to a fusion of oppressive boredom and its positive correlative, a yearning for excitement to break the tedium of life. Not unlike Roquentin in Sartre's *Nausea*, Stavrogin experiences the world as fundamentally alien to his consciousness of self. Dostoevsky ties Stavrogin's atheism, as well as his rejection of all traditional authority, to his condition of embittered uprootedness. His total loss of self-involvement, so characteristic of the emancipated intellectual, generates cynicism and an irresistible desire for scandal to cover up the spiritual burdens of Nothingness.

Oblomov's boredom is far less sensational, though it is of particular significance as a corrective to the Protestant ethos of salvation through industriousness. Goncharov's masterpiece was welcomed by many critics as an unmasking of Russia's superfluous men who had resisted participating in the practical tasks facing their native land. On the one hand, according to the critics, individuals were stifled by circumstance; on the other, they used it as a pretext for self-indulgence and the cultivation of irresponsible nonchalance. Oblomov, representative of the landed gentry, can be viewed as an unwitting celebration of this state of affairs, but he can also be seen as a knowing protest against the frenetic hustle and bustle of technology with its unmistakable contempt for the arts of leisure and the wisdom of occasional resignation. In disdaining to rise from his couch, Oblomov displays a healthy if eccentric respect for indolence as against the constant fretting inseparable from careerism. His grotesque inertia suggests an affirmation of human dignity in a period of history obsessed with creating fools' paradises by dint of unceasing noise and agitation.

For Tolstoy, as for Rousseau, there is a fateful correlation between the refinements of civilization and the moral corruption of man, of which the widespread acuity of boredom is but one of many manifestations. Not only in "The Death of Ivan Ilyich" but in all his major fiction, the author of *War and Peace* launches his fiercest attacks against that Western culture in which he himself was steeped. It is easy enough to note inconsistencies in his theoretical position as well as in his personal conduct, but conventional faultfinding scarcely does justice to his amazing sensitivity toward the problem of total cultural rationalization, which in our own century has assumed monstrous proportions. While in Russia Slavophiles fought with their opponents over the merits of Westernization, the West by and large was complacently confident of its own future and invincibility. Only a few exceptional voices raised cries of alarm. But Tolstoy and his contemporaries, tantalizingly perched between Russia with her backward social order and a progressive West glorying in its scientific and cultural triumphs, were in a remarkable position to note the threatening ambiguities of modern culture. Whatever their final evaluations of advanced technology and its moral ramifications, on visits abroad they could not help but contrast conditions at home with enlightened circumstances in the West.

Tolstoy's veneration of the Russian peasant rested on his belief in the *muzhik*'s moral superiority over the European lower classes. In spite of his intimate acquaintance with and frequent revulsion from the intractable habits of the *muzhik*, Tolstoy was at one with Dostoevsky and Herzen in ascribing to him a unique sincerity and steadfastness of character. But beyond the chauvinistic considerations that may have induced him to prefer peasant simplicity to the bourgeois ethos, Tolstoy shared with such thinkers of Western Europe as Kierkegaard, Nietzsche, and Marx a profound mistrust of philosophical abstractions divorced from the concreteness of life. For him, as for them, the conceptual vocabulary of the Encyclopedists—law, order, history, and universal rationality—inadequately rendered the actualities of lived experience. The anarchical tendencies in his thought, as in that of Bakunin, have very close affinity with the radical individualism of the classic Existentialists. Just as many of his psychological insights are genuinely pre-Freudian in their sensitivity to the tensions between spontaneity and contrivance in human behavior, so, analogously, can his overall critique of modern Western civilization, independent of its Slavophile overtones, be understood as an existential judgment on the bystander mentality of technological man.[1] If Tolstoy himself approached madness in his doubts about the desirability of Russia's catching up with the West, his negative stance toward the threat of depersonalization in the Russia of the future completely transcends the immediate causes and motives which gave rise to this rejection.

By a curious dialectic, the horrors wrought in civilized Germany in the twentieth century, not to speak of enlightened Russia after the overthrow of the tsars, exceeded in bestiality the sloth, drunkenness, subservience, and indignity suffered before the advent of the age of the masses. Tolstoy, the intermittent champion of progressive education, was aware at the same time of the sense in which man is uneducable. It is in these ambivalent terms of admiration for and recoil from European culture that Gogol's far-fetched generalizations about national character or Tolstoy's and Dostoevsky's hyperboles begin to illuminate their morbid visions of modernity, whether enthroned in democratic or totalitarian societies. The uneasiness of non-civilization is obvious, but that of civilization has become transparent only in our own times.

In Gogol's remarkable tales, the unpredictable has a way of breaking the continuity of experience to embarrass any theological or philosophical belief in preestablished harmonies. The Absurd for Gogol humiliates the intellectual's pretensions to postulate a synthesis between thought and action, much as Kierkegaard's attack on Hegel undermined the claims of the System to have healed the rift between practice and principle. Gogol's splendid architecture of confusion exposes the radical contingency of lived experience, often so painfully untidy and so different from the necessities rationalists like to claim for reality. *Gogolesque* means that nothing about the human condition should be taken for granted, given the interplay of the seemingly natural regularities of experience and the "thunderbolts out of the blue" which constantly shatter man's best-laid plans.[2]

Dostoevsky's insight on the subject of the Irrational is somewhat different. The Underground Man is only one of a number of negative heroes in his fiction whose acute interpretations of the world around them do not carry over self-referentially into their own situations. They are unable to regard themselves as others see them, while they view other men with breath-taking keenness. Sooner or later they discover in themselves an unhealable rift between obsessions with self and clairvoyant observation, which reason alone is powerless to overcome. From the Underground Man's brilliant mockery of the Idea of Progress to Ivan Karamazov's probing atheism, Dostoevsky confronts us with a series of intellectual malcontents, if not villains, who, while unable to come to terms with themselves, manage to understand the dilemmas of modernity with frightening incisiveness. Peter Verkhovensky and Raskolnikov shed far more light on Russia's desperate political situation than the saintly Prince Myshkin, who in the end becomes a destructive force in spite of himself, or the Pollyanna-like Alyosha Karamazov, who also is unable to redeem the broken icon.

Since he is not a nineteenth-century novelist, Solzhenitsyn's inclusion in this study requires a word of explanation. Aside from the topical interests his works have aroused both in the Soviet Union and in the West, and the accompanying notoriety so embarrassing to his government's philosophy of culture, Solzhenitsyn is squarely in the great tradition of existential Russian prose fiction and possibly represents its culmination in and for our time. Harassed and exiled like so many of his predecessors, Solzhenitsyn bears witness in his works to the dehumanization of man by bureaucratic terror and lunacy. Whatever the literary influences upon the Soviet novelist may have been, there are striking parallels between Dostoevsky's *Notes from the House of the Dead* and Solzhenitsyn's preoccupation with life in Stalin's prison camps and hospitals. Solzhenitsyn's analysis of freedom under enforced confinement and isolation profoundly supplements related discussions in "The Legend of the Grand Inquisitor" and *The Devils.* Moreover, like Gogol, Solzhenitsyn is fascinated and horror-struck by the grotesqueries of officialdom, particularly as they emerge in the concept of the *sharashka* in *The First Circle.*[3] Over and over again he calls our attention to the inversions and perversions of Reason, curiously accentuated by Stalin's paranoia and the whole totalitarian machinery of the Soviet state, presiding over the liquidation and degradation of its finest citizens.

Another recurring aspect of Solzhenitsyn's thought is his rejection of all absolutes as comprising a violation of spontaneous life. Here too he is in the company of Gogol, Dostoevsky, and Tolstoy, who, each in his own way, broke with orthodox ideology or academic philosophy in favor of individual open-endedness [4] In his heart-rending vignettes of victims of Stalinism, personal concern and perspective invariably triumph over the rule of dogmatic tyranny and insensitive collectivism. No group of writers has written more perceptively about the inside meanings of suffering than the Russians, and Solzhenitsyn continues this tradition. Not only does he explore repeatedly the experience of dying and enforced isolation for a wide gallery of human beings but he proceeds to raise even more delicate issues along the same lines when, for example, in *The Cancer Ward* he puzzles over the situation of a young woman losing her breast, a loss which to her is as important as losing her life. All the bathing suits in the world, past, present, and future, which she conjures up in a desperate flight from her fate, Solzhenitsyn suggests to us, cannot relieve her *Angst*.

But, above all, the existentiality of Solzhenitsyn's fiction lies in his awareness of senseless cruelty in everyday affairs. Man's infinite capacity for tormenting himself and others permeates every page of *The Cancer Ward*, *The First Circle*, and *One Day in the Life of Ivan Denisovich*. It reaches a climax in the last chapter of *The Cancer Ward*: the hero, Oleg, just released from the hospital and about to return to his place of permanent exile in a remote province, takes a walk through the zoo in the city from which his train is scheduled to depart. He has been through the camps and their horrors; he is dying of cancer, though it may have been temporarily arrested; he has even lost his sexual potency, if not libido, as a consequence of the treatments he received; and he has really nothing to look forward to in whatever time remains to him. Nevertheless, without the benefit of Marxist dialectics, as interpreted by the Party, he has preserved both his humanity and his sanity. Close to the entrance of the zoo he notices a monkey cage with a notice to the effect that the animal was gratuitously blinded by some visitor who threw tobacco in its eyes. In the last sentence of his novel, Solzhenitsyn comments that the symbolic senselessness of this deed is life writ small.

The foregoing examples should serve not only to illuminate in a preliminary way the theses of this study but also to justify the application of the term "existential" to a body of literature which was written prior to the establishment of any school of existential thought, be it German or French, atheistic or religious, phenomenological or radically empirical. The themes of intuitive existentialism were not the exclusive preserve of philosophers in revolt against orthodox theories of human rationality. In addition to such exceptional thinkers as Kierkegaard and Nietzsche, there are also isolated figures, such as Hölderlin and Herman Melville, with their untimely presentiment of dread and despair. What underscores the achievement of the Russian novelists, however, is the cumulative and collective focus on the spiritual crisis of modern man.

Each chapter which follows is prefaced by a few observations on the timelessness and timeliness of the problem to be examined in juxtaposition with the work of a major Russian novelist. In addition, the theme in question is connected with a central preoccupation of philosophers of *Existenz* or of proto-existentialists, like Pascal. Thus I hope to suggest a significant overlap between the mainstream of classical Russian fiction and the universe of existential discourse. The body of each chapter explores some aspect of the existentiality of selected works of the writer under consideration.

In the concluding chapter, I venture certain generalizations about conditions in nineteenth-century Russia which predisposed its major novelists to examine the horizons of their lived experience from an existential point of view. While I do not claim to provide the reader with an original interpretation of Russian prose fiction, the clarification of its existential import points to at least one striking conclusion. Just as Kierkegaard, Nietzsche, and Ortega y Gasset somehow juxtaposed extreme elitism in politics with the most radical insights into the human condition, Gogol, Dostoevsky, and Tolstoy preserved a religious cast of mind in the very process of confronting us with the most unorthodox awareness of life's terrors and deceptions. In brief, with notable exceptions, such as Sartre, the commitment of the existential mind to radicalism in thought is no necessary handmaiden to radicalism in politics.

The Russian tradition is frequently identified with the celebration of life *per se*. From an existential point of view, it would be truer to remark that its reaffirmation of hope invariably commingles with the realization of despair, much like Ravel's "La Valse," which begins as an innocent Viennese waltz, and without ever sacrificing its intrinsic happy rhythm, dialectically transforms itself into ghastly and garish parodies of the original.

The Broken Icon

CHAPTER 1

Gogol and the Absurd

"He was one of those grotesquely odd creatures who are only possible in Russia where life is so odd as to be grotesque. He was a man gifted by nature, yet he spent his whole life in absurd actions, often almost crimes."

ALEXANDER HERZEN
My Past and Thoughts

Introduction

OF THE NUMEROUS designations given to our times, none seems more appropriate than the Age of Absurdity. The Absurd today encompasses a multitude of events ranging from Hitler's Final Solution to Karl Barth's *deus absconditus*, the dialogue in *Waiting for Godot*, the attempt to win guerrilla wars by conventional military means, the reverse racism of American blacks, and, among other cultural phenomena, drive-in churches. It is infinitely curious to discover how our streamlined, technological civilization generates and supports some of the most bizarre patterns of behavior in history.

The concept of absurdity almost invariably hinges on some glaring discrepancy between expectation and fulfillment, promise and delivery, conventionality and sincerity, or, in Freudian terms, the reality and the pleasure principle. Either a totally ordered universe or a completely random one would be free from the Absurd. Inasmuch as human experience encompasses principles and rules as well as disorders and exceptions, life without the Absurd is but another disembodied notion, appealing to dogmatic

I

2 · *The Broken Icon*

metaphysicians, revealing to psychiatrists, and impossible in the light of man's disposition to envelop the immediacy of existence with the abstractions of reason. The resuscitation of the myth of Sisyphus in our time merely underscores the timelessness of the problem.

There are at least two types of absurdity, formal and situational, though the dividing line between the two is not always clear-cut. Formal absurdity is rooted in logical inconsistency or semantic incongruity, by which primitive rules of correct thinking and speaking are misused. Situational absurdity revolves around discrepancies in our lived experience, by which our most justified expectations of the plausible are violated by daemonic twists of accidental occurrences.

A significant feature of such formal absurdities as married bachelors or Epimenides the Cretan who asserted that all Cretans are liars is their susceptibility to resolution by logical analysis. The latter example, to be sure, has an existential self-referential element which no "hierarchy theory" can explain away.[1] Frequently an important component of an absurd statement is a discrepancy between the character of the person who utters it and its content. Of course, even the Devil can quote Scripture, just as avowed pacifists have advocated violent means to bring about non-violent ends. Another instance of formal absurdity is to be found in the type of paradox where the application of logic to experience appears deliberately confusing. For example, at a dinner party in a restaurant, A orders tomato juice for his first course, B decides on grapefruit juice, whereupon C observes that in that case he will opt for orange juice, as if a matter of taste was dictated by a concept of necessity.[2] This produces a farcical effect, marking the transition from the Absurd in the sphere of pure Reason to its manifestations in the realm of contingency. In both cases, it is worth noting, a seemingly coherent framework of understanding proves vulnerable to jarring disruptions. The idea of internal consistency is unattainable in situations where human emotion and aspiration play a central role. The course of experience suggests the intrusion of the improbable against the presumption of universal predictability. Accordingly, a wise man will not be inordinately surprised by the sudden occurrences of what is least expected.

At the start of *Madame Bovary*, Flaubert gives an unforgettable description of Charles Bovary's cap. Making him look ridiculous in the eyes of his schoolmates, this cap foreshadows the lack of wits which subsequently proves his undoing.[3] How absurd that a schoolboy's headgear should tell the story of his life. Needless to remark, life is full of coincidences where seemingly fortuitous details disclose the heart of the matter. Hegel ascribed such happenings to the "cunning of Reason," while overlooking the ramifications of this notion for his own System. As the late David Owen pointed out in his book on charity in England, a philanthropist may bequeath a sum of money for the purchase of faggots with which to burn heretics. This is but one of the hundred contradictions in human affairs whose truth was so eloquently proclaimed by Pascal. Who among us is not a mixture of inconsistencies? Changes of mind surprise only those unable to accept the burden of the unexpected as natural. The confluence of depths and heights with the odiousness of the obvious and the repugnance of the mean and the low constitutes one of the main sources of the Absurd in human experience.

The banality of ordinary life and our frantic attempts to cover it up with pleasing rhetoric also furnish innumerable illustrations of the Absurd. Silence offends us, even though it be the sole appropriate response in certain situations. Thus, as in the dramas of the Absurd, human beings constantly make mindless observations about things and themselves. The import of their platitudinous remarks lies in the frustrated attempt at verbalization in order to compensate for an unendurable vacancy of feeling and faith. Often we make fools of ourselves less by taking the serious frivolously than by bestowing upon the trite a false solemnity. An example is the phenomenon of sports announcers endlessly talking about nothing to kill time in a spirit of simulated earnestness and reasonableness.

A further exhibit of the Absurd derives from our misuse of the concept of necessity. We speak of having a duty to love others, of getting married by a certain age if we are to be judged normal, of justifying our moods and preferences, when in fact there can be no such duty, short of hypocrisy, unless desire and want are in accord with it, when nobody really knows what normalcy is, and when, for example, an attempted justification of trust is tantamount to a declaration of its absence. How absurd is the confusion of convention with "right reason" and, in turn, of "right reason" with truth! Too often we pretend that our preferred way of doing things or thinking through a problem is apodictically compelling, though as Pascal observed, a difference of one degree of latitude or longitude could obvert our entire ontic stance. Not merely the length of Cleopatra's nose is a matter of chance rather than of preordained design. The vanity of human reason, however, shrinks from such an admission, choosing instead to embroider the contingent with fictitious imperativeness.

The bourgeois cult of respectability, so splendidly catalogued by Flaubert in *Bouvard et Pécuchet,* forms a seminal testament to a distinctively recent form of fraudulent reasoning and vulgar play-acting. Taking a longer view, one would have to grant that at all times the ceremonial and ritualistic facets of living tend to be sublimated into highly questionable verities. The recognition of the genuine absurdity of our morals and manners presupposes an ability to laugh at ourselves which pretentious men, not least among them bureaucrats, can rarely cultivate. This self-centered antipathy to levity in our behavior is one of the strongest links between absurdity, banality, and bureaucracy. How seriously Eichmann took himself in drawing up plans for the transportation of European Jewry to the death camps![4] The performance, as well as the manner in which it was planned and subsequently recounted at the trial, would have been a real challenge to the author of *Dead Souls* and *The Inspector General.*

The thin line separating formal from situational absurdity is nowhere better illustrated than by the *reductio ad absurdum* argument. A familiar case of this argument is the kind of category mistake resulting from an infinite regress, where a child asks his mother "Who created God?" As Hume pointed out in his *Dialogues Concerning Natural Religion*, it is absurd to seek a self-sufficient cause for the chain of finite causes and effects constituting the world as we know it. Nevertheless, Paul Tillich, in *The Courage to Be*, sought to surmount this absurdity by postulating a God beyond God. On the assumption of the first premise of the cosmological argument for the existence of God —that every cause is also the effect of a previous cause, *ad infini-*

tum—the child is perfectly justified in asking for the cause of the Uncaused Cause. But the second premise of this argument—that the infinite chain of causes must be broken at some point—cannot be reconciled with the first, thus reducing the whole to an exercise in futility.

The late Professor C. I. Lewis was fond of citing a variant of the *reductio* which hinges on the acceptance of the framework of discourse in which certain questions may be put. Hence, according to Lewis, for a believer in Kant's primacy of the moral life to insist on an obligation for obeying the categorical imperative is comparable to a logician questioning the law of non-contradiction in the course of advancing a new logical theory. There is nothing wrong with rejecting the law of non-contradiction if the individual is prepared to be comfortably illogical, just as there is nothing wrong with an immoral or amoral agent doing at all times as he pleases. On the other hand, it would be absurd for someone who derives joy through immediate gratification to claim that his particular response to experience is a mere expression of feeling and not a theoretical statement. While no one can quarrel with his state of mind, his assertion would be inconsistent with his awareness of ecstasy as uncontaminated "firstness."

Unlike soaring metaphysicians and poets, Gogol focused his attention on the minutiae of formal and situational absurdity. The tailor in "The Overcoat" drinking heavily at first only on great holidays but then on all days marked by a cross (almost all days on the Russian calendar are so marked); a character in *Dead Souls* trying to account for some evil by linking it waywardly with the circumstance that someone is German; Major Kovalev rediscovering his vanished nose walking along the Nevsky Prospect—these incredible illuminations of disorder amid seemingly unshakable evidence to the contrary emphasize the haphazard nature of our lot in space and time.

The uniqueness of Gogol's achievement lies not least in his juxtaposition of detailed descriptions of apparent trivia with sweeping pronouncements about such grandiose issues as national character, historical destiny, and, on another level, the risks involved in smoking a pipe. In marked contrast to the school of *Kleinmalerei* in German fiction of the last century, Gogol is never content to enunciate the petty for its own sake. Beyond suggesting the incongruities of common sense and daily experience, Gogol gives further expression to our absurd postures by setting them against lofty ideas and pseudo-arguments, which endow them with a fleeting aura of irresistible persuasiveness.

The discussion to follow will focus on three distinct, but inseparable, aspects of the Absurd in Gogol's fiction. In the first section, I consider the dimension of situational absurdity as embodied in many of Gogol's plots. Section two follows the theme of bureaucracy in conjunction with absurdity. Finally, the discussion turns to formal absurdity as a central component in Gogol's art. Here I am concerned with such devices as generalizations and questionable explanations, which Gogol uses to point up the absurd element in man's condition.

Situational Absurdity

Among the numerous objections leveled by Kierkegaard against the Hegelian System, none seems more valid than his claim for an inherent incongruity of any ideal structure of thought and the confused actuality experienced as real by flesh-and-blood human beings. From Hegel's eternal point of view, Kierkegaard concedes, the fleeting moments of our temporal condition are indeed insignificant when opposed to the dialectician's possession of pure consistency and unfailing coherence. Inasmuch as the run of finite observers are not privileged to look at things from the dazzling heights of consciousness *per se* without succumbing to an "Icarus complex," their constitutional attachment to the trivial as of utmost importance for them commands not only our respect but also our reflective humility as subjective knowers in and of the human scene. It is all very well for Hegel to despise the non-heroic passions of those who do not make world history, the victims of processes beyond their comprehension, but such metaphysical *hubris* scarcely assuages their suffering nor does it justify it to any clear-headed mind contemplating its destiny in the maze of the World Spirit mysteriously working out a remote salvation. On occasion Hegel himself saw this clearly enough.[5] Nevertheless, his insistence on objectivity as hypostatized from the facts of ordinary life prevented him from giving situational absurdity (e.g., banality) its due. Within the lofty regions of the Concept he reconciles all conflicting concrete universals and smooths over the sharp edges of individual failure or frustration. Although Kierkegaard tended to remain abstract himself even while disavowing Hegelianism, his reflections on life retain a degree of lifelikeness rare among both critics and advocates of German speculative philosophy.

A) PLOTS AND SETTINGS

The System bears no more resemblance to what goes on in the world than it does to the *Lebenswelt* of Gogol. Doubtless the author of *Dead Souls* had this discrepancy in mind when, at the start of the seventh chapter of his masterpiece, he took time out from narration to apologize to his readers for attempting to beguile them with trivialities instead of casting a more traditional spell with sublime truths and ethereal metaphors.[6] Gogol's attachment to the banal as a legitimate subject of prose fiction interestingly supplements Kierkegaard's depiction of the subjective thinker as inescapably immersed *in medias res.*[7]

With tongue in cheek, Gogol voices his envious admiration of those fortunate authors whose heroes dwell in the rarefied atmosphere of Beautiful Souls striving for some Absolute. He, on the other hand, like a classical scholar condemned to provide exegeses of Plato's Form of the Ugly, is obliged to use his poetic license for the creation of mediocrities.

But not such is the lot and different is the fate of the writer who has dared to bring out all the things that are before man's eyes at every minute, yet which his unheeding eyes see not—all that fearsome, overwhelming slimy morass of minutiae that have bogged down our life, all that lurks deep within the cold, broken, workaday characters with which our earthly path, at times woeful and dreary, swarms. Different is the fate of the writer who has dared, as if with the puissance of an implacable burin, to bring out all these things in bold and vivid relief before the eyes of all men![8]

If only he could remain faithful to the highest expectations of his refined reading public, Gogol protests somewhat feebly, though not without flights of lyrical hyperbole, before replunging into the everyday adventures of his anti-hero. Chichikov's "ultimate concern" is neither Tillich's Ground of Being nor the God beyond the God of Christianity but merely lots of money and the respectability it can purchase in anonymous provincial capitals. Chichikov is a perverse Puritan who expends time and effort on shoddy deals only to miss making the kingdom of heaven on earth by a hair's breadth. His ambition to project an image of prosperity sustained by a share of the real thing is enveloped by Gogol in layers of meticulous detail about such intrinsically unexciting subjects as underwear and *eau de cologne*, and then again elevated to universal import by virtue of generalizations on the human condition, which oddly combine homespun truths and falsities, piercing insights and blatant distortions.

Chichikov's moral stature matches his career in being consistently undistinguished. Not for him the saintly excesses of Myshkin or the egotistical elitism of Raskolnikov: instead, he professes a refined gentility which enables him to preserve the proprieties while giving free rein to selfish impulses. His exploitation of others, far from being crude, is conducted with unexceptional correctness and occasional touches of humane solicitude. His meals, so lovingly described by Gogol, attest to a capacity for sensual enjoyment strikingly deficient in the anti-heroes of twentieth-century tales of the Absurd.

As he was driving up to the tavern, Chichikov ordered Seliphan to stop for two reasons: on the one hand, to give the horses a chance to rest, and, on the other, to have a bite of something and fortify himself as well . . . But you take some of these fair-to-middlin' gentlemen, who will call for ham at one stage-post, a suckling pig at a second, and at a third for a slice of sturgeon, or some sort of sausage baked with onions and then, as if they hadn't eaten a thing all day, will sit down at a full table, at any hour you like, and tackle starlet chowder, with eelpouts and soft roe, so hot it hisses and burbles as they take it into their mouths, followed, as a sort of chaser, by a fish pie with millet porridge, or cabbage dumplings, or a pie baked of young catfish, so that even an onlooker must needs work up an appetite—now, these gentlemen really are enjoying an enviable gift from Heaven![9]

The plot of *Dead Souls* provides an example of Gogol's straddling the fence between the concrete particular and the hypothetical universal. On the one hand, he depicts conditions in rural Russia of his time with compelling accuracy; on the other, he invents situations and characters which border on the miraculous and yet, perhaps just as miraculously, enable us to realize that "suspension of disbelief" which endows the wildest flights of imagination with plausibility. Generations of readers, including the most learned expositors of this most remarkable of novels, have asked themselves whether in fact Chichikov might have got away with his fantastic scheme had he not foolishly betrayed himself by talking too indiscreetly and out of character to Nozdrev.

The irony of Chichikov's downfall is all the more bitter for the fact that, as Chichikov himself is aware, Nozdrev is a fool who does not even realize what he himself is saying or doing. His actions are totally impulsive and devoid of rational import. Analogous to his lack of theoretical reason in seeking the true explanation (for example, Chichikov's reasons for collecting dead serfs) is his deficiency in practical reason, which constantly leads him into dubious enterprises and attempted swindles. Only in a world where anything can occur can such a man serve as an instrument of poetic justice.

Gogol's brilliant juxtaposing of dead souls as a quasi-feasible business venture and as a symptom of moral corruption and corruptibility is, to adapt his own way of stating things, neither too outlandish nor too common. Probably these events would not have happened, conceivably they might have happened, but whether they did or not, their significance as a parable of deception and self-deception remains compelling. When Sobakevich, one of the landowners, speaks of his deceased serfs as if they were still alive, affectionately recording their faults and strong points, pondering their whereabouts at the present time, Chichikov himself begins to wonder whether the logic of things has broken down completely.

"Really, now, what is he up to?" thought Chichikov, "Is he taking me for a fool, or what?" and then added, out loud: "I find it strange, really, it seems as if we were going through some sort of theatrical performance or a comedy; I can't explain it any other way. You are, it seems, a man who is quite intelligent, possessing knowledge and an education. Why, the matter under discussion has no more substance than a puff of air! What can such stuff be worth? Who needs it?"[10]

On the basis of extraordinary assumptions—such as Chichikov's ingenious scheme—one could be driven to the espousal of far-fetched yet persuasive conclusions. Logical validity need not entail empirical truth. Hence, Gogol's favorite practice of deducing improbable conclusions from false or bizarre premises permits him to invest his fantastic tale with an irreproachable air of cogency.

As the anti-hero of *Dead Souls* is a self-conscious impostor who projects his low fantasies on a gullible society, so his counterpart in *The Inspector General* does precisely the same but, though far more successful in the end, without any deliberate intent. Although Khlestakov, in marked contrast to Chichikov, is too stupid to scheme, both of them find themselves major participants in absurd situations. In his novel, Gogol staggers the imagination by investing the hierarchy of Russian serfdom with the vision of middle-class success, while in his comedy he plays off conventional apprehensions of normalcy against the intractable unpredictability of human affairs.

The tyranny of common sense is dramatically dethroned in both works. In a world in which Chichikov's acquaintances could, through the spread of rumor, come to regard him as Napoleon in disguise, it is not surprising that an entire town's administration would be deceived by the facile posings of a ne'er-do-well feebly yet adequately emulating an *incognito* official. Terror rooted in guilt has so warped the officials' collective judgment that they can no longer respond critically to the unsuspected.[11]

Once the crucial mistake of identifying Khlestakov with the dreaded Inspector General has been made, every subsequent act of folly and humiliation follows quite predictably. Nothing is more natural than the kowtowing of ambitious flunkies to the highest authority, especially when they know themselves to be tainted by gross malpractice and hence vulnerable to extreme penalties. Into this explicable scene of servile ingratiation and Habsburg deviousness in Russian dress, Gogol interpolates the fantasies of Khlestakov, the Mayor and his wife, and the other officials. The Mayor, for example, looks forward to the day when, through the intercession of Khlestakov, he will dine in a general's uniform at the Governor's table while the mayors of other towns will have to stand at attention during the entire meal. Partly egged on by his stupid if ambitious wife, he dreams of cutting down to size his former colleagues and threatening subordinates by virtue of the weight of his newly gained son-in-law's influence at court. The daydreaming of the Mayor and Khlestakov, set against their crass pragmatism, once more illustrates a world of which the interfusion of forgetfulness and calculation constitutes not the least daemonic aspect.

However rich and varied the fantasies of the protagonists in *The Inspector General*, they never assume the commanding position of the hero's obsession in "The Overcoat." Akakiy Akakievich fixes his heart and mind on the procurement of an outer garment not simply to protect him against the beastly cold of St. Petersburg but to satisfy an all-consuming passion.

Akakiy Akakievich is highly idiosyncratic, like so many characters in classical Russian fiction. His love for his occupation as a copyist leaves him outside of what is usually called "the mainstream of normal behavior." Gogol presents him as deriving a considerable amount of satisfaction from his "unfreedom" in the civil service. Reduced to the level of an office marionette, he nevertheless enjoys his drudgery. Deeply attached to his duties, he takes home extra work, so as not to be away from it for long.[12]

Nonetheless, there is a tremendous void in his life. These feelings of emptiness manifest themselves in his responses to the new coat. As the tailor expounds the special features of the coat, he casts a spell over Akakiy Akakievich. The latter's obsession with this garment exceeds all utilitarian considerations, including those of desperate need.

To tell the truth, he found it at first rather difficult to get used to these privations, but after a while it became a habit and went smoothly enough—he even became quite accustomed to being hungry in the evening; on the other hand, he had spiritual nourishment, for he carried ever in his thoughts the idea of his future overcoat. His whole existence had in a sense become fuller, as though he had married, as though some other person were present with him, as though he were no longer alone but an agreeable companion had consented to walk the path of life hand in hand with him, and that companion was none other than the new overcoat with its thick padding and its strong, durable lining. He became, as it were, more alive, even more strong-willed, like a man who has set before himself a definite goal. Uncertainty, indecision, in fact all the hesitating and vague characteristics, vanished from his face and his manners.[13]

The subsequent theft of the overcoat is more a fatal blow to his ego than the loss of a necessity. Since life without his new overcoat is not worth living, he dies soon thereafter.

If the first two dimensions of situational absurdity in "The Overcoat" revolve around the hero's strange attachment to an uncreative job and an even stranger affection for a material object, the third embraces his supernatural interference in the workings of this world. Akakiy Akakievich's demise is followed by reports of coat-snatching, which build up to a confrontation between the specter of the dead clerk and the official who had refused to listen to him. One night, as the official is riding in his carriage, he finds himself in the company of a ghost, whom he recognizes as Akakiy Akakievich, and who deprives him of his own garment.

Yet another example of situational absurdity in Gogol is the story "The Nose." In contrast to the other stories, including "The Diary of a Madman," in which the protagonist is clearly bereft of his senses, Major Kovalev's trials and tribulations with his vanished nose embody a dual absurdity. Here one encounters a fantastic mixture of absurdity-in-the-real-world and phantasmagorical absurdity-beyond-credibility. For example, the fantasies of Khlestakov are developed against a background of intelligible order, of legality and moral corruption. Similarly, Akakiy Akakievich is consumed by the pursuit of neurotic desires all too familiar to the lonely inhabitants of this world. The assumption of organic wholeness by a detached nose, on the other hand, is inherently absurd. Nevertheless, Gogol succeeds in giving even this narrative the illusion of plausibility. It is precisely the unquestioned normalcy of the setting that makes the reader wonder with David Hume whether we are justified in believing that the sun will rise again tomorrow, however predictably it has done so in the past. More intensely than any other narrative, "The Nose" points up Gogol's fascination with "radical contingency" in human experience. By persuading his reader to take an odd imaginative somersault, Gogol exposes the precariousness of our most deeply ingrained customs and expectations.

It is also worth noting here that while the story is told in a comic vein, this coexists somewhat uneasily with the dread involved in finding oneself without a nose or finding a nose within a piece of bread. Especially for those who correlate human freedom with total unpredictability, Gogol's "Nose" serves as an excellent object lesson in the limits of ascertainable coherence. In opposition to the fatalists, he allows for "thunderbolts out of the blue" to uncover the tyranny of conventional wisdom. At the same time, in opposition to the libertarians, he dramatizes the logic of madness as a terrible threat to the integrated personality.

In contrast to Hegel, Gogol repeatedly suggests that our reading of monumental history may deceive us into underestimating the thrust of trifles as historical determinants. Dazzled by the image of "the *Weltgeist* on horseback" (Napoleon), Hegel would have been hard put to admit that a quarrel between two sausage-makers could touch off a cataclysmic change.

Good old people! But my account of them is approaching a very melancholy incident which transformed forever the life of that peaceful nook. This incident is the more impressive because it arose from such an insignificant cause. But such is the strange order of things; trifling causes have always given rise to great events, and on the other hand great undertakings frequently end in insignificant results. Some military leader rallies all the forces of his state, carries on a war for several years, his generals cover themselves with glory; and in the end it all results in gaining a bit of land in which there is not room to plant a potato; while sometimes two sausage-makers of two towns quarrel over some nonsense, and in the end the towns are drawn into the quarrel, then villages, and then the whole kingdom.[14]

As a corrective to the hero-worship of the nineteenth century, the mistaking of Chichikov for Napoleon in the closing chapters of *Dead Souls* constitutes a sort of therapeutic absurdity to the pretensions of speculative reason to tell us, in Ranke's celebrated phrase, *wie es eigentlich gewesen.*

B) SYCOPHANTS AND OFFICIALS

Although bureaucratic absurdity is a special case of situational absurdity, the prominent place it occupies in Gogol's fiction (as well as in Russian history) merits special attention. While the emerging Russian intelligentsia drew its chief inspiration first from the writings of French *philosophes* and subsequently from those of the German poetic and Idealistic philosophers, the successors of Peter the Great found in the Prussian civil service a model worthy of their most ambitious emulation. In his history of the tsarist secret police, Sidney Monas points out that the parade drills of Nicholas I exceeded in blind devotion to discipline even those of his Prussian cousins.[15] The exploited clerks and humiliated generals who populate the pages of Gogol and Dostoevsky are but one reflection of this gigantic machinery, which has dominated Russian life for over two centuries. It is, of course, possible to say a great deal in its favor, but, so far as the negative hero in Russian and Soviet literature is concerned, it is fair to generalize that administrative absurdity and cruelty rather than administrative efficiency and justice have been the dominant note struck by his creators. One could almost speak of a tradition ranging from Gogol's fantasy-ridden bureaucrats to Solzhenitsyn's functionaries exercising their power with incredible stupidity and callousness—a tradition which embraces the farce as well as the tragedy of administrative absurdity in its repeated manifestations in Russian life.

The distinguishing marks of administrative absurdity may be enumerated as follows. First, cast in the role of a civil servant or public official, the administrator is tempted to take himself more seriously than his position warrants. Whether he wears a special uniform or, American style, presides arrogantly over a magnificent desk, his assigned rank in a hierarchy is apt to conceal both from himself and from his colleagues the negligibility of his talents, frequently compounded by mammoth incompetence masquerading as imperturbability under pressure. There results an absurd discrepancy between the trappings of his office and his individual character. As a class, bureaucrats naturally prefer to forget that their position in a given hierarchy, far from being the function of their native abilities, is a reflection of their simple-mindedness and spinelessness.

The second characteristic of bureaucratic absurdity grows out of the corruptibility of a decent individual by his position of power. Thus many an American college dean has been molded into a liar by the responsibilities of his office, so at odds with his

personal integrity. There is something ludicrous about the acceptance of public trust undermining an individual's personal integrity, the sort of phenomenon Reinhold Niebuhr had in mind
when he juxtaposed moral man and immoral society.[16]

A third dimension of administrative absurdity revolves around
the fact that the administrator is often a mere tool, powerless in
the face of his superiors, a victim of invisible circumstances,
which determine the course of his action in a particular case.
Detached from the System as a whole, any of its parts would
shrivel to insignificance, while the System itself may be little
more than one of accidental coherence.

Finally, bureaucratic absurdity frequently takes the form of
dehumanization in which the public role of the authority is dras-
tically divorced from its private dispositions and sentiments. On
this score, all men are divided into inferiors and superiors and
treated merely in accordance with their degree of influence in
the organization. Here, to be is to be the value of a vacancy or a
promotion. It is interesting to note that Tolstoy's Ivan Ilyich no
less than Akakiy Akakievich's boss could be a very decent fellow
when not acting officially.

The absurdity of administrative language lies in its studied
noncommittal quality. Almost nothing is said which cannot be
revised to fit the exigencies of the shifting moment. In order to
endow the organization with maximum flexibility, all declarations
made in its name must be capable of being adjusted to its compelling needs. In Mozart's *Così fan tutte* and *Le Nozze di Figaro*,
the legalistic jargon of the marriage official characteristically
serves to throw everyone into a state of unrelieved confusion and
wry amusement.

According to Kierkegaard, men acquire authentic being by
involving themselves in crucial decisions affecting their own lives
and the lives of those in their care. In administrative bureaucracies,
on the other hand, men in office acquire responsibility and prestige
by blindly submitting to manipulation which they would never toler-
ate in their private lives. Herein lies the gist of their absurd
predicament and ours. If children are authentic by displaying a
lack of conscious control, and Kierkegaardian individuals by
choosing themselves as responsible moral agents, bureaucrats
attain authenticity only through an excess of political acumen.

The gulf between the spontaneity of a child and the artifice of a bureaucrat partly conveys the pathos of administrative absurdity.

Examples of bureaucratic absurdity are everywhere. A department chairman at a university lies to a colleague about the latter's prospects for promotion and tenure because the dean for whom the chairman must cover up had lied to him in turn; the Vietnam peace negotiations in Paris are snarled because the various parties to the dispute cannot agree on a mutually satisfactory seating arrangement at the conference table. Gogol doubtless would have felt very much at home amid these vignettes of bureaucratic etiquette drawn from the contemporary scene. Although, in his brief stint as professor of history at St. Petersburg University, Gogol was spared the humiliation suffered by the philosophy department —having a general appointed as its head—he could not help but acquire an intimate knowledge of the conjunction of hierarchical self-glorification and dazzling ineptitude. Oddly enough, it fell to this enigmatic conservative to establish a powerful literary tradition directed against the sycophants and officials of tsarism.

In his works, Gogol touches on a wide spectrum of administrative distortion in human affairs.[17] Take, for example, the Mayor in *The Inspector General*: no less corrupt than the other town officials, he nevertheless attempts to project to Khlestakov an official attitude of integrity (as though his public image bore no relation to his private conscience). Similarly, Chichikov proves himself a zealous investigator of customs violations before accepting bribes in a higher official position which devolves upon him as a reward for his conscientious labors. At an earlier stage in his career, during a governmental reform, the future trader in dead souls had made his peace with the new order by being careful only to pocket his self-assessed share of the bribes left by his clients, the remainder being duly conveyed to his superiors. Far more dehumanizing than Chichikov's connivances is the posture of the official to whom Akakiy Akakievich turns for help in his distress about his stolen overcoat. This "important personage's" three codes of behavior—one toward his equals, another toward his superiors, and a third toward his inferiors in the hierarchy—make him completely incapable of responding to our poor clerk's plight with even a pretension of sympathy. Anyone in the position of a copying clerk has the anonymity of a mere instrument in the eyes of the official.[18] However, Gogol adds, significantly, as a private individual he was a very decent man, just as Chichikov does not begrudge an occasional coin to a beggar when his mood is right.

Gogol's characters are literally obsessed with the importance of rank, from Khlestakov's fantasy of dining in the palace to the mad diarist, a clerk, who persuades himself that he is the King of Spain. The hero of "The Nose" also dreams of climbing the bureaucratic ladder and the Mayor in *The Inspector General*, as was noted earlier, sees himself in the dress uniform of a general, lording it over his subordinates. Chichikov's attitude toward others is almost determined by their individual official stations and titles. In brief, long before Kafka's nightmarish visions of anonymous bureaucrats terrorizing the community, long before *Growing Up Absurd*, Parkinson's Law, the Peter Principle, and the whole contemporary gamut of procedural method and substantive madness, Gogol intuitively grasped this conjunction as symptomatic of a world run amuck. Gogol's Russia was, in many respects, the least modern of European societies, yet its contradictions between rich and poor, educated and ignorant, disturbingly anticipated many of the anachronisms of our own technological society

Formal Absurdity

The conjunction of sweeping generalizations with pseudo-explanations may be construed as a distortion of the traditional philosophical quest for true models of explanation leading to the formulation of general laws or principles from which singular instances of a phenomenon may be logically deduced. In this connection, it is not irrelevant to point out that this quest has been far from successful. Explanations of Napoleon's triumphs and downfall, to take a classic example, for all the intellectual sophistication of contemporary historians, still do not conspicuously exceed in imperativeness the caricatures of textbook accounts offered by Tolstoy in the epilogue in *War and Peace*. No one can claim to know whether the Napoleon story was unique and hence immune to being comprehended under some universal pattern of decline and fall applying to each and every dictator; whether it was a blending of particulars and general principles and, if so, how the two can be separated; or whether Napoleon's career is only a rare instance of the general—subject, in principle, to Nietzsche's idea of the Eternal Return.

Given this uncertainty, it follows that Gogol's sweeping generalizations and pseudo-explanations, save for the transparently ludicrous ones, may be viewed as commonsense formulations not necessarily devoid of some cognitive significance. To the extent that phenomena have fugitive causes they most assuredly fall into the province of Gogol's imaginative concern. The focus of this concern is of course not identical with that of the professional epistemologist in quest of exact empirical knowledge, but rather with that of the ordinary citizen, intellectually perplexed and morally upset by the incongruities of human fortune. For Gogol, as for most of the religious existentialists of a later day, it is the hiddenness of Providence juxtaposed with radical contingency which, above all, calls into question any comprehensively intellectual vision of our experience.

A) SWEEPING GENERALIZATIONS

As every schoolboy knows, hasty generalizations are to be spurned and avoided—this too a generalization challenged by its own import. Some generalizations, like "all equilateral triangles are equiangular," are formally true, just as others, like "all grocers are thieves," are patently false. Tautologies add nothing to our empirical knowledge, inasmuch as the predicate is inherent by definition or stipulation in the subject; though we may learn something from the process of spelling out the multiple implications of the *definiendum*. On the other hand, ludicrous assertions about a large class of individuals varying considerably among themselves only poison the already combative atmosphere of human interrelationships by exacerbating the scapegoat mentality. A more problematic case is the familiar "all men are mortal," which Tolstoy criticizes from an existential point of view in his "Death of Ivan Ilyich."[19] He does so not because there is some slight possibility of the hypothetical universal proving false (assuming for the moment revolutionary developments in biology), but rather on the ground that the death of an individual or, more precisely, his actual dying and his attitude toward this boundary experience, are obscured by the tone of a noncommittal sweeping statement, however true in itself. To be sure, this is less a logical objection to the major premise of a syllogism than a plea for self-referential discrimination on occasions when existential facts override those of formal logic.

Contrary to a widely held belief, great thinkers have often been unabashed generalizers. It is precisely the unbalanced character of their radical theses which, by provoking sharp legitimate disagreement, carries the movement of thought to previously untouched facets of experience. Hence an obvious rebuttal to any imaginative insight is to point out its oversimplifying tendencies. Thus Marx is ingeniously misleading in imputing all human exploitation to the dialectics of the class struggle in history, and, by the same token, Freud can scarcely maintain that the conflicts of infantile sexuality are the sole determinants of every dilemma of culture and civilization. The more fruitful for the reinterpretation of human experience a generalization turns out to be, the fewer the chances of its being unassailably accurate. A difficult problem requires a one-sided focus if the point to be made is not to be swallowed up by an endless string of qualifications whose disarming air of objectivity all too often is nothing more than a screen for mental exhaustion or indifference.

As previously noted, Gogol made the exploration of the minute his special task. Reason did not return to him the compliment it paid Hegel when, having looked at the world rationally, the German philosopher found that it gazed back upon him in the same manner. Gogol, on the contrary, found himself confronted by an inexhaustible variety of unnecessary facts which, far from adding up to a single coherent pattern, underscored the radically contingent quality of lived experience. It would appear well-nigh impossible to arrive at generalizations from detached noses walking around as state councilors, ghostly clerks stealing overcoats on the Nevsky Prospect, traders in dead souls, and madmen fancying themselves in the role of the King of Spain. At first glance nothing seems more incongruous than Gogol's interest in the logic of explanation and generalization. Even if a small-time house painter did become the Chancellor of the Third Reich (a

German *tour de force* worthy of "The Diary of a Madman"), and even if Freud has in the meantime shed a great deal of light on the truth value of detached noses parading in dress uniform in our dreams, Gogol's world of strange obsessions and premonitions, of thunderbolts out of the blue and daemonic supervention in the realm of the banal, scarcely invites the pontifical pronouncements of a Goethe. Where the Eternal Feminine draws men into folly instead of into heaven and where absurdity takes precedence over virtue in human conduct, the bold and broad statements of speculative reason seem peculiarly vulnerable.

In many of his works Gogol devises a striking number of generalizations in order to caricature and illumine our claims to know things as a whole. As a structural device the Gogolesque generalization undercuts the tyranny of the trivial by relating it rather ambiguously to the explanatory power, real or imagined, of the universal. At the same time Gogol provides his readers with a commentary, be it ironic, serious, facetious, or even inconsistent, on the unusual experiences which are the lot of his heroes. As a result, the inexplicable becomes partly explicable and the tensions between imagined reasonable demands from life and how life is actually lived are accentuated to a degree where we must reexamine the tired assumptions guiding our view of the pedestrian flow of things.

"But let us abandon these reflections. They are out of keeping here. Besides I am not fond of reflections, so long as they get no further than being reflections." With this existentialist sentiment Gogol concludes his above-mentioned generalization about trivial causes in history kindling monumental effects, like premonitions of death induced by the off-handish behavior of a cat.[20] Gogol's reflections, admittedly, always have a bearing on our first-hand knowledge of life. Whether their mood be whimsical, satirical, self-mocking, totally absurd, dead earnest, or a combination of some of these attitudes, they form a vivid contrast to his meticulous attention to detail.[21]

The generalizations can be divided primarily into those which express his own philosophy and those which he treated facetiously —at least as articles of personal belief. Nabokov's contention that crediting a writer like Gogol with having had ideas is tantamount to casting aspersions on his pure literary gifts simply is not borne out by the evidence. Not merely in his *Selected Passages from Correspondence with Friends* but in the plays and tales themselves, Gogol, however unphilosophical in his method, touches on weighty issues. It is worth remembering in this connection that poet-thinkers like Rousseau and Nietzsche, by producing an argument for their assertions only on the rarest occasions, nevertheless did more to advance our knowledge of the human heart than the vast majority of disciplined scholars. Analogously, Gogol, for all his levity and superficial playfulness, manages to shed remarkable light on the anomalies and anachronisms of human conduct. His refusal to come out and tell us in so many sententious words that working in bureaucratic offices is apt to have a dehumanizing effect on men or that the inexplicable deserves the respect of reasonable beings, does not imply his indifference to these questions. On the contrary, his point of view on these and related matters is unmistakably communicated in his fiction both non-discursively through image and metaphor and non-tendentiously through generalization and hyperbole. Like the *Noumenal* in Kant overcoming the tyranny of the *Phenomenal*, in which freedom and responsibility are ruled out by the causal nexus, Gogol's generalizations may be said to resemble transcendental disruptions of "everydayness" which weaken the hold of the banal on us: now illuminating the curriculum of a finishing school for girls as a paradigm of hierarchical pretension, now hinting at the superiority of Russian national characteristics by defining the essence of various ethnic groups in terms of conspicuous incidentals (as if we could grasp the personality of Socrates by the shape of his nose).

In his generalization about life as subject to the intrusion of at least one luminous joy into a man's career, however drab and routine it may be the rest of the time, Gogol asserts his faith in singular redemptive moments amid our experience of the world as a terrestrial prison.

Everywhere in life, no matter where it may run its course, whether amid its harsh, raspingly poor, and squalidly mildewing lowly ranks, or amid its monotonously frigid and depressingly tidy upper classes— everywhere, if it be but once, man is fated to meet a phenomenon that is unlike all that which he may have chanced to meet hitherto; which, if but once, will awaken within him an emotion that is unlike all those which he is fated to experience all life long. Everywhere, running counter to all the sorrows of which our life is compact, a glittering joy will gaily flash by, as, at times, a glittering equipage with gold on its gear, with its picturesque horses, and sparkling because of its gleaming plate-glass, will suddenly, unexpectedly, speed by some backwoods poverty-stricken hamlet that had never beheld anything but a country-cart, and for a long while the muzhiks stand there, their mouths gaping and without putting on their doffed headgear again, even though the wondrous equipage has long since whirled away and vanished out of sight.[22]

Short of being carried away into the Faustian realm of everlasting bliss in temporal form, Gogol steers clear of the Schopenhauerian view whereby the prospect of any happiness for man stands condemned by the paradox of satisfied desire, according to which there is no alternative to frustration or jadedness. While he was too pessimistic about the human condition to gloss over its intractable limiting factors on the attainment of dependable bliss, Gogol's agonizing concentration on the trivial as a continuous instrument of enslavement is reconcilable with falling in love, reading *Anna Karenina* for the first time, or whatever other experience may serve as an occasion for self-forgetfulness in a transport of unsolicited delight. Even those of us incapable of experiencing mystical ecstasies are likely to recall an incident in which the clock stood still and in the course of which we were not bored.

A common feature of existential thought is its combative stance toward the bourgeois ethos, that mode of existence often, though perhaps a bit unjustly, identified with an exaggerated sense of security and a smug arrogance. From Kierkegaard's attack on Christians in Christendom as irreligiously objective to Sartre's self-accusations for being a man of letters in violent times, a whole tradition emphasizing man *in extremis* has evolved— partially as a corrective, one is tempted to conjecture, to the liberal ideal of non-partisan tolerance. It is interesting to note how Gogol's distinction between the "misery and glory of man" revolves around this specific dichotomy.

And therein was clearly evinced what kind of creature man is: he is wise, he is clever and sensible in all things that pertain to others but not to his own self. What circumspect, firm counsel he will supply you with on the difficult occasions of life! "What a wide-awake head he's got on his shoulders!" shouts the mob. "What a steadfast character!" But let some calamity come swooping down upon this wide-awake head, and should it befall him to be placed himself in the difficult occasions of life, why, where in the world has his character gone to? The steadfast man of action is totally at a loss and has turned out to be a pitiful little poltroon, an insignificant, weak babe, or simply, as a Nozdrev puts it, a horse's tail.[23]

As long as things do not pertain directly to himself, which is to say, as long as he can view them with the sagacious detachment of a classical philosopher, man does indeed measure up to the contemplative ideal of which Pico della Mirandola spoke so eloquently. But let him be caught in a dilemma and his much-vaunted dignity is likely to give way to panic and fuming despair. A chasm divides the love of God in whitewashed churches from its human efficacy in crucial boundary situations—say, in the face of death—where the conditions for abstract rejoicing no longer prevail. "Physician heal thyself" has proved an injunction of strikingly little force in man's quest for self-understanding, particularly when the climate is unfavorable to reciprocal action.

A related existential incongruity centers on man's inconsistent credulousness. Again and again he will ignore or pass over truths which might alleviate his worldly plight, only to succumb to the lure of nonsense or fakery when something serious is at stake.

Strange people, these Messieurs the bureaucrats—and, with them, all the other ranks as well. For they knew very well that Nozdrev was a liar, that one couldn't believe him—not in a single word he uttered, not in the least trifle—and yet, just the same, they had recourse to him. There, go and cope with man! Man does not believe in God, but he does believe that if the bridge of his nose itches he is inevitably slated to die soon; he will pass over the creation of a poet, a creation as clear as the day, all permeated with the accord and lofty wisdom of simplicity, but will eagerly pounce upon a work wherein some successful charlatan talks a lot of rot, tells a pack of lies, distorts nature and turns it inside out, and this will prove to his liking, and he will set up a shout: "Here it is, here is a genuine knowledge of the secrets of the heart!" All his life he doesn't value doctors at more than a bent pin, but in the upshot turns to some old conjure-woman who heals through whispered spells and gobbets of spit, or better still, he will devise for himself some decoction or other out of who knows what rubbish which, God knows why, he will consider the sovereign cure for what ails him.[24]

Gullibility and scrupulosity, far from being always at odds in man's makeup, come rather oddly together depending, to use the telling phrase of William James, on whether he is more afraid of going to hell or of making a mistake. Elsewhere in *Dead Souls* Gogol repeatedly touches on the spread of false rumors in human affairs. Perfectly hard-boiled citizens are prepared to believe that Chichikov is Napoleon in disguise or some other unlikely character merely because the liar Nozdrev inadvertently discredited his seemingly innocent purchase of deceased serfs. Also worth noting in this connection is the Mayor's speech in *The Inspector General* in which, under the pretext of official correctness, he lies to Khlestakov and, conceivably, to himself about his unsullied devotion to duty. However, as Gogol makes clear, it is not only bureaucrats who, having uncritically damned all physicians, run to quacks in an emergency.

Generalizations in Gogol's fiction therapeutically clash with his painstaking enumeration of seemingly irrelevant detail. Thus the absurdly lengthy accounts of Chichikov's meals or possessions are relieved by hyperbolic expressions of proclaimed wisdom: the acid truth of the concrete refined and qualified by the soaring truth of the universal. Neither by itself can do justice to the constant commingling of triteness and illumination in human experience. Together they mirror one of the dominant contradictions in our makeup: our unselective greed for sensation and perception with our irrepressible quest for meaningful, transcendent self-assertion.

B) PSEUDO-EXPLANATIONS

Pseudo-explanations fall into three main classes. First, there is the mythical variety, according to which an unverifiable entity, such as the *deus absconditus* of Christian theology, is invoked to account for specified effects. The second type, while partially based on discernible evidence, proceeds to make claims for its particular arrangement of the evidence which transcend whatever explanatory powers it may possess. This kind of explanation has an undeniable air of plausibility which, however, conceals the ways in which contrary evidence has been strained, if not totally suppressed. Finally, there are existential pseudo-explanations, characterized by a confusion of a branch of knowledge with a mode of life or, as it were, by categorical inappropriateness. From the positivistic point of view this variety of pseudo-explanation rests on the confusion of fact with value or attitude with belief. From an existential point of view it is grounded in over-assessment of intellect as a self-sufficient arbiter of all human disputes.

Pseudo-explanations are rarely unambiguously false. In fact, given our limited knowledge of human behavior combined with our passion for self-righteousness and our preference for ego-reinforcing states of mind, it would be out of character for us to entertain accounts of events utterly devoid of either self-interest or a modicum of truth. Often we are simply ignorant of how the facts fit a specific theory, so, naturally, we choose the theory which will fit the facts without unnecessarily wounding our pride, especially where our powers of judgment are challenged. A lack of clear-cut answers invariably turns out to be fertile soil for gratifying speculations. Frequently, we lack the time or the energy to cull the appropriate types of explanations from counter-intuitive alternatives. Since we are both prejudiced participants and impartial witnesses in life (so that our most precise reasoning continues to be governed by preconceptions and hidden hopes and fears), and since our knowledge of many things and relationships remains at best extremely spotty, very few of our explanations can be expected to stand the test of ideal verifiability or falsifiability. Furthermore, positivists themselves have failed to justify their own criteria of truth.[25] In a world in which rationality means one thing to politicians, another to physicists, something else again to fools and/or madmen, the *prima facie* absurdity of Gogol's pseudo-explanation is not wholly deficient in the therapeutic value of "learned ignorance."

Possibly the best-known example of pseudo-explanation in Gogol's work is the totally nonsensical connection drawn in *The Inspector General* between the assessor's alcoholic breath and his having been dropped on the floor by his nurse during his infancy.

THE MAYOR: . . . And as for your assessor . . . of course he is a man who understands his business, but he smells as though he has

just come out of a distillery—that's not quite proper either. I meant
to speak about it long ago, but my attention was always diverted by
something else, I don't know what. Something can be done for it if,
as he says, it is his natural smell; he might be advised to try onion or
garlic or something. Christian Ivanovich might give him some drug
for it.

AMMOS FIODOROVICH: No, there is nothing you can do for it: he
says his nurse dropped him as a baby and he has smelled a little of
vodka ever since.[26]

By the farthest stretch of the imagination, these two events
remain unrelated. Still, one may wonder whether the sociology of
alcoholism in our time has advanced much beyond positing this
sort of absurd conjecture, which at least has the merit of professing witty ignorance. In this light Gogol's memorable *bon mot*
represents a highly stylized expression of Fate concealed behind
a mask of incredulous laughter. The Mayor, at any rate, accepts
this explanation with the comment that there is nothing to be
done about it anyway. It is worth noting in this connection that
the virtual absence of all plausibility in an explanation is as rare
a phenomenon as conclusive certainty. Chichikov's attribution of
his backache to the sedentary mode of life, although almost
equally preposterous coming from a man who never sits still, at
least has the merit of psycnosomatic suggestiveness. His self-
diagnosis lends itself to ceremonial small-talk, whereas Ammos
Fiodorovich's account commands definitive silence.

A more plausible example of pseudo-explanation is the derivation of Akakiy Akakievich's surname in "The Overcoat."

This clerk's surname was Bashmachkin. From the very name it is
clear that it must have been derived from a shoe (bashmak); but
when and under what circumstances it was derived from a shoe, it
is impossible to say. Both his father and his grandfather and even
his brother-in-law, and all the Bashmachkins without exception wore
boots, which they simply resoled two or three times a year.[27]

Having declared the impossibility of determining the exact derivation of Akakiy Akakievich's surname, Gogol proceeds to confuse
the issue by introducing extraneous data which have no bearing
on the question. The name Bashmachkin implies that some
ancestor of Akakiy Akakievich was a shoemaker. The footwear

of his relatives has no connection with either the occupations of Bashmachkin's ancestors or the derivation of his surname. Thus the juxtaposition of these two sentences, one perfectly reasonable and the other completely irrelevant, establishes a pseudo-logical link between them which the reader finds difficult to sever.

Similarly uncompelling but faintly plausible is Manilov's *non sequitur* on the health-giving powers of pipe smoking.

... they say that pipe-smoking gives one asthma.

Allow me to inform you that that is a prejudice. I even believe that to smoke a pipe is far healthier than to snuff tobacco. We had a lieutenant in our regiment who never let a pipe out of his mouth, not only at table but even, if I may be allowed to say it, in all other places. And now he's forty and over but, God be thanked, he's in such good health that it couldn't be better.[28]

Manilov's imputation that the lieutenant's ripe and hearty middle age is due to his constant smoking is manifestly unsupported by sufficient evidence. A negative correlation between indulgence in tobacco and the preservation of health, moreover, makes a good deal of sense today. Manilov's judgment that smoking a pipe is far healthier than snuffing tobacco endows his broader generalization with the additional thrust of a subtle comparison. To be sure, he fails to demonstrate his point, if only by not taking into account the multiplicity of pertinent variables affecting the situation, but he does go through the motions of presenting an argument, however specious and ultimately unconvincing. Nor, it is worth keeping in mind, is the possibility ruled out by his failure to establish it as compelling, that pipe smoking may, under certain circumstances, have beneficial health effects as in the case of a particular individual such as the lieutenant. In our own sophisticated time it has often been asserted that the late Sir Winston Churchill's robust constitution was favorably influenced in its longevity both by his daily intake of Scotch whisky and by his enormous consumption of cigars. Summing up the whole complicated business, Chichikov's acceptance of the "inexplicable" may be as close an approximation to the truth as anyone has been able to achieve.

In Gogol's characterization of Ivan Ivanovich as "an excellent man," a phrase repeated three times, there is a striking incon-

gruity between the assertion of moral irreproachability and the
failure to mention a single character trait corroborating it.[29]
Instead, we are treated to a lyrical passage stressing, irrelevantly,
Ivan Ivanovich's house and its surroundings, his way of eating
melons, and the way other people regard his mode of life. Not a
single concrete instance of his supposed excellence is given. These
good moral qualities dangle whimsically, as it were, from Ivan's
luscious fruit trees and other precious possessions. By playing
upon the widespread confusion of conventional rhetoric (what
Heidegger calls *Das Man*, the voice of the mob) with authentic
moral discrimination, Gogol unmasks the emptiness of worldly
success vis-à-vis a true estimate of human integrity. From the
prevailing point of view in most societies the association of Ivan's
prosperity with his being a quite remarkable fellow is indisputably
plausible.

Unlike Ivan Ivanovich, the hero of "The Diary of a Madman"
completely loses touch with reality. Once Poprishchin sees himself
as the King of Spain, no shred of contradictory evidence is allowed to undermine this fantastic redefinition of his role in life.

> Spain is a strange land! When we went into the first room I saw a
> number of people with shaven heads. I guessed at once that these
> were either grandees or soldiers because they do shave their heads. I
> thought the behaviour of the High Chancellor, who led me by the
> hand, extremely strange. He thrust me into a little room and said:
> "Sit there, and if you persist in calling yourself King Ferdinand,
> I'll knock the inclination out of you." But knowing that this was only
> to try me I answered in the negative, whereupon the Chancellor hit
> me twice on the back with a stick, and it hurt so that I almost cried
> out, but I restrained myself remembering that this is the custom of
> chivalry on receiving any exalted dignity, for customs of chivalry per-
> sist in Spain to this day.[30]

Drawn with striking precision from false premises, his conclusions
are as formally valid as they are empirically false. Probably the
climax of this discrepancy between having lost touch with reality
and thinking coherently in terms of his new *Lebenswelt* occurs
when he interprets the painful blow administered by the keeper
as an initiation into an esoteric order of knighthood. Gogol's insight into the interpenetration of insanity and lucidity would not
be lost on the historian of enlightened Western civilization in its

recent phases. While Hitler was riding the crest of glory, even the minority of more decent Germans still in Germany sometimes asked themselves whether it might not be they who were going out of their minds. The compellingness with which madmen have advanced their arguments has not infrequently had a dazzling effect on men with less certain notions about ends and means.

The madness unleashed by Stalin on Gogol's countrymen had all the marks of the great writer's understanding of the Absurd. Trumped-up accusations, great show trials, formalized confessions explaining nothing—all these manipulated by a vast bureaucracy of terrified officials and sycophants. The setting of these activities is one or another Five-Year Plan, presumably implementing the perfectibility of man and society. A veneer of normal growth and production often lends an air of total unreality to the plots with which the victims are charged. So violent have been the distortions of reason that even those who risked their lives in making the Revolution are no longer immune from extermination. For all his clairvoyance about the absurdities of life in general and of Russia in particular, Gogol loved both too much to envisage the unrelieved terror of Stalin's utopia. Yet, among the lesser absurdities of our century, he, to use Alexander Blok's telling phrase, might well have laughed through tears over the following incident: in her memoir *Hope Against Hope*, Nadezhda Mandelstam, relates how her husband, the famous poet Osip Mandelstam, was interrogated in the Lubianka by a specialist in literary matters and personalities. His patronymic "Christoforovich" was identical with that of the head of Nicholas I's Third Section.

CHAPTER 2

Dostoevsky and the Intellectuals

"To know the good is to do the good."

SOCRATES

"Man is a crook; and a crook is he who says so."

Crime and Punishment

Introduction

EVEN IF HE WAS NOT the first intellectual, Socrates (and the Socratic paradoxes) marks a watershed in defining this hazardous calling. His dialectical hairsplitting, his excoriation of the Establishment of his day, and his belief in the examined life as the only one worth living became staples of intellectual respectability. Most important, Socrates set out to solve the insoluble problems of existence by subjecting them to rational analysis.

Not all philosophers are intellectuals, many of them being interested solely in narrowly technical questions, and the converse of this is equally true. Many intellectuals plunge into action without having given sufficient thought to their reasons for so doing. While Nietzsche and Kierkegaard had little use for the Socratic mission to save mankind from ignorance by argument alone, as Existentialists they could not help but admire the manner in which he carried out this task, not least for personally exposing himself to the risks implicit in his mission. He, at any rate, cannot be accused of failing to implement in decisive action what he stood for as a thinker, whereas subsequent intellectuals have too often come to grief over this challenge of "duplication."[1]

What intellectuals have in common besides a generalized love for the life of the mind is a tremendous capacity for self-laceration. Hence one finds in their careers certain recurring patterns of inconsistency, in addition to those contradictions which man as such is apt to exhibit. Socrates himself could never bridge the gap between the tragic sense of life as revealed in the dramas of Aeschylus and Sophocles and his own, often seemingly uncircumscribed confidence in the power of reason to overcome every exigency and contingency. On the other hand, such critics as Nietzsche, Kierkegaard, Bergson, and William James all too frequently concealed their own intellectuality from themselves when launching their polemics against the primacy of intellect as seminally embodied in the Socratic tradition. The miracle of Socrates the intellectual was a rare combination of self-scrutiny with conceptual rigor. By putting himself on the line against the tyranny of counterfeit conventions in morality and religion, he dramatized the dilemmas of intellectuality. Time and again, in the history of Western civilization at least, intellectuals have assumed the Socratic burden of balancing the dictates of clarity and precision with the requirements of sincerity and faith.

Any plausible generalization about intellectuals will call attention to their perennial contempt for Philistines and fools. Whether Marxist or *Action Française*, Socratic or Nietzschean, Hamlet-like or Trotskyite, the intellectual seems inexorably condemned to separation if not isolation from the run of ordinary men. This dichotomy takes on tragic proportions when he professes to be the spokesman for suffering humanity at large.[2] The most sophisticated ideology cannot gloss over the fact that the majority of men have no inclination for critical thinking, an activity at which the intellectual excels, irrespective of his specific vision of humanity. In this Socratic sense of privileged understanding, the intellectual perforce cuts himself off from the majority in the very process of articulating their resentments and grievances against society. Marx could not bring himself to admit openly that a reflective capitalist could understand him better than the exploited proletarian whose chains Marx was determined to break.

In brief, whatever their ideological differences, intellectuals are united as a group by virtue of their groping for truth.

Not surprisingly, and not unjustly, intellectuals have been repeatedly attacked for their condescension toward the unreflective and for their arrogant aloofness from the miseries of other mortals. The tension between involvement and discernment reaches a breaking point when intellectuals blame themselves for not "going out to the people" in the correct spirit of sympathetic identification with their aspirations. Refined theoretical distinctions between force and violence formulated by intellectuals *engagés* in their studies are apt to lose their persuasiveness in the face of riots and demonstrations.

Most men act conventionally, even in reacting against conventions, whereas the *bona fide* intellectual will test the authenticity of the conventional as such. Almost invariably he will be misunderstood by most of his contemporaries. If he retreats from the world, he betrays his vocation as a reformer; if, on the other hand, he joins its battles without exercising his vaunted powers of dispassionate analysis, he invites a fateful suspension of conviction.

The gulf dividing the intellectual from persons unskilled in autonomous thinking bears directly on a host of related problems about his character and usefulness. It has been argued, for example, that his unqualified allegiance to theorizing often goes hand in hand with an insensitivity—bordering on cruelty—to the suffering of individuals. From a purely intellectual point of view, imperfection of any sort is unforgivable; this is an attitude implying a basic lack of compassion. It is precisely the dreams of radical utopians which allow virtually no loopholes for the frailty of men. Along the same lines runs the intellectual's insistence on order and control, so strikingly at odds with man's untidy habits. History shows that the intellectual's exaggerated faith in persuasion is all too frequently superseded by violent eruptions beyond the scope of self-conscious planning and that some of mankind's noblest goals are attained independently of any dialectical interplay of ends and means. It is illuminating to recall here the condemned Socrates, mercilessly mocking the joys and pleasures of temporal existence, and Lenin's bitter hostility toward all deviationists, however courageously they had fought at his side before the Revolution. A good deal of evidence suggests that intellectuality, threatened by the contradictions of reality, exhibits a dogmatic stance no less terrible in its contempt for human weakness than the willful denial of existential truth in the face of what William James called "the sentiment of rationality."[3]

The occasional commensurability of logic with life has no doubt had a spellbinding effect on the intellectual, in making him underestimate the role of the fortuitous and of passion in each human endeavor. His ambition to remake the world into an earthly paradise is apt to obscure the difficulties of changing himself. If the unexamined life is not worth living, the examined life offers no foolproof happiness and virtue. This disturbing reflection lies at the heart of the intellectual's dilemma, in his efforts to confer upon humanitarian impulses the mantle of self-evident truths.

The modern intellectual, the subject of Dostoevsky's probing analysis, comprises a special problem. He shares with his predecessors a critical perspective predicated on the detachment of consciousness from the everyday world. However, his status after the French Revolution undergoes important changes. On the one hand, it becomes strengthened through the great political upheavals which he helped to prepare by justifying and disseminating the ideological principles on which they rest. In marked contrast to Socrates' struggles, the *philosophes*, for a few decades at any rate, could count on a favorable *Zeitgeist* to support their cries for reform of the prevailing Establishment. In other words, whereas the death of Socrates remained basically a personal triumph, the death of Voltaire was almost immediately accompanied by far-reaching changes in the whole structure of European society. Never again have intellectuals been so successful in translating their ideas into influential, widely accepted truths and public works of historical import. On the other hand, events soon revealed serious weaknesses in their armor, resulting in a crisis of confidence and inducing grave doubts, which are still unresolved. Goya's famous caricature of reason devouring her own children epitomizes the predicament of the intellectual after the Reign of Terror. It was one thing to unmask the evils of Versailles and to project a new order for an emancipated society, quite another to come to terms with the realities of the freedom from over-thrown authorities once it had been obtained. The assumption so dear to the *philosophes*, that the wave of the future was bound to be ameliorative and felicitous, simply did not pass the test of time and experience. Although this realization was not necessarily immediate, the torments and hesitations of Romantic poets and intellectuals in the first decades of the nineteenth century already expressed a more somber mood, not infrequently touching on despair. Once again Hamlet's question of whether it was worth-while to act at all imposed itself on a generation of intellectuals still very much under the shadow of unilateral progress through, to use the current phrase, radical demythologization on all fronts. Dostoevsky's disinherited intellectual was not merely a figment of his imagination nor, for that matter, a Russian oddity.

No doubt conditions in Russia were peculiar. Even in Prussia the legitimate existence of the intellectual had been grudgingly acknowledged, not to speak of the situation in England and France where, in spite of his ideological setbacks and occasional harassment, he had stored up considerable credit. But the Russian autocracy, seemingly invulnerable to liberalizing reforms, barely tolerated critical thinking on any issue affecting society and the state. Though the libraries of its aristocrats were well stocked with the most revolutionary literature of the eighteenth century, only at their personal peril with the threat of exile or worse, could the ideas therein be openly discussed or taken seriously as potential instruments of influence and power. Catherine the Great had been an intellectual of sorts (a second-rate mind conversant with first-rate ideas), yet she made certain that her daring cor-respondence with the *philosophes* would not be misconstrued as an invitation to fundamental changes in the pervasive control she exercised over her subjects. Nevertheless, when all due allow-ances have been made for the differences between Western Europe and tsarist Russia, the problems of the intellectual in both were not really too dissimilar. Here as there his implicit atheism and explicit humanism gave serious offense to established tradition. By acting rashly he made a fool of himself and sub-verted his cause; by failing to act he betrayed his calling and showed himself a coward in his own eyes as well as in the eyes of those counting on him to relieve their misery. His ineffectuality should not necessarily be attributed to lapses of nerve. While intelligence is neither a substitute for, nor a guarantee of character, it is also true that the more critical a person's intelligence, the more alternatives he will entertain, and the more hesitant he will be to commit himself unilaterally to one of them. Too often intellectuals crave a life of action precisely because they can no longer bear the burden of carefully weighing conflicting goals, each in its own way partly appealing and partly repugnant. Conversely, the intellectual savors his alienation from the scene of unavoidable involvement insofar as he must coolly examine the evidence supporting or invalidating each hypothesis. Thus paralysis of effort on his part is not necessarily a consequence of acquiescence to the *status quo* or of self-indulgence. The contemplative life inseparably linked to intellectuality functions as a restraint on unbridled bursts of activity.

An illuminating analysis of the problems of the modern intellectual is given by Turgenev in his essay "Hamlet and Don Quixote." While seeing the literary intellectual under the spell of Hamlet's vacillations, he nevertheless prefers his own equivocal creation, the scientific nihilist Bazarov, whose dedication to action and reticence looms much larger in the end than the soliloquies of the tormented Dane.

Dostoevsky as Devil's Advocate

The existential critique of intellectuality is a dominant theme in Dostoevsky's fiction. While conventional criticism has called attention to his love of native soil, Christ, and tradition as against his contempt for the rational spirit of the Enlightenment, such a view fails to take into account Dostoevsky's tendency to doubt his own most cherished convictions and even to "soil his own nest" for the sake of sharpening the issues tormenting him and his heroes. In this respect much like Kierkegaard, who throughout his writings adduces reasons for not becoming a Christian, Dostoevsky had a special genius for playing off his second thoughts against his professions of faith.[4]

In considering the role of daemonic advocacy in Dostoevsky's work, one must make a distinction, of which Dostoevsky himself

was probably not unaware. On the one hand, as a person perennially divided against himself, Dostoevsky unselfconsciously
embodied the Pascalian maxim that "a hundred contradictions
can be true"; on the other, as a highly self-conscious artist, he
deliberately strengthened the position of his adversaries in the
very act of explicating his own. In other words, a fruitful
approach to the meaning of his fiction must reckon both with the
open-endedness of the various modes of life experienced by his
characters, colliding with one another in perpetual tension, and
with Dostoevsky's personal conflicts and unresolved questioning.
He took to the task of being the "devil's advocate" like fish to
water by virtue of his predisposition to suffer the dialectic of
opposites in his own psychic makeup. At the same time, as a
writer and psychologist of genius he was moved to represent the
ideological conflicts of interest and knowledge which, on numerous occasions, went against the grain of his longing for conclusive
certainty.

One may wonder how intellectuals like Dostoevsky, Kierkegaard, Nietzsche, Tolstoy, and other non-academic existentialists
can reconcile inconsistencies in their lives and thought with the
imperative demand of intellectuality for precision and lucidity.[5]
Only on the assumption that our conscious intentions may be
superseded by unconscious desires is it possible for a Dostoevsky
to play the part of a double agent in articulating the case of the
opposition with greater intensity and persuasiveness than the
thesis he is determined to demonstrate. By nature as well as by
circumstance he was singled out to dramatize contrariness for
generations of intellectuals, whose commitment to truth and justice was no less problematic than their hatred of cant and
institutionalized falsehood.

When a thinker changes his mind he contradicts himself only
insofar as he gives up one position on a subject for another, with
the latter conceivably entailing the negation of the former. For
Nietzsche, fools alone were impervious to such shifts of opinion
in a lifetime of experience and reflection. Since intellectuals as
well as philosophers are foolish at least part of the time, Nietzsche
did not find it at all surprising that an uncritical veneration of
consistency for its own sake was often made to serve as evidence
for intellectual respectability. Dostoevsky's conversion to Christianity during his exile in Siberia doubtless compromised his

radical past as a member of the Petrashevsky circle, though considered biographically it is not at all an unintelligible development. Whether or not this turning point in his life constitutes a betrayal of his primordial sympathy for "the insulted and the injured" remains problematic. Shestov, for his part, is inclined to argue that Dostoevsky, like his Underground Man, came to be more interested in a cup of tea than in the survival of the universe at large.[6] Should Shestov's analysis be only halfway correct, this would mean that the humane passages throughout Dostoevsky's middle- and late-period writings only serve as a kind of frosting on the cake to divert the reader from his explosively radical conclusions about the human condition which, in a curious paradoxical way, are far more radical than anything the young writer showed to Belinsky, who was enraptured over a new dimension of critical realism in *Poor Folk*.

The apparent contradiction in Dostoevsky's development from dissenting intellectual to defender of Orthodoxy should not obscure the unusual complexity of his nature, misjudged equally by friend and foe. One does not have to be sentenced to death and reprieved at the last moment, or suffer epileptic attacks, to become intimately acquainted with the strains and stresses of emotional turmoil. Dostoevsky, whose father was murdered by his peasants when the future author was a youth, experienced more than his share of crises. Even if he had been spared some of them, it seems likely that his psychological makeup would still have drawn him to the fascinating horror of human motives and moods in perennial conflict. The appeal of this spectacle of men at the same time loving and hating, admiring and envying, hoping and fearing was reinforced, as it were, by Dostoevsky's private experiences and by a seemingly inborn proclivity to react impetuously and tumultuously to everything. The justly celebrated observation in *The Brothers Karamazov* to the effect that a man setting out to emulate the Madonna ends up acting like Mephistopheles might well serve as an epitaph for Dostoevsky's own emotional double-mindedness. The inseparable greatness and misery of man as proclaimed by Pascal was not only the Russian novelist's special field of literary inquiry but also the cross he bore with remarkable courage in Siberia as well as in the gambling casinos of Baden-Baden.

Those critics who see considerable significance, usually of an ominous variety, in Dostoevsky's fideism bolster their case by seizing upon only the more obvious side of his development as a thinker. In point of fact, he professed hatred of the West while adoring Beethoven's piano sonatas and the Raphael Madonna in Dresden; he was a Christian who did not believe in God, or, at least, whose concept of Christ had as much in common with that of a Unitarian minister as with that alive in any more orthodox tradition of Christian belief; and he became a publicist whose hysterical and sententious pronouncements in his *Diary of a Writer* belied the open-endedness of his psychological genius as well as the unrelieved skepticism embodied in his fiction. Such contradictions do indeed cast a shadow on his single-mindedness, though an accusation of anti-intellectualism is still not necessarily in order. In *The Devils*, which contains his scurrilous attack on political radicals, he still manages to distinguish socialists from scoundrels and, what is more, to offer a convincing apology for the reasonableness of being civil, even though conventionality is essentially indefensible by reason. Two young radicals come to the momentous conclusion that the venerable Russian custom of serving tea should not hold for gatherings of revolutionaries, since it involves wasting too much time on the irrelevant. As Pascal had observed, no custom can stand the test of analysis better than any other custom. A genuine intellectual like Dostoevsky, by virtue of not committing the error of confusing logic with life, revitalizes this insight as he elevates tea drinking to a ceremonial gesture of congeniality beyond the scope of revolutionary reason and its utopian blueprints for human perfection.[7] The teenager in that scene in *The Devils* who becomes agitated about superfluous diversions from revolutionary politics is the modern irrationalist *par excellence*.

Shestov, probably the most existentially oriented critic of classical Russian fiction, argues persuasively that the reader should not confuse the lofty ideas and ideals of Dostoevsky, Tolstoy, and *mutatis mutandis*, of Nietzsche and Kierkegaard, with their revolutionary impact on European thought and literature.[8] So far as Dostoevsky is concerned, even today reputable critics like Robert Lord fail to distinguish his religious rhetoric from those underground ideas which represent his unique legacy.[9] Shestov rightly calls our attention to the anti-Christianity of Kierkegaard, the "human all too human" quality of Nietzsche's major writings so strikingly at odds with the oracular hysteria of Zarathustra and the myth of the Overman, and also, in the same connection, to Tolstoy's cruelty, which often makes a mockery of the very ideals (such as family happiness) he would seem to profess in *Anna Karenina* and elsewhere.

Like Dostoevsky, according to Shestov, these thinker-poets, however radical in their innermost thoughts and feelings, simply could not bring themselves, out of fear or whatever motive (not excluding an ambiguous relationship to their own break with the past), to give a consistent presentation to their reading public of what they meant to say. Far from casting any aspersions on their original genius, far from blaming them for occasional flirtations with consensus politics and religion, Shestov discerns their peculiar greatness in the advancement of ideas which their Victorian contemporaries, for example, enveloped in an impenetrable fog of complacency and pervasive dullness, could not even ape, much less develop on their own. Nonetheless, especially for the student of Dostoevsky's attitude toward the intellectuals, it becomes indispensable in the line of Shestov's critique to weed out what he calls "the babble of Alyosha" from the *Hintergedanken* of the Underground Man, Raskolnikov, Prince Myshkin, Kirilov, Shatov, Stavrogin, and Ivan Karamazov—to mention the major protagonists of Dostoevsky's vision of modern man's dread and homelessness.

It is within the framework of this Shestovian context that the approach to Dostoevsky and the intellectuals followed in this chapter should be understood. In brief, Dostoevsky played the devil's advocate in this fictional representation of intellectuals, first, because he was divided himself on the subject, and second, because he did not dare to expose his reading public to the full force of his nihilistic ruminations. To be sure, allowances must be made, as Shestov makes them himself, for changes in Dostoevsky's development from a pre-exilic author sympathetic to various radical causes to a post-exilic conservative thoroughly disillusioned, as Nietzsche and Kierkegaard had also become, with socialism, democracy, and the tyranny of the majority. At the same time Dostoevsky never ceased to feel compassion for the plight of the poor and harassed. But when all this is said and done, the overriding thrust of his fiction is a relentless questioning, so distinctively typical of radical Russian intellectuals in the nineteenth century and beyond, of every preconception in the vocabulary of uplifting talk and edifying action. Just as he discarded the inanities of the felicific calculus and the general welfare, Dostoevsky spared no oversimplification of human life including the Christian from his destructive pursuit of cant and commonplace wisdom.

Shestov is fond of dwelling on the previously mentioned notes from underground, according to which the whole world can go to blazes so long as the Underground Man is assured his cup of hot tea. The critic discerns in this shocking pronouncement a turning point in Dostoevsky's own career from a Dickensian lover of the humiliated *en masse* to a revolutionary realist on the incorrigibility of man. With all due allowances for Shestov's bias in advancing such an interpretation, it is not incompatible with an apocryphal incident attributed to the publisher Alexander Suvorin. While visiting Dostoevsky's apartment at the height of the terror against Alexander II, he asked Dostoevsky whether he would be prepared to turn in two suspicious-looking nihilists lurking on the streets nearby. In the spirit of the Underground Man, rather than that of Alyosha or Father Zosima, the author of *Crime and Punishment* replied no, giving as his reason that, his personal views notwithstanding, he would not care to be hounded by the liberal press for besmirching the name of the Russian intelligentsia.

Underground Man: The Intellectual as Voyeur

The classical philosophers of Greece were probably too sanguine in their then revolutionary belief that the liberating effects of the pursuit of knowledge would be unequivocally positive. The Socratic identity of knowledge and virtue, Aristotle's enthronement of curiosity, and Plato's notion of an elite of philosopher-kings immune to the baser impulses of our nature, reinforce each other as links in the same chain of privileged intellectual faculties. Without belittling the contribution of these giants to the development of civilization, one may with hindsight suggest, as Sophocles had already done in *Oedipus Rex*, that in certain situations the unexamined life is left well enough alone.

Dostoevsky's Underground Man paradigmatically exhibits the tensions of the intellectual as a daring voyeur; conquering new territory, setting straight his erring contemporaries yet at the same time revealing an archetypal failure on the part of a superior intellect in being unable to live in harmony with himself. In *Notes from Underground* Dostoevsky dramatizes the excessive burdens of an individual who asks more questions than his capacity for suffering allows. Not unlike the atheistic element in Job's faith is the Underground Man's relentless pursuit of enlightenment (beclouded in his case by an excess of malice).[10]

Had Dostoevsky wished to portray the Underground Man as utterly vile, he would scarcely have made him the mouthpiece of some of his own favorite ideas, such as the inviolability of individual experience threatened by the tyranny of statistical fact, the polarity of extreme self-consciousness and the capacity for action, and the right to rebel both against futurist chimeras and all-inclusive mandates of necessity. On the other hand, these insights into nineteenth-century reality, which permit the Underground Man to judge his contemporaries in the light of Dostoevsky's own concepts, do not enable him to extricate himself from his personal agony. Strangely echoing the life of Baudelaire is the Underground Man's irrepressible intelligence linked to a passion for immorality. His deliberate espousal of self-abasement, while making it possible for him to see through the Crystal Palace, never provides him with a vision of the stars. Like many intellectuals outside and inside the Establishment, he combines an obsessive preoccupation with himself with a clear-sighted grasp of world events which affect him only vicariously. A consequence of this is his incapacity to bridge the gap between sound clinical observation and self-referential appropriation. His perceptions of the agony of the world offer no relief for his private anguish. Similarly Karl Marx was offended by his fellow men while pinpointing their road to disaster in strikingly vivid terms. A marked affinity for the discernment of human weakness often goes hand in hand with a delight in cruel mockery.

Dostoevsky's hero, completely fed up with the conventional world of sanctimonious fools and calculating hypocrites, decides on a strategy of "internal emigration" to the Underground—a not wholly figurative expression for extreme loneliness. Instead of following the herd, he is guided by his own instincts for remaining himself. This self, to be sure, is sick and very much aware of the malady afflicting it. Thus Dostoevsky develops an intriguing image of the dissolving bourgeois ethos in nineteenth-century society as shrewdly observed by a distraught individualist in a total state of exile. From his slanted vantage point, the Underground Man nevertheless feels empowered to diagnose the ills of his age.

After all, to maintain even this theory of the regeneration of mankind by means of its own advantage, is, after all, to my mind almost the same thing as—as to claim, for instance, with Buckle, that through civilization mankind becomes softer, and consequently less bloodthirsty, and less fitted for warfare. Logically it does not seem to follow from his arguments. But man is so fond of systems and abstract deductions that he is ready to distort the truth intentionally, he is ready to deny what he can see and hear just to justify his logic. I take this example because it is the most glaring instance of it. Only look about you: blood is being spilled in streams, and in the merriest way, as though it were champagne. Take the whole of the nineteenth century in which Buckle lived. Take Napoleon—both the Great and the present one. Take North America—the eternal union. Take farcical Schleswig-Holstein. And what is it that civilization softens in us? Civilization only produces a greater variety of sensations in man—and absolutely nothing more. And through the development of this variety, man may even come to find enjoyment in bloodshed. After all, it has already happened to him. Have you noticed that the subtlest gentlemen, to whom the various Attilas and Stenka Razins could never hold a candle, and if they are not so conspicuous as the Attilas and Stenka Razins it is precisely because they are so often met with, are so ordinary and have become so familiar to us. In any case if civilization has not made man more bloodthirsty, it has at least made him more abominably, more loathsomely bloodthirsty than before. Formerly he saw justice in bloodshed and with his conscience at peace exterminated whomever he thought he should. And now while we consider bloodshed an abomination, we nevertheless engage in this abomination and even more than ever before. Which is worse? Decide that for yourselves.[11]

So far as his own sickness is concerned, it revolves around a hypersensitivity to real or imagined slights, compounded by the sort of thinking about oneself which never leads to action or choice but, as Kierkegaard analyzed it in *The Sickness unto Death*, to a growing despair (paradoxically tinged with joy) over one's own despair.[12] As he permits us to enter the labyrinthine realm of his internal contradictions and inconsistencies, of mixed feelings about everything, and of enormous resentment against the enigmatic turns of experience, we soon realize that here is a man who will under no conceivable conditions cure himself, his animadversions to the contrary merely augmenting his rudimentary spite. And yet we also learn to respect his honesty about his hounded self, his insistence on calling things by their right names, and his refusal to give lip service to any genteel tradition which might induce in him a complacent mood of innocence. If the Underground Man is inordinately harsh on the foibles of his age, he is no less unsparing in unmasking his particular frustrations and disguises. Precisely herein lies a significant part of his role as intellectual voyeur probing previously uncharted depths of malice and contrariness.

Lamenting what he wants, desiring what will give offense to him, humiliated by motions of gratitude or affection, the Underground Man brings into the open a dimension of true feeling. As he would insist himself, he is not a laboratory case but an individual (however nasty and eccentric), provocatively challenging the self-deception of his peers. But when he uses Liza as a live subject for his psychological experiments, his daring glimpses into the pit of human folly become irredeemably stained with a foul odor of betrayal and debasement. It is one thing to use oneself as a guinea pig for principled cruelty, another to manipulate a fellow human being whose sensibility is indisputably affronted by such action. The Underground Man provides a terrifying example of the martyr as scoundrel in a desperate diversion from the loneliness he requires to attain his goal of breaking through façades.

In his exploration of the unconscious, his investigations into the criminal personality, and his probings of the extremes of human experience, Dostoevsky himself was an intellectual voyeur in the positive sense of that calling. The dream sequences in *Crime and Punishment* undoubtedly served as a catalyst in the birth of depth psychology. At the same time, however, Dostoevsky, like his Underground Man, paid a heavy price for these insights into the twilight zones of the psyche. He did not, of course, become a clairvoyant scoundrel in the manner of his hero, but his dealings with Turgenev and many of his relationships with friends and fellow writers disclose a pattern of disingenuousness strikingly at odds with the irresistible authenticity of his fiction. It may be argued that his virulent anti-Semitism, his chauvinism, and his occasional outbursts of jealous frenzy called into question the lofty ideas permeating his work. On the other hand, the Dostoevskyan insinuation that intellectual voyeurs cannot be balanced personalities in which the respective demands of character and intelligence are predictably given their due may point to a truth as pertinent to certain aspects of his own life as to that of the Underground Man. Possibly a modern writer must have a streak of cruelty in himself in order to expose the cruelty of the world with relentless candor.

On this subject of Dostoevsky's split consciousness no more intellectually stimulating discussion might be cited than Joseph Frank's "Nihilism and *Notes from Underground*."[13] Frank contends that in the *Notes* Dostoevsky develops a kind of dialectical interplay between the idealism of the 1830s and '40s and the radicalism of the '60s and '70s: in other words, between the conflicting aspirations of Dostoevsky's own career as a writer. It is characteristic of Dostoevsky that neither one of these two strains is either whitewashed or utterly condemned. According to Frank, the Liza episode, while ridiculing the preposterous overtones of Romantic idealization so widespread among the first two generations of Russian intelligentsia, at the same time pays its due to a fundamental respect for human decency. Obversely, the Underground Man's dreadful observation that he is prepared to see the world end in fire and brimstone so long as he can enjoy his cup of tea goes hand in hand with dazzling insights into idealistic self-deception. I agree with Frank that in this brilliant parody Dostoevsky once and for all settled his score with his contemporaries both on the Right and the Left. More specifically: to puncture the illusions of nineteenth-century liberalism from the inside out proved a task beyond the high-minded but incredibly naïve reasonableness of J. S. Mill. Dostoevsky's insistence on man's proclivity to act against his enlightened self-concern remains the keenest counterargument to any gospel of humanitarianism as the catalyst of our salvation.

Stepan Verkhovensky: The Intellectual as Connoisseur

A memorable scene in *The Devils* shows Stepan Verkhovensky taking leave of his bourgeois comforts, for which he had had to pay such humiliating penalties, and striking out on Russia's infinite open road toward a dignified though miserable death far removed from his natural habitat. What a contrast between Gogol's troika at the end of *Dead Souls* hurtling toward the promised Russian scene of tomorrow and Stepan Verkhovensky on foot, dragging his tired frame away from his insufferable humiliations in the hope of finding a decent spot to rest and recover his strength—a futile hope, as it turns out.

Dostoevsky does not tell us whether Stepan Verkhovensky read or lectured on Schiller's *Aesthetic Education*, but there can be little question that this unfortunate retired professor, the kept man of Stavrogin's mother and the father of the nihilist, Peter Verkhovensky, was given to imbibing and regurgitating some of the German dramatist's ideas on the cultivation of beautiful souls. As a younger man he had written a poem, which, contrary to his misguided fears, aroused no interest on the part of the government, though it provided him locally with the reputation of a martyr. His exaggerated enjoyment of his literary achievement made him somewhat ridiculous in the eyes of his circle.

The elder Verkhovensky is an example of Kierkegaard's aesthetic intellectualism for which Dostoevsky, like Kierkegaard himself, had a good deal more sympathy than his satiric treatment of it might lead the reader to believe. Their recourse to caricature on this topic partially belies a deep-seated affection for this mode of understanding the world and the self. Not only were they most responsive to the charm and delights of aesthetic intellectualism, but in the very process of revealing its hazards and faults, they themselves indulged in its pleasures and, above all, ideologically favored some of its features in opposition to the spreading gospel of Utilitarianism.

Neither the daemonic masculinity of Don Giovanni nor the innocent sensual gratification of Papageno, two of Kierkegaard's mythical figures at the "aesthetic stage on life's way," quite fits Stepan Verkhovensky. It would also be far-fetched to speak of any resemblance with Dr. Faustus, except for their shared love of learning. More to the point would be an analogy with innumerable academicians who enjoy their glass of wine together with interminable talk about the enduring questions of mankind —men who would never accept an existence like that of Kierkegaard's anxiety-ridden individual. Stepan Verkhovensky is a genuinely cultured person, but what he cannot do is to make up his mind conclusively on any subject and to act firmly in accordance with such a decision. Although his heart is in the right place and his sympathies engaged in the broad issues of the day, whenever a crisis arises he vacillates until the matter is decided, so to speak, by its own momentum, or he retreats to his study where, over a bottle of wine, he talks the dilemma to death in congenial company. No doubt Stepan's personal circumstances, such as his emotional and financial dependence on Varvara Petrovna, play a role in shaping the unreality of his style of life, but anyone who is acquainted with universities can recognize in him an archetypal member of the community of scholars. The intellectual as an aficionado of high-mindedness and John Stuart Mill's "higher pleasures" easily finds himself transfixed by the disinterested pleasures of serene contemplation. As a result of such seduction,[14] he may find it impossible to negotiate the chasm between the mandates of the liberal imagination and the exigencies of life.

It is a common characteristic of intellectual aesthetes to profess a liking for things which make no existential difference to them; to cultivate preciosity as a substitute for precision; and to ask too many questions which have already been answered or to which the answer will prove resoundingly inconsequential. In Stepan Verkhovensky's case, his natural attraction to erudite, high-sounding phrases has been accentuated by his lack of success in building a career for himself. All the efforts of his formidable patroness are inadequate to bring him once again to the forefront of public attention he had held for a short interval as a young aspiring lecturer on history and literature at the university.

The loosely defined narrator in *The Devils*, who enjoys the confidence of a large assortment of townspeople, also introduces us to the sufferings and tribulations of the ridiculous Stepan. There are, on the one hand, his pretentious use of French, his chronic indecisiveness, and his unceasing complaints about the unchangeable. However, on the other, there are his undeniable intelligence and good taste, his capacity for renunciation, triumphantly vindicated by his tragic finale, and, in spite of his overall weakness and lack of diligence, his fundamental decency. He plays the fool too much, but he is neither stupid nor wicked. That such a *Schöngeistler* should become the tutor of Nicholas Stavrogin and the father of Peter Verkhovensky is one of Dostoevsky's master strokes of characterization.

While Dostoevsky obviously takes delight in exploiting this irony for his own ideological purposes, it remains too often overlooked that Stepan Verkhovensky voices ideas and sentiments in surprising agreement with the author's. In the spread of utilitarian doctrine, which he has the courage to attack in front of a hostile audience, Stepan Verkhovensky discerns possibilities for human debasement tragically realized in the Soviet Union in the wake of the Bolshevik Revolution.

"And I maintain," Mr. Verkhovensky squealed, beside himself with excitement, "and I maintain that Shakespeare and Raphael are higher than the emancipation of the serfs, higher than nationalism, higher than socialism, higher than the younger generation, higher than chemistry, higher even than almost all humanity, for they are the fruit of all mankind, and perhaps the highest fruition that can possibly exist. A form of beauty already attained, but for the attaining of which I should perhaps not consent to live. Oh Lord," he cried, throwing up his hands, "ten years ago I said the same thing from the platform in Petersburg, in exactly the same words, and they did not understand it in exactly the same way, they laughed and booed as now; you little men, what is it you lack still, that you don't understand? Why, do you realize, do you realize that mankind can get along without the Englishman, without Germany, too, and most certainly without the Russians—it can get along without science, without bread, but without beauty it cannot carry on, for then there will be nothing more to do in the world! The whole mystery is there, the whole of history is there! Even science could not exist a moment without beauty—do you know that, you who are laughing at me? It will sink into dark ignorance—you won't invent a nail even! I shan't give in!" he shouted idiotically in conclusion, and banged his fist on the table with all his might.[15]

If boots be more important than Shakespeare and if, moreover, the enjoyment of Shakespeare must pass the test of social use-

fulness, the functionaries sooner or later will elevate themselves
to judges of aesthetic taste. Thus the radical intelligentsia destroys
the intellectual elite. Everything is subordinated to pragmatic
usefulness as defined by ideological zeal. Throughout his career
as a polemicist, Dostoevsky, like Stepan Verkhovensky, affirmed
the autonomy of artistic creation against the social-political
fanaticism of Chernyshevsky and his "new men."[16]

This, in brief, is the background of Stepan Verkhovensky's
unsuspected heroism. Browbeaten, often uncomprehending, deficient in single-mindedness, much of the time intellectually mud-
dle-headed, aesthetically self-indulgent, Stepan, nevertheless, in
the greatest crisis of his life, sticks to his guns and lives the
proposition that freedom is not the sole prerogative of embattled
radicals. If he himself is too much of a dabbler, his adversaries
are worse off by not even being in a position to lose confidence
in what escaped them from the beginning. Stepan, at least, knows
Shakespeare's enchantment, though his own boots may have to
be tied for him by a servant.

Dostoevsky's ambivalent attitude toward Stepan Verkhovensky—now affectionately chiding him for his ridiculous dreams,
his impracticality, and his addiction to creature comforts, now
praising him for his dignified deportment under extreme stress,
his dedication to Beauty, and his steadfast character only super-
ficially compromised by parasitic impulses—is a reflection of the
author's own outlook. In marked contrast on this issue to Kierkegaard, who, following his conversion, postulated an exclusive
disjunction between the aesthetic and the ethical-religious as
understood in Christian terms, Dostoevsky remained loyal to his
youthful ideal of Eternal Beauty, however distorted by professional aesthetes posing as dependable guides to the life of the
Spirit.[17] Born into the golden generation of the Russian intelligentsia, Dostoevsky grew up on a diet of Schiller, whose dramas,
particularly *The Robbers*, had lasting influence on his mind. Martin Malia has thoroughly explored the pervasive fascination which
this major German poet held for the outstanding Russian writers
and publicists of the thirties and forties. Suffice it to remark here
that the heady mixture of Kantian deontological ethics and
Romantic excitability and grandeur interweaving in his best work
provided adequate justification for the pursuit of literature in
perilous times. From Gogol's "Overcoat," which he is reputed to

have read more than a hundred times, Dostoevsky derived his understanding of literature *engagé*—a mandate not to refine the suffering of human beings into rarefied images sharply detached from the felt experiences of everyday existence. At the same time, prodded by his anti-utilitarianism and by his devotion to Schiller, Dostoevsky resisted the temptation of using literature as a mere tool of propaganda. He saw no Kierkegaardian chasm between being a man of letters and a man of the spirit.

Ivan Karamazov: The Intellectual as Unbeliever

The garrulous Stepan Verkhovensky fighting the Philistines of his day and the monologic Underground Man in his battle against uncritical optimism have in common a spirit of opposition to popular idols, characteristic of most intellectuals in modern times and certainly shared by their creator, even as he made his peace with the state. Not unlike Ivan Karamazov, perhaps the keenest devil's advocate in Dostoevsky's impressive catalogue of Pyrrhic villains, Dostoevsky himself could never accept fully the political and religious ideals of Orthodoxy, much as he tried in his non-fiction to acclaim the virtues of inherited legacies. Ominous as the link between socialism and atheism may have appeared at times to the author of "The Legend of the Grand Inquisitor," the sustained critique of theodicy which runs through his works, from *Notes from the House of the Dead* to "The Dream of a Ridiculous Man" and, of course, through *The Brothers Karamazov*, bewilders the faithful and comforts the godless. If Hume,[18] in the *Dialogues Concerning Natural Religion*, is as much Demea as Philo, by the same token, Dostoevsky's sympathies for Ivan Karamazov are just as pronounced as his respect for Zosima and Alyosha.[19] In both cases there is an unexpected conjunction of extreme skepticism and faith. Possibly a key to this spiritual overlap is given in a recent work by the eminent philosopher Ernst Bloch. In his book entitled *Atheismus im Christentum* (Frankfurt am Main, 1968) he traces certain organic interconnections between orthodox theism and its seeming antithesis, atheism. He maintains that belief and doubt, far from being mutually exclusive, have often been consonant in the Judaic-Christian religious consciousness. This insight is substantiated by his root metaphor of Christ on the Cross beseeching God to let Him know why He was forsaken or, in the Old Testament, by the example of Jehovah praising Job for not having listened to the consolations of his friends—persuasive advocates of Divine Providence. Such an interpretation of religious truth in inseparable conflict with knowing skepticism seems particularly germane to the spiritual tribulations of Ivan Karamazov.

Just prior to recounting "The Legend of the Grand Inquisitor," a chromatic fantasy and fugue in the Russian manner on the theme of double betrayal, Ivan speaks to Alyosha of one of Dostoevsky's obsessive motifs—the suffering endured by children. Ivan claims not to understand how, in a world presided over by a Supreme Intelligence, children can become the victims of deliberate outrages. To be sure, the argument from design has always broken down for non-believers, but whatever cogency it may possess is thoroughly undermined by acts of senseless cruelty.[20] It is in the context of relating the death of a small boy torn to pieces by wild dogs in front of his mother that Ivan makes his famous offer to return his ticket to the source of all our "blessings."

"I don't want harmony. From love for humanity I don't want it. I would rather be left with the unavenged suffering. I would rather remain with my unavenged suffering and unsatisfied indignation, *even if I were wrong.* Besides, too high a price is asked for harmony; it's beyond our means to pay so much to enter on it. And so I hasten to give back my entrance ticket, and if I am an honest man I am bound to give it back as soon as possible. And that I am doing. It's not God that I don't accept, Alyosha, only I most respectfully return Him the ticket."[21]

Granted that systematic theologians may succeed in their own eyes in reconciling the presence of God with every conceivable horror of existence, Ivan, without explicitly denying a Creator, rejects any such sophistry—espousing instead the "permanent possibility" of existential rebellion regarding this issue.[22] Alyosha, as is usual in these controversies with his brother, fails to come up with a compelling counter-argument, save to affirm, rather platitudinously, the regenerative sap of life. Thus the Russian Voltaire, as Dostoevsky called himself on occasion, formulates the prelude to Ivan Karamazov's version of one of the travesties of Western Christendom, the Inquisition.

Ivan's brother listens spellbound to the description of events in Seville during the Inquisition, excitedly prodding his blasphemous narrator to tell more and to tell it more rapidly. This undisguised desire on Alyosha's part for Ivan to divulge the most destructive evidence against the good faith of the Roman ecclesiastical Establishment, which for all its singularity also bore considerable resemblance to the Russian Orthodox Church, and, beyond that, to invite criticism of Christ Himself, supports the suspicion that Dostoevsky was playing with fire when he created his parable of the "double-cross" at the heart of Christian claims to a monopoly on purity and truth. To say the least: Dostoevsky's Alyosha "listened with the third ear" to Ivan's flow of subversive musings.

The Grand Inquisitor has convincing reasons on his side. His opposition to demythologization, individual responsibility, and the suspension of the miraculous probably meets with the approval of the majority of men past and present.[23] A Kierkegaard, another Christian intellectual *manqué*, could appreciate the depths of the offense of Christ hiding His power from the masses and hence forcing them to rely on "evidence unseen" for their "leap of faith," but the vast number of baptized Christians would lose their faith in a flash without some promise of stones being turned into bread, of God taking the side of whatever armed might backs their cause in the world, and of the miraculous superimposing itself in some manner on the harshness of actuality. The Inquisitor is historically right in insisting that the awesome burdens of the Christian religion cannot be borne in their naked relentlessness by frail, sinful, mortal flesh. As Plato had already observed in his *Republic*, the wisest rulers in the world must resort to "noble lies" in properly governing their subjects. The frightening cynicism of the Grand Inquisitor manifests itself in the contrast between the robes of his office and the Person he claims to represent on earth through his Church. On the other hand, the "shock of recognition" induced by a churchman as *Realpolitiker* may itself be a symptom of overintellectuality. Why, for instance, should Kierkegaard have been so appalled by the obvious fact that only a few Christians at any time, not merely in the nineteenth century, sought martyrdom rather than relief and comfort? Christ's Christianity, beautifully expounded by the Inquisitor, has but rarely had an irresistible appeal. Were Christians to be given their dreadful freedom *en masse*, in accordance with Christ's injunctions, the chances are that Christianity would soon vanish.

The final vindication of Christ in "The Legend of the Grand Inquisitor" is no more convincing than the final vindication of Jehovah in the Book of Job. Obedience to impossible imperatives is just as ahistorical as the restoration to an old man of his health, his family, and his possessions—not least because he is no longer young enough to enjoy them as he did before. Perhaps the most legendary implication of the "Legend" is the supposition that the Church would not rearrest Christ within a day of his release from prison. It is one thing for the Grand Inquisitor as a human being to be shaken by Christ's kiss, quite another for any high official of the Church to contemplate in the long run the triumph of individual freedom over institutional charity.

Ivan Karamazov is the indisputable hero of *The Brothers Karamazov*. It is he who raises the awkward questions that no one answers; it is through him that Dostoevsky recounts the tale which signifies more than any other that is related in the book, with the possible exception of Ivan's encounter with the Devil; and it is he who gives the lie to any simplistic theistic response to the human predicament. This is not to minimize Ivan's personal tragedy. Like Raskolnikov he is driven to the edge of total despair, and like Stavrogin he might choose to commit suicide. The unresolved conflicts in the novel seem to bear out Shestov's contention that Dostoevsky, for all his talk about loving humanity and Christ, identified most closely with the spiritual nonconformist of his narrative. In any event, like the Underground Man, Ivan Karamazov dramatizes most persuasively our modern predicament of abandonment and alienation. While Dimitri goes off to Siberia to do penance, and while Alyosha speaks endlessly of the virtues of Christian compassion, Ivan remains faithful to his father in confronting reality with rebellious passion and skepticism. In this regard Ivan Karamazov has much in common with his creator.

The Devils: *The Intellectual as Revolutionary*

The socialist dream which Dostoevsky discarded during his exile in Siberia would, if realized, have made the likes of him superfluous. In its conception of the radically transformed society, the activist intelligentsia did not envisage the prospect of individuals in rebellion against the future *status quo*. In line with the teachings of Utopian socialists, post-tsarist Russia was to be a technological paradise, freed from the manipulations of unjust exploiters, as well as from the private broodings of disaffected intellectuals. Dostoevsky, who believed that spiritual suffering was not solely a by-product of poor social engineering, repudiated any notion to the effect that if the best thinking in its entirety at a particular stage of human development were taken into account and implemented, the collective sanity of mankind would thereby be assured.

Herzen and Bakunin, who like Dostoevsky belonged to the idealistic generation of the intelligentsia, in varying degrees shared his skepticism in regard to the possibility of viewing all human problems merely as social issues. These exceptional men deplored the extremes of Russian backwardness as much as any of their Marxist successors. Nevertheless, while suffering exile and persecution for their efforts to bring about sweeping reform, even if this required recourse to violence, they were not taken in by the platitudes of sociologism, a disease which afflicted later generations of intellectual revolutionaries. To be sure, they entertained woolly ideas of their own, like Herzen's idealization of the peasant commune and Bakunin's infatuation with creative destructiveness as a method of bringing about constructive novelty, but the overriding objective of their political radicalism, after all due allowances for the differences between them have been made, was to liberate every future fellow Russian from the overseer mentality not only of the tsar but of all despots, Grand Inquisitors, sadistic and greedy landowners, corrupt parliamentary politicians, and other such authoritarian personalities.[24] It is safe to conjecture that Dostoevsky preserved a lifelong sympathy for the Russian intelligentsia in its attempts to assuage or eliminate arbitary force in human affairs. On the other hand, he rebuffed the nihilistic schemes of the radicals of the late sixties and seventies. These self-styled elitists of the people, Dostoevsky felt, would sooner, rather than later, sacrifice their innate idealism for the delights of manipulation and skulduggery. (They hated Turgenev's characterization of Bazarov for what they felt to be its undue emphasis on his idiosyncrasies, which diluted his revolutionary zeal.)[25] Still and all, the radical intelligentsia in *The Devils* taken collectively, for all the terrible faults attributed to it by the author, is rich precisely in those irrepressible eccentricities which distinguish a human being from a mere party member. Clearly Dostoevsky committed many an injustice in grappling with his themes. However, the psychological novelist in him would not consistently defer to the engaged polemicist when it came to conceiving the major characters in this powerful novel. And so, once again, Shatov, Kirilov, Stavrogin, and Peter Verkhovensky confront us as revolutionary intellectuals—not merely as archetypal embodiments of evil but as complex individuals in whom the conflicting motives and aims of strident political action permit no end to ideology or personal skepticism. Where the intellectual as revolutionary does fail for Dostoevsky is in his blindness to the consequences of his actions, both for himself and for those he seeks to redeem from themselves. This discrepancy between ideal and reality in the pursuit of the millennium is the focal point of Dostoevsky's literary treatment of the third generation of the Russian intelligentsia.

Imagine an academic administrator holding a reception for new members of the faculty at one of America's prestigious institutions of higher learning. This particular administrator is famous not least for his reiterated remark that no one can pull him by the nose—an awe-inspiring profession of power. Suddenly, in the midst of the stiff, gossipy gaiety so typical of these functions, Professor Nicholas Stavrogin, recently returned from his sixth trip to Russia in four years, casually walks up to the said administrator and pulls him around the room by the nose. Having made his existential point, Professor Stavrogin proceeds to take his leave, while the learned faculty and their wives revel in feelings of self-congratulatory outrage. On the following day Stavrogin is called on the carpet by the provost in charge of academic affairs, an old Menshevik who has always had a special place in his heart for him. He tells Stavrogin that all he needs to do to assuage the offended administrator and the other guests is to take another leave of absence to Russia and to send a note of apology to his insulted colleague. But, once again, unexpectedly, Professor Stavrogin walks up to the provost and bites off a piece of his ear. He is dismissed on the spot for moral turpitude. After a week or so under the care of the university physician, he is on his way to Minsk. Thus, transposed to the present age, Dostoevsky introduces us to his charismatic revolutionary.

Stavrogin, the Anti-Christ figure of Dostoevsky's demythologized parable of Christ driving out the devils from the possessed man into the pigs, radiates irresistible charm by virtue of an uncanny fusion of unapproachability and passionate presence. His criminal impulses and amorous adventures interfere with his competence as the leader of the revolutionary group. Yet, by a freakish coincidence, they endow him with human traits which the dedicated radicals in history seem to have lost entirely in the course of their indoctrination into party discipline. Stavrogin yawns while the young nihilists talk the wave of the future to death; he is bored to distraction not only by Peter Verkhovensky's fanatic adulation of him as the great leader of tomorrow but by most conversations which endow destructive fervor with moral righteousness. He is quite capable of cracking jokes about the use of umbrellas in human affairs—a far cry from a doctrinaire ideologist taking the latest interpretation of Marxism with unrelieved seriousness. When Stavrogin visits Switzerland he thinks of other matters besides exploring and undermining the structure of Russian autocracy.[26]

If one grants Stavrogin's monstrous personality, there remains the puzzle of Shatov, who considers himself Stavrogin's disciple and voices a number of his ideas. Shatov, as well as Peter Verkhovensky, is somewhat unnerved by Stavrogin's inclination to disavow responsibility for disseminating these notions. Indeed, herein may lie the clue to Stavrogin's failure to be a successful revolutionary: his ironic vacillations, no less than his private indiscretions, do not exactly reinforce the kind of blind obedience necessary for carrying out a revolution. Whatever charges may be leveled against Stavrogin, he cannot be accused of encouraging cliquish applause. His mocking despair saves him from the *hubris* of the commissar, even as it drives him to suicide. His sense of the ludicrous is too strong to permit him to occupy himself exclusively with radical politics. Many intellectuals similarly deficient in single- or simple-mindedness, without Stavrogin's burden of personal guilt, have likewise found it impossible to play God to the masses without introducing diversionary interludes into their acts. These distractions, at any rate, break the spell of total surrender to The Cause.

Peter Verkhovensky, Stavrogin's leading lieutenant, is very different from his master. An instinctive activist, he does not allow himself to be deflected from the goals of the revolutionaries by any scruples, selfish in the narrow sense or intellectual. The Revolution and its wide ramifications absorb his every waking hour. The gift of ruthlessness he brings to its fulfillment does him credit in his chosen role, though on the surface, at any rate, it appears to accentuate a streak of vulgarity in his makeup quite alien to his spiritual benefactor, Stavrogin. It is worth noting in this connection how skillfully Dostoevsky suggests the contrast between Stavrogin's intermittent adherence to a code of "civilized" behavior and Verkhovensky's undeviating brutality in his relationships with others. The latter speaks to his father as if he were little more than a stupid nuisance, whereas Stavrogin, though a psychopath, for the most part displays or dissimulates some respect for his mother's feelings of shock and concern over his eccentric conduct, and in general maintains a respectful distance from the professional anti-manners of embattled radicals working under him. Nevertheless it is through Verkhovensky that Dostoevsky voices his justly famous prophecy of a perverted "age of the masses."[27] While Stavrogin listens aghast, Verkhovensky expounds to him his theory of a great man coming out of hiding to impose a regime of terror on his self-deceived subjects, the like of which it would be hard to match with any historical precedent. According to Verkhovensky, the whole point is to let the masses have the illusion of becoming politically emancipated in the process of restoring a new elitism more terrible than the older varieties by virtue of its apparent popular consent. It is in this context that Verkhovensky outlines the daemonic transition from absolute freedom to total tyranny.[28]

"We shall proclaim destruction—why? why?—well, because the idea is so fascinating! But—we must get a little exercise. We'll have a few fires—we'll spread a few legends. Every mangy little group will be useful. I shall find you such keen fellows in each of these groups that they'll be glad to do some shooting and will be grateful for the honour. Very well, then, so an upheaval will start. There's going to be such a to-do as the world has never seen. Russia will become shrouded in a fog, the earth will weep for its old gods. And it will be then that we shall let loose—whom?"

"Whom?"

"Ivan the Crown-prince."

"Who-om?"

"Ivan the Crown-prince. You! You!"

Stavrogin thought for a moment.

"A pretender?" he asked suddenly, gazing at the madman in sheer amazement. "Oh, so that's your plan, is it?"

"We shall say that he is in hiding," Verkhovensky said quietly, in a sort of amorous whisper, as through he really were drunk. "Do you know what the expression in hiding means? But he will appear. He will appear. We shall spread a legend which will be much better than that of the sect of the castrates. He exists, but no one has ever seen him. Oh, what a wonderful legend one could spread! And the main thing is—a new force is coming. And that's what they want. That's what they are weeping for. After all, what does socialism amount to? It has destroyed the old forces, but hasn't put any new ones in their place. But here we have a force, a tremendous force, something unheard of. We need only one lever to lift up the earth. Everything will rise up!"[29]

Numerous critics of *The Devils* have warned contemporary readers against harboring associations of Stalin and a Verkhovensky–Stavrogin, an obvious bow to intellectual caution which unnecessarily denudes this passage of its truly prophetic dimension. Whether or not Dostoevsky had something like Stalin's purges in mind is irrelevant. What counts are his insights into the mentality of an unrepresentative proletarian elite which, passionately in love with power for its own sake, uses the frustrations and resentments of the underprivileged majority to elevate itself to a commanding position over their destiny in the misleading guise of liberators from autocratic oppression. The original motives of these radicals may be quite unobjectionable, but before long they find themselves ensnared in an ambience of venom and terror which they can no longer control or transmute. Admittedly, Verkhovensky's version of the great Revolution represents a distortion of the Ideal. But that is precisely Dostoevsky's point: to warn against the distortion of the noblest Ideals that results from the endless complexities of human existence under a "final solution" which may transgress against every vestige of decency and dignity. Peter Verkhovensky's worshipful attitude toward Stavrogin is certainly not the appropriate response of the People's General to his Commander-in-Chief, given the democratic aspirations of the participants, but then neither was Stalin's personality cult. This sort of thing is quite apt to occur when modern man makes revolution, and, more-over, it is also the sort of thing many intellectuals committed to revolution are quite apt to forget in the intoxication of becoming historically significant. Peter Verkhovensky's failure can be attributed to the *Zeitgeist* of his day, not yet ready to reward him for his deviousness. Clearly Dostoevsky meant us to respect his knowledge of what it takes to initiate a "revolt of the masses" in the name of a potential dictator, who differs from the tsar by being more competent than his predecessor. A self-confessed scoundrel rather than a socialist, Verkhovensky leaves the con-nections, if any, between these two a wide-open question.

Shatov, the deviationist from the group singled out for execu-tion, comes closer than any other member of the cell to express-ing Dostoevsky's own political philosophy. This simply would not make sense on the premise of Dostoevsky's pervasive anti-intel-lectualism, since Shatov before and after his conversion is an intellectual. But, as we have seen in case after case, Dostoevsky, far from condemning the life of the mind out of hand, only takes strong exception to what he regards as its undue excesses and hazardous perversions in the concrete life of man. Shatov believes in the distinctive national destinies of peoples. Not at all narrowly chauvinistic, giving due credit to the French, Germans, English, etc., in advancing civilization in their particular fashion, he feels that Russia has a historical destiny of her own, distinct from but not necessarily in conflict with the achievements of other nations. This, incidentally, had also been the view of Hegel, for whom Dostoevsky maintained a lifelong respect, not devoid, to be sure, of reservations congruous with Kierkegaard's in reviewing the achievements of the great German philosopher.[30] Unless a people is aware of a special calling, its energies will be dissipated in sundry directions to no monumental effect. The cosmopolitanism of the jet-set, to transpose Shatov's bias, is unlikely to yield supreme works of art or produce a lasting impact on the human spirit. Through Shatov, Dostoevsky raises the question of whether the undeniable evils of aggressive nationalism are necessarily more destructive in the long run than the faceless vacuity resulting from man's dislodgement from any parochial ties. (Jacob Burckhardt, who certainly cannot be accused of Slavophilism, speculated two decades earlier whether the triumphs of Greek civilization could have been realized apart from the Greeks' antipathy to alien or barbarian influences.) Shatov's murder is a consequence of a basic conflict between the international dictates of intelligentsia radicalism and the consciousness common to most men of belonging to one or another minority with its peculiar emotional attraction, quite aside from its historical uniqueness or ideological persuasiveness. A large measure of the tragic dilemma of Russian Communism in the twentieth century has revolved around Shatov's fateful disjunction of national pride and transcendent radicalism. If Stavrogin is too ironic for the good of fermenting revolution and Peter Verkhovensky too much of an exhibitionist, Shatov's dismal end both as a revolutionary and as a human being is rooted in an idealistic stance he stubbornly assumes toward irreconcilables—a stance curiously in harmony with Hegel's Absolute. In the last analysis he represents the duped intellectual who, as it were, never quite comprehends that for the radical intelligentsia to make concessions is tantamount to self-betrayal.

Among Dostoevsky's unnerving collection of *déclassé* intellectuals, none is more radical or insightful than Kirilov. Loosely but crucially affiliated with the ideologues of Revolution, his radicalism and intelligence are metaphysically rather than politically oriented. Consistent with his attitude of indifference toward living or not living, Kirilov offers to commit suicide to cover up the conspirators' plot against Shatov. His belief that true freedom lies beyond despair or exuberance has early Nietzschean–Schopenhauerian overtones far removed, in any event, from the customary rhetoric of revolutionary politics in which Kirilov's involvement is peripheral at best. He does not believe, for example, that atheists any more than orthodox worshipers have reached his stage of spiritual development, inasmuch as both camps continue to cling inordinately to the lure of the trivial. Kirilov himself gives the lie to any deranged death-wish underlying his bizarre philosophy of life. He loves to play ball with a little girl or watch the leaves turn, and he experiences a mysterious unity with Being which could be construed as religious ecstasy in reverse, much like Heidegger's evocation of the powers of Nothingness in *Sein und Zeit*.

All the doors there were unlocked and not even closed. The passage and the first two rooms were dark, but there was a light burning in the last room where Kirilov lived and had his tea. Laughter and some very curious cries could be heard coming from it. Stavrogin went straight towards the lighted room, but stopped in the doorway without going in. There was tea on the table. In the middle of the room stood the old woman, the landlord's relative, bareheaded and wearing only a petticoat, a pair of shoes on bare feet, and a hare-skin jacket. In her arms she held an eighteen-months-old baby with nothing on but a shirt, its little legs bare, its cheeks flushed, and its white hair ruffled. It had apparently just been taken out of its cradle, for there were still tears in its eyes; but at that moment it was stretching out its little arms, clapping its hands, and laughing, as children do, with a sob in its voice. Kirilov was bouncing a red India-rubber ball on the floor before it; the ball bounced up to the ceiling and back again, the baby crying, "Baw! Baw!" Kirilov catching the "baw" and giving it to the baby, who threw it clumsily with its little hands, and Kirilov ran to pick it up again.[13]

Indeed, this general imperturbability stands out as a shattering antithesis of Peter Verkhovensky's reckless impatience. Kirilov's passion for disassociation remains hidden behind a disciplined exterior mode of existence. For those not privy to his thoughts he could easily pass as a respectable civil servant.

By a stroke of literary genius Dostoevsky created this metaphysical nihilist as a corrective to the shallow revolutionary zeal of those rebels the majority of whom, if successful, would only pour old wine into proletarian bottles. Kirilov, on the other hand, answers the question whether a man can mean what he says by translating his convictions into action. Dostoevsky obviously disapproves of the substance of Kirilov's thought, but just as unmistakably admires his personal honesty and unshakable integrity. Moreover, Kirilov would never do as a comrade or commissar, for there is an insuperable obstacle in the innermost reaches of his heart and mind to lording it over others. Like a great artist who performs for the benefit of listeners he knows to be deficient in taste and perception, but whom he cannot begrudge the kindness of background support, Kirilov gives up his life for a nest of fanatics, knowing all the time that they don't understand his gratitude for their unwitting cooperation in his attempted conquest of death. Of such stuff, one scarcely needs to add, the leaders of the masses have not been made so far.

In a remarkable passage in *From the Other Shore* Herzen makes the following comparison between professional revolutionaries and genuine free men:

> With all that, *they* are more modern than we, more useful, because closer to reality. They will find more sympathy among the masses, they are more needed. The masses want to stay the hand that impudently snatches from them the bread they have earned— that is their fundamental desire. They are indifferent to individual freedom, to freedom of speech; the masses love authority. They are still dazzled by the arrogant glitter of power, they are affronted by the sight of someone who stands apart. By equality, they understand equality of oppression; afraid of monopolies and privileges, they look askance at talent and allow no one not to do what they do. The masses want a social government that would govern *for* them, and not like this existing one, *against* them. To govern themselves doesn't enter their heads. That is why the *liberators* are much closer to the present revolutions than any *free man* could be. A free man may be totally useless, but it does not follow from this that he should act against his convictions.[32]

Just as the mature Herzen looked askance at the professional liberators of mankind who found no time to liberate themselves, the mature Dostoevsky recognized that the death of the Christian God, far from leading modern man to the earthly paradise, was likely to lead to universalized megalomania, where every human being regards himself as godlike merely by virtue of being alive. While the death of God does not strictly entail comprehensive permissiveness, given the hypothetical imperatives of society and the fear of ostracism, historically the breakdown of all standards, so poignantly hinted at by Ivan Karamazov, has indeed characterized our twentieth-century experience, from the *avant-garde* in the arts to the horrors of Stalin's and Hitler's concentration camps. There is in fact scarcely a realm of life and thought in our day untouched by a reckless spirit of experimentation which as often as not is tantamount to a scandalous betrayal of decency and integrity. Whether it be teachers making a mockery of learning by dissociating discussion of substantive issues from the indispensable tools of logical analysis or some related aberration of intelligence, Dostoevsky's prophecies of the abuse of Reason and related virtues of civilization have never been so timely as now. However diabolical he may have conceived his devil's advocates to be, the voice of persuasion with which he allowed them to speak in his novels testifies, rather plausibly, to his own existential dialectic, placing him squarely in the great Russian tradition of skeptical idealists.

Beyond a shadow of a doubt, Dostoevsky himself was tempted by the voices he excoriated in his intellectual "villains." In questions of psychology he was, next to Nietzsche, the subtlest voyeur in the nineteenth century; his attractions to and investigations of the emotionally disturbed remain unsurpassed in the history of modern fiction. Moreover, he was a self-confessed aesthete not only as a professional writer giving form to his ideas and perception but as a fancier of discursive prose, dialectics, and sensual pleasures. As a young revolutionary he was a member of the Petrashevsky circle and, however fleeting and half-hearted his involvement in extreme political radicalism may have been, he preserved a sympathetic understanding for the "humiliated and offended." As one tempted by unbelief, he did not hesitate to plumb the depths of a universe indifferent to the welfare of humanity, his efforts to overcome such doubts not to the contrary. Above all, he laid bare in his fiction the antinomies of the intellectual life without glossing over the difficulties inherent in the proposed solutions, including his own.[33]

CHAPTER 3

Goncharov and the Spectrum
of Boredom

"I do not care for anything. I do not care to ride, for the exercise is
too violent. I do not care to walk, walking is too strenuous. I do not
care to lie down, for I should either have to remain lying, and I do not
care to do that, or I should have to get up again; and I do not care
to do that either. *Summa summarum*: I do not care at all.

"When I get up in the morning, I go straight back to bed again. I feel
best in the evening when I put out the light and pull the eiderdown
over my head. Then I sit up again, look about the room with indescribable
satisfaction; and so good night, down under the eiderdown."

KIERKEGAARD
"Diapsalmata" in *Either/Or*

Introduction

ONE OF MAN'S OVERRIDING metaphysical needs is to avert boredom or to make himself useful. The acedia[1] of the twentieth
century is the experience of "being condemned to freedom" in a
world seemingly devoid of objective values. From the Romantics'
preoccupation with ennui, a mixture of free-floating disenchantment and world-weariness, to the interminable dreariness of
"waiting for Godot" under the aspect of absurdity, the modern
intellectual's inability to "kill time" in good spirits characterizes
a most crucial aspect of his general disillusionment.

But not only intellectuals are hyperafflicted with boredom in
the twentieth century. Particularly in highly technological societies, where the majority of the population has attained an
unprecedented freedom from drudgery, the problem of excess

leisure time is experienced as being no less tormenting than the Marxist problem of alienated labor. Where the created products of man disclose themselves as instruments of tyranny and disintegration on the one hand, his newly won freedom to relax from his labors tends to be an enslavement to the emptiness of unfulfilled time on the other. Moreover, the philosophical nihilism of our foremost literary intellectuals reflects the subversion of such traditional articles of bourgeois faith as "salvation through work" or "getting to the top" by virtue of unflagging ambition. Boredom today links the manic activity of the technocrats, in frantic pursuit of self-destruction, with the revolt of the existentialists, anxiously diagnosing the human condition as dreadfully free.[2] One of its major components is in the moral and intellectual apathy without which the horrors of recent world history cannot be explained. And it seems as pertinent to the present-day adolescent's obsessive desire for uninterrupted pleasure (which somehow always eludes him because he desires it too much) as to the cosmological despair of the poet "desiring desire" (in Tolstoy's phrase) amid the shifting relativities of history and the neutrality of nature.[3]

Being bored has always had the dialectical character of "there is nothing of interest to do" and "there is too much of interest to do" joined in contradiction. Hence the immemorial roots in common between "country bumpkins" and "city slickers." In the modern world it is the irrepressible drive for all-encompassing change and the profound disappointments and setbacks which accompany such change that foster its peculiar vulnerability to the agonies of boredom. Like schoolchildren after school is out, we moderns, having looked forward so long to the ideal vacation from necessity, find ourselves faced instead with interminable afternoons, groping for "do-it-yourself" projects to keep from reflecting on our plight.

The problem of boredom in the Western world can be summarized by a single paradox: the paradox of emancipation. Whether it be the emancipated woman experiencing the sexual act as a disappointing bore (because she doesn't experience orgasm), the emancipated worker despairing of his leisure time (because he doesn't experience pleasant relaxation), or the emancipated masses alienated from each other and from themselves (because any feeling of genuine community has virtually disappeared), the paradox of liberation haunts the liberated with troubles at least as severe as the ones they presumably left behind. The ways of analytic reason are inadequate to provide man with a *raison d'être*. To be sure, they have done a great deal to alleviate concrete grievances and injustices and, as one might put it, to make life easier. But just as doing metaethics is not only no substitute for but has no vital connection with being moral, the deepest reasons a man might have for not committing suicide lie beyond any calculus yet devised by philosophers or theologians.

On the supposition that the outbreak of World War I could have been prevented and that William James's proposal for a "moral equivalent of war" had been implemented by the total application of modern technology to the advancement of justice and prosperity everywhere, what would there be left to make life interesting today? As it is, while the underdeveloped world suffers from the drabness of underprivilege, the sophisticated intellectual complains despairingly about spiritual emptiness. There is more than a little irony in the social-economic aspirations of "backward" peoples in our time trying to catch up with our privileged *tedium vitae*, as if Western civilization in its most recent manifestations displayed any emulative balance between security and creativity. It would appear to be a sad truth that life can be as meaningless in an affluent industrialized society as it was brutal in the Hobbesian "state of nature."

The intensity with which boredom is experienced by contemporary Western man is on a deeper level a consequence of his disavowal of the possibility of all novelty—from unbelief in theistic miracles (the raising of the dead) to lack of faith in the realization of secular utopias (the establishment of a classless society). Having rejected the article of faith that Christ came into the world but once to redeem us through history from the tyranny of natural cyclical processes (according to which there can never be anything new under the sun), he is at the same time unable to remythologize the world along Nietzschean lines and thus discern a degree of divinity in the repetitive movements of seasonal change. We neither can love Fate as some ancients may have been able to do, nor can we find adequate consolation for being scientifically determined in any eschatology transcending this determination. Alienated from *natura naturans* by an all-encroaching technology, disenchanted with every major historical mode of thinking—from the Kingdom of God to *Walden Two*—few are left who put any credence either in the uniqueness of a person or that of an event different from those we recall again and again. Today the visions of the technocrats are as discredited for us as those of the Calvinists were for Voltaire. If we have nothing better to look forward to than Orwell's *1984*, for example, it is little wonder that we are bored to the depth of our being, the reduction of individuals to mere vehicles of social usefulness reinforcing this message on the most inescapable plane of daily experience. The dullness of the characters in Chernyshevsky's *What Is to Be Done?* is perhaps less significantly a result of his aesthetic failure as a novelist than an unwitting triumph of his nightmarish projection of meaningless human toil and, even worse, of insufferably tedious talk. His lovers seeking a rationale for falling in or out of love mock that element of spontaneity without which human existence degenerates into a mechanical farce.

Some Elementary Notions of Boredom

Manifestations of boredom invariably embrace both a state of mind and a situation. Where the disparity between the consciousness of boredom and the context in which it arises is glaring, the kind of boredom at issue appears of particular interest. Analogous to the already classic distinction between fear and dread in existentialist literature, the most problematic boredom man must cope with is inexplicable in terms of public evidence.[4] Like the lonely man in a crowd, it is the bored individual in the middle of Manhattan who constitutes the paradigm of this human affliction. Whereas it is "normal" to be bored on holidays in our post-religious culture, to suffer boredom amid all the bustle of business is regarded with grave suspicions of stand-offishness, if not outright disloyalty. Yet few things are more distinctly human than the negative capacity of an individual suddenly to lose all interest in what fascinates his neighbors. The chances are that most men never truly admit to themselves why they are bored, thus making them doubly eager to attribute their mood to some flaw in their environment. On the other hand, insofar as there is a constant interplay between our moods and our *Lebenswelt,* our span of attention is surely influenced by environmental factors. Undergraduates may be bored with a lecture on "seeming to see" at any time, but their concern with the passing of the hour will be especially intense at eight o'clock in the morning. While vitality by itself is no guarantee of sustaining interest, it helps to feel alive at a civilized hour of the day to see a point in "seeming to see." The spectrum of boredom passes from "bores" who are never bored with themselves to psychopaths capable of doing anything precisely because they find their own lives so excruciatingly unexciting. Nero, we are told, set fire to Rome because he had nothing better to do. And Wittgenstein, reputedly, could not abide the talk in Oxbridge common rooms because its major purpose was to elicit applause for verbal virtuosity. Ordinary boredom is related in one way or another to these legendary cases.

What probably constitutes the most prosaic experience of being bored is a consequence of frustration. Against his avowed intentions the individual is prevented from doing things which he anticipates would hold his interest. Life in the "provinces" is emblematic of this state of affairs. Its failure to offer the mind adequate possibilities of diversion has often been likened to a "living death," a sort of fixed vegetative existence. Since the Industrial Revolution the irresistible appeal of cities for each younger generation has, apart from social-economic reasons, been associated with the excitement generally ascribed to urban life. To be sure, frustration is no respecter of suburban limits or, for that matter, of historical development. But the place where most things are going on is Moscow rather than Minsk, Paris rather than Aix-en-Provence, New York rather than Bismarck, North Dakota. And insofar as profane boredom (in contrast to spiritual boredom which is an ethical-religious problem) cries out for relief from the tyranny of uneventfulness, the modern city is the best place to provide it. The existential irony is that the unnerving hustle and bustle of city life may prove just as boring in its own way as the oppressive peace and quiet of the countryside. Man is bored not only when there is nothing to do, but also when there is too much, or when everything waiting to be done has lost its luster. Had Chekhov's three sisters finally got to Moscow they might well have longed for the eternal freshness of the seasons on the land. As it is, they are left smarting under the cyclical yoke of rural dispensation.

Whereas rural boredom rests peculiarly on frustration, urban boredom is closely linked with disenchantment. The sensibility of city dwellers tends to be dulled by an embarrassment of riches in their immediate environment. Either they have difficulty making up their minds what *not* to do, become bored with having to decide, and end up by doing nothing, or there is nothing left for them to find new and exciting, and they dream of returning to a golden age of pastoral. In his elucidation of satisfied desire, Schopenhauer has given us seminal insights into the oscillations between the boredom of frustration and the boredom of satiety. Accordingly, man can only be happily discontented when he feels himself to be freely striving for what must always elude his complete possession. The boredom of the rich who cannot become rich again may be viewed as an act of revenge on the part of the dialectic against the boredom of the poor who dream of not having to seek wealth. Analogously, the restlessness of the alienated urban intellectual, bored, as Dostoevsky knew so well, with the splendors of St. Petersburg, and thus motivated to go "underground," is contrapuntal to the restlessness of Chekhov's three sisters desperately pining for Moscow, bored with the tedium of provincial society, and driven to live in a speculative future. It is worth noting that both boredom as frustration and boredom as disenchantment are instances of a sense of futility which threatens to overwhelm man whenever he realizes that his presence in the world is *de trop*.

In his classical account of boredom in the *Pensées*, Pascal observed that it is neither the "chase" alone nor the "quarry" itself which can satisfy man's desire for *not* just having been there and gone. At a minimum there must always be a simulated struggle and a simulated reward to keep us from feeling super-fluous. Man, Pascal argues, will gamble or hunt if and only if the illusion of victory, however Pyrrhic, is somehow preserved. In other words, even to play just for the fun of playing games requires a mock element of seriousness to hold our interest. Men will enjoy their work if and only if they sense some necessity for performing it. Nevertheless, much as they may complain about being in harness, the boredom accruing from excess leisure is apt to be just as problematic as the less opaque boredom of alienated labor. A person without a role, whether rich or poor, is especially vulnerable to boredom. Hence well-off matrons, who turn to social work after their children leave home, rarely manage to fill the resultant lacunae in their lives unless they can invent the equivalent of a paycheck or some other therapeutic substitute for punching a clock. In order not to suffer boredom it may be better to be the Sartrean waiter, frozen in his professional role, than the Beckettian "waiter for Godot."

People in society will often profess to despise the conscious roles they must play in order to make a living. They may resent having to appear likable to their superiors or they may feel enslaved by the rigid schedule of the working day, but no sooner do they retire than they despair of having too many possibilities to choose from or even of being deprived of the regularized joys of pretension. Being entirely on their own makes them restless and bored, even though it would seem to be the long-awaited emancipation from drab routine. Save for the very few who are genuinely absorbed in their activity or sustained by their vanity, the majority of mankind must feel under some form of external pressure in order to labor with a sense of meaningfulness. Thus it comes about that the amateur of independent means is no less subject to boredom than the proverbial civil servant, the one confronted by empty hours, the other by inane ledgers. Boredom as bondage to drudgery and boredom as bondage to the uncommitted life are both instances of man's ambivalent desire to "dance in chains."

The ironies of rural and urban boredom as well as those of occupational and leisured boredom yield to some measure of situational relief. To paraphrase Kierkegaard: there is always apt to be some temporary way out of these contradictions, some comic interlude between bouts of self-weariness. This, however, does not apply to the jaded feelings of spiritual boredom which transform the whole world of the individual into a "wasteland" of striving. Here it is no longer a question of providing the proper occupational therapy or, as the case may be, a convivial change of scenery, but rather one of a Nietzschean "transvaluation of values," of reanimating the person's understanding of reality.[5] Contempt for the world is a "root metaphor" in the history of human thought. And, especially where such a mood remains untranscended, the burden of cosmological boredom becomes almost too painful to bear. Why indeed should anyone care about anything in a universe that presents itself to Reason as indifferent if not hostile? The contemporary "theater of the Absurd" represents far more than the pathology of catatonic lack of response. From Spinoza to Wittgenstein the negation of facts as vehicles of significant meaning for man has been a dominant undercurrent of the keenest philosophical reflection. The heroic effort of the German Idealists to counter it by advancing a rational theology in which *Geist* takes the place of God failed. Hume related that once outside his study he could divert his mind from the nihilistic implications of his epistemology by playing billiards. But he knew, just as the less placid Nietzsche and Wittgenstein did, that even if the existence of the external world could be proven, the necessity of man to inhabit and amend it remained most problematical. What makes cosmological boredom so hard to bear for post-Christians is their post-pagan memories of Providence. Modern philosophy has succeeded in eradicating theodicy from our minds but not from our hearts.

Historically, it is not without irony that the Enlightenment should have harbored within itself a wave of ennui so formidable that it remains unspent to the present time. While the "idea of progress" seemed to triumph over Pascal's conception of the "misery of man even in his greatness," Rousseau questioned the future happiness of the human race, though he himself played a major role in establishing its theoretical foundation. (Oddly enough, boredom in the eighteenth century came to be known as the "British malady.") It is of course not in the least surprising that profound disenchantment with the world will spur profound disenchantment with oneself. For the gist of ennui is a bittersweet discontent with having been cast into the worst of all possible worlds. Hence the characteristic longing among its victims for distant times and places or for their own annihilation amid the terrors of actuality. When a man is bored with himself he is bored with what interests him the most, and the resulting despair makes him capable of committing any crime. Kierke-gaard in his *Concluding Unscientific Postscript* has depicted the bored individual as carrying the attitudes of the laboratory into his life to the point where he can condemn humanity to death for the sake of rigorous science. He becomes a kind of parody of the objective thinker, "a transcendental ego" estranged from the world as well as from his concrete self. There would appear to be a correlation between intense introspection and a pronounced susceptibility to the agonies of spiritual boredom. The wide-spread diffusion of "spleen" among thinkers and writers since the eighteenth century is probably related to the glorification of the Cartesian *cogito*, which in its lonely splendor will commence to feed on itself. Swift's self-hatred and Dr. Johnson's melancholy appear, when put in this context, as the legacy of rationalism to Romantic disillusionment. Their creative genius and their moral fortitude should not blind us to the "void inside" whose undertone is unmistakable in their finest work.

From the foregoing it should at least be clearer why boredom is such a live issue today. Man's potential enslavement to auto-mation engenders the kind of technological boredom Chaplin immortalized in *Modern Times*, wherein the mechanical cycles of assembly-line production are juxtaposed with the worker as a sort of anti-hero in a pointless process. On the other hand, the banality associated with the same cocktail parties in the same big cities of the world suggests the eschatological boredom of those who must keep busy doing nothing in order to have no time left for self-examination. T. S. Eliot gives us a striking poetical description of the twaddle which eschatalogical boredom helps to foster:

> In the room the women come and go
> Talking of Michelangelo

The Lived Experience of Boredom

The phenomenon of boredom transcends the strains and stresses endemic to bourgeois and communist societies in the twentieth century. One has only to think of children bored because not sufficiently fussed over, of old men literally dying because they have no decisions left to make, or of the depressed "sick unto death" with their overinvolvement with themselves, to visualize the universal dimension of the problem. The apprehension of boredom always depends on a person's character and temperament. At the same time there would appear to be special factors in the milieu of modernity which predispose us in different ways to find less and less (including ourselves) of any vital interest.

Time drags not only for those who are bored. Peculiar to the time experience is the absence of any suspense or threat whose relief under ordinary circumstances would be instrumental in restoring the normal flow of events. Instead, for no good apparent reason, our everyday preoccupations suddenly lose their luster, plunging us into a state of depression in which days never end, tomorrows and yesterdays appear identical, and nothing engrosses us any longer. Given this state of mind, even sleep can become boring and sleeplessness a temporary diversion. Yet strangely enough, this slow passing of time can also prove enjoyable when the individual is able to feel that he could have chosen not to go along with it. Doing nothing worthwhile gracefully is an aristocratic art. Egalitarian activists will never comprehend it. Authentic lovers of boredom have always known how to play aimlessly with balloons and how not to worry about worrying. They make a virtue of time dragging, whereas the overanxious cannot stand the boredom of its echoless silences. All temperamental differences aside, the "Protestant ethic" is far less compatible with the delightful aspects of boredom than is the wisdom of the Mediterranean peoples, who can take small things seriously and big issues frivolously.

The silences of the bored resemble those implausible snatches of dialogue in a typical drama of the Absurd. Any attempted conceptualization of the feeling that there is nothing left worth saying ironically clashes with the desire to communicate this very feeling. Hence the relapse into baby talk, the constant reiteration of banalities, or the poses of "making conversation." When one is bored one is inclined to say anything to conceal the desperate apprehension that there is nothing to say. Whereas bores talk like books (as the Germans put it), the bored themselves are prone to seek unconsciousness either in the futility of their gestures or in the randomness of their assertions.

An integral part of growing old is the loss of expectations. As the horizons of the future shrink, coping with the "specious present" arouses less and less zest. There is too little time left to look forward to very much. Even the ambivalent prospects of repetition and recollection are diminished for the aging. Their "remembrance of things past" almost excludes what they will have experienced another day. Whereas a young woman can redecorate her home in anticipation of future recollections of happiness, an old woman can do the same for hers only in anticipation of death. And what, she may ask herself, is the point of that? *Das Nichts nichtet* (the force of Nothingness is to negate everything) is Heidegger's pregnant phrase for the time experience of irreversible dissolution as a part of human existence. Because man's essence is so indefinable, he is ever threatened with boredom by a future which appears too nebulous or too fixed. Dangling between the certainty of death and the impenetrable possibilities of coincidence, he is apt to cling to any diversion as a promising sign of novelty. In short, human existence as such does not entail the experiences of feeling alive. Those who are not sustained by this experience die of boredom.[6]

Literary-Historical Expressions of Boredom

Though boredom is universal, its dominant form in any culture will be contextually determined. While a fusion of despondency and sloth is not confined to the Middle Ages, acedia is no longer an issue in an age pursuing technological rather than spiritual progress. In the seventeenth century Pascal identified boredom with the need of the dominant aristocracy to seek constant distraction—in other words, to get away from themselves by doing anything short of spending that celebrated half hour of solitude in an empty room. Since the Enlightenment, ennui has menaced generations of writers and artists.[7] Life imitated art when Werther's *Weltschmerz* served as a catalyst for a great many suicides and attacks of neurasthenia. Its victims proved at the same time its most eloquent interpreters, wavering schizophrenically between what would later become the demands of Byronic detachment and the infinite passion of Kierkegaard. The "gospel of work" as propounded by Carlyle was intended to overcome the agonies of Romantic boredom.[8] And while it may have succeeded in doing so in the case of a Carlyle, it was patently inadequate to cope with "the myth of Sisyphus" so symbolic of boredom in the twentieth century. For what is the point of sheer becoming without any prospects of genuine fulfillment? Camus's Stranger, already an archetypal figure, fails to intervene to stop two cases of gratuitous cruelty, one to a dog and the other to a girl he knows, not because he is sadistic, but because he is ultimately unconcerned. Neither what Heidegger calls *Sorge* nor what Sartre calls *engagement* has penetrated his indifference toward everything and everybody, including himself.

So far, cultural historians have not succeeded in attaching a label to a variety of boredom widely diffused among the sons and daughters of the bourgeoisie from roughly the second half of the nineteenth century to the holocaustic year 1914. This type of boredom lies somewhere between the free-floating introspection of Romantic passion and the burdensome leisure of the *nouveaux riches*. While the sweet anguish of ennui was occasioned by fruitless longing for the Unattainable, the boredom peculiar to the middle class was induced by an idolatry of the respectable, the conventional, and the mediocre. Whereas an Onegin's listlessness is aristocratic and Jimmy Porter's (relieved by flashes of sardonic humor) proletarian, the banalities uttered by Monsieur Homais in *Madame Bovary* are devoid of all poetic quality; in short, they are typically *bourgeois*. A Sunday with the Clapham Sect, a meal at the Buddenbrooks', a walk with Simone de Beauvoir and her parents through the Bois de Boulogne—each of these situations exemplifies all that is hostile to vitality, sparkle, and spontaneity. Instead we get the familiar syndrome of bourgeois boredom: lack of imagination, compulsive thrift, and an uncritical optimism regarding the established order. Where Onegin yawns mellifluously and the hero of *Look Back in Anger* vents his infinite *ressentiment*, the archetypal bourgeois expresses his boredom by making money and good impressions, talking cant, and doing his utmost to prevent his neighbors from enjoying being alive any more than he does himself. In the name of respectability he aims to divest human experience of all unruly elements. His attachment to routine is classically described as "never having been sick or missed a day's work" (Gregor Samsa prior to his metamorphosis), never having been tormented by the demands of personal judgment (Babbitt), and never having been carried away even in sexual passion (the bourgeois lovers in D. H. Lawrence). In contrast to the "superfluous" aristocrat who is too bored to do anything, the bored bourgeois feels himself menaced by the prospects of genuine leisure. And thus his happiness becomes contingent on not having any time left for doing the things he professes to enjoy. Even the forlorn souls in the drama of the Absurd are capable of responding to gallows humor, while the bored bourgeois does not crack a smile in the middle of his frantic absorption in busyness and business.

Anhedonia[9]

Although this type of self-destructive boredom proliferated in the second half of the nineteenth century, the discussion focuses on an archetypal embodiment of spleen and torpor, unequalled even by Baudelaire's *Season in Hell.* Stavrogin is not only, as we have already seen, Peter Verkhovensky's Messiah, but also a tormented individual, almost crazed by his condition of uprootedness and boredom. The accentuation of boredom, so tragically exhibited by Stavrogin, has become a common factor in our radically demythologized culture. According to Heidegger's analysis in *Sein und Zeit,* the modern intellectual becomes bored with himself, not least on account of having killed Nature[10] by virtue of asserting the primacy of scientific abstractions at the cost of appropriating direct lived experience. It is worth noting that Heidegger, an atheistic existentialist, shares Dostoevsky's contempt for those whom the gods have deserted and who can no longer take any pride in their local associations and traditions. Both these writers, if from distinct perspectives, suggest an organic connection between the ravages of spiritual boredom and the "disinherited mind" of the scientific intellectual perhaps unwittingly soiling his own nest by rationalizing every fact of significant experience.

Nicholas Stavrogin carries this cult of dispassionate objectivity to an extreme by detaching his own stake from the thrust of his most persuasive arguments. When he can no longer bear the burden of himself, he decides to visit the monk Tikhon, his spiritual antithesis. He finds that he feels rather ill at ease in Tikhon's presence. On the one hand, he looks at things far too abstractly to confide in anyone, least of all in a monk; on the other, his very appearance at the monastery underscores his need to unburden himself of guilt. And thus, in the wake of a pre-liminary exchange of banter, Stavrogin hands Tikhon three to five sheets of paper (there are two versions of his Confession, whose contents Dostoevsky agreed not to disclose in the narrative of *The Devils* as it appeared during his lifetime).

Stavrogin begins his Confession by relating—"*I could have hanged myself out of sheer boredom*"—how, in order to find distraction from a life of dissipation in St. Petersburg, he impli-cated his landlady's twelve-year-old daughter, a girl named Matryoshka, in a theft he knew she had not committed. As a consequence of being led on by Stavrogin, her mother cruelly thrashes the reticent Matryoshka in his presence. Even now, characteristically, he refuses to intervene. "I remember that I was then seriously preoccupied with theology," he remarks. "It distracted me a little but afterwards things became even more boring. As to my political view, I just felt I'd have liked to put gunpowder under the four corners of the world and blow the whole thing sky-high—if it had only been worth the trouble. But even if I had done it, I would have done it without malice, simply out of boredom."

It is worth noting that Stavrogin's boredom is far from being solely "subjective." Rather his whole world of ideas and intentions has become stale to him *within* the context of his everyday activi-ties. In other words, not only is Stavrogin's psyche disturbed by what might be called a sickness of soul but this disturbance reaches out, so to speak, to distort his whole sense of reality. Dostoevsky ingeniously suggests how his boredom comes to corrode everything he touches, which is another way of saying that self-hatred and world-hatred are in the last analysis inseparable. His desire to blow up the world could be character-ized as a potential act of gratuitous folly.

The next time Stavrogin is alone with Matryoshka sne allows

him to have sexual intercourse with her—from another point of view, he rapes her. Like everyone else who comes in contact with Stavrogin, the girl is fascinated by him, no less so for his having been a far from guiltless witness to her recent humiliation at the hands of her mother. Matryoshka flings her arms around Stavrogin's neck in a gesture of reconciliation, and Stavrogin proceeds to violate her. Consequently she falls critically ill. "I offered to call a doctor and pay for the visit," Stavrogin recalls at this point. But when she is better and he sees her next, he doesn't address as much as a single word to her:

> She suddenly began shaking her head the way simple, common people do to mark their disapproval of you. Then, incongruously, she raised her little fist and shook it at me threateningly from where she stood. At first her gesture struck me as funny, but after a while I couldn't stand it any more. I got up and took a step towards her. There was an expression of despair on her face that was quite unimaginable in a child. She kept shaking her head reproachfully and threatening me with her fist. I spoke to her then, softly and kindly, because I was afraid of her, but I soon realized that she didn't hear me and that frightened me even more.

Thereupon, as Stavrogin half dozes while reading a newspaper, Matryoshka hangs herself in the closet behind his armchair. "The main trouble was that I found life so boring that it drove me mad."

Thenceforth Stavrogin could not find any peace of mind, though his powers of analytical reasoning remained unimpaired.[11]

> A couple of years ago, passing a station store in Frankfurt, I saw, among other things, the picture of a small girl very richly dressed. She reminded me of Matryoshka. I bought it and when I returned to my hotel I placed it on the mantelpiece. I left it there without moving it and without as much as glancing at it, and when I left Frankfurt I forgot to take it with me . . . I mention that to prove again how clear my recollections are and with what detachment I can view them. I could reject them wholesale at will. Reminiscing has always bored me.

Having pondered this, Tikhon remarks:

> Apparently men cannot without impunity become alien in their own land. There is one torture devised for those who have torn themselves

away from their native soil—it is boredom and the inability to do anything try as they may to keep busy.

Even before reading Stavrogin's Confession, Tikhon had pointed to "indifference" (William James called it alienation from "the world of the streets") as the root of Stavrogin's torment:

"Tell me now, is it possible to believe in the Devil without believing in God?" Stavrogin asked, laughing.

"Very possible indeed—happens all the time," Tikhon said, raising his eyes and smiling.

"And I'll bet you consider that form of belief more worthy of respect than complete disbelief?" Stavrogin said, laughing loudly.

"No, on the contrary, I feel that absolute atheism is more worthy of respect than worldly indifference," Tikhon said in a light and cheerful tone, but at the same time darting a worried look at his visitor.

"I see—so that's how you feel. You know, you really puzzle me."

"Whatever you say, a complete atheist still stands on the next-to-the-top rung of the ladder of perfect faith. He may take the last step; and he may not—who knows? But the indifferent, they certainly have no faith, only an ugly fear—and only the more sensitive of them have that."

Clearly Dostoevsky is at pains to relate Stavrogin's boredom to his alienation from God, society, and traditional values. His self-destruction is intended to symbolize the emancipated Westerner whose paramount authority is his detached intellect. In identifying Stavrogin's monstrous behavior with the distortions of clinical objectivity, Dostoevsky was of course grinding one of his favorite axes. Its constructive antidote is his emphasis on a return to Holy Russia as a means of Stavrogin's hypothetical redemption. But, as has already been shown, Dostoevsky's great creations always transcend his special pleading. While in his portrait of Stavrogin we may discount his idealization of Orthodox Russian religiosity and his general predisposition to romanticize what he himself, if only in certain moments, yearned to become, his psychological insights into Stavrogin's boredom as distinctive of detached self-consciousness hating itself remain uncanny.

Stavrogin sees through the illusions entertained by his own disciples. He admits to himself that wishful thinking will not bring about a new order, however desirable it may appear. So far as he himself is concerned, he looks for something to do that will not be eroded by his critical intelligence. At one and the same time nothing finite can relieve his *tedium vitae*, while he dreads infinite intervals of time without any possibility of time-lessness. For Stavrogin no news is bad news and any news is better than none. And since in Sartrean fashion ("condemned to be free") he has to make his own news, he seizes avidly upon any occasion to relieve the dull pattern of day-by-day events. What stares him in the face is unrelieved contingency: Hume's dangling external world emptied of love and logic. Thus he is metaphysically bored, bored with the gnawing awareness of "there being plenty of nothing." He turns to dissipation for an anodyne, but not being a sybarite, he cannot enjoy losing him-self in mere pleasure. Not being a pragmatist either, he proceeds to act outrageously in society.

Oblomovitis

Of the legion of Superfluous Men in nineteenth-century Rus-sian literature, none has cast as dazzling a spell on posterity as the figure of Oblomov—a thorn in the eyes of the "peripatetics" (the disciples of Calvin and Carlyle) bent on changing the world at all costs and by all means. In the heterogeneous company of Rudin, Pechorin, and Onegin, Oblomov is an atypical specimen of humanity, idiosyncratic to the core, and strikingly different from this illustrious group by virtue of being happy most of the time.

As a cheerful eccentric in classical Russian fiction Oblomov is the Kierkegaardian Exception to the Exception.[12] Supine on his celebrated couch, enveloped in the soft contours of his spacious dressing gown, dreaming of his idyllic childhood in Oblomovka, attended by his servant, the cunningly stupid Zakhar, and later by a loving wife, provided with a cuisine which might well be the envy of professional gourmets, Oblomov is a picture of unruffled calm amid the storms of daily existence. Until he succumbs to a heart attack brought on, it would appear, by overeating and lack of exercise, Oblomov retains the courage of his convictions and, unlike Marxists, Christians, and other incorrigible teleologists, leaves this life a consistent and contented deontologist.[13] While Superfluous Men in classical Russian literature almost by definition fret, mope, and sigh, aching to get to the barricades or to play some useful role in running and streamlining the affairs of their luckless country, Oblomov, who at the first opportunity impetuously resigned from the civil service, delights in his superfluity as a gift of the gods.

"A dozen places in one day—poor fellow!" thought Oblomov. "What a life!" He shrugged his shoulders. "Where is the man? He splinters and scatters himself—for what? Of course, it's not bad to look in at the theater, or to fall in love with someone like Lydia . . . she is charming. To be in the country with her, picking flowers, boating . . . very pleasant. But a dozen calls a day—poor fellow!" he concluded, turning over on his back, glad that he had no such empty desires and thoughts, that he was not dashing about, but lying right where he was, preserving his human dignity and peace.

"You're sunk, my dear friend; you're up to your ears in it," thought Oblomov, as he watched him go out. "Deaf, dumb, and blind to everything else in the world . . . But he'll be a big man; in time he'll hold a position of authority, with high rank in the service. He's what is called a careerist. But how little of the man himself is required for it! He'll live out his life, and many things within him will never be awakened. And meanwhile he goes on working from twelve to five in the office, from eight to twelve at home—the unfortunate man!"

It was with a sense of calm delight that he realized he could stay in bed from nine to three, and from eight to nine; and he was gratified to think that he did not have to run about making reports and writing papers, but could give free play to his feelings and imagination.[14]

We first encounter Oblomov in his element, that is to say, supine, though going through the motions of finding sufficient incentive to assume an upright posture—a special prerogative of *Homo sapiens*. His futile efforts in this direction strongly suggest a paralysis of will or a daemonic apathy beyond the scope of common sense. Unless Oblomov's affairs on his estate are taken in hand, he won't be able to pay his bills; and unless he makes proper arrangements, he will have to move—a thought which fills him with absolute terror. Lying there in his dusty and neglected quarters, surrounded by unopened books and papers, evidently helpless to help himself, Oblomov does not initially inspire his spectator-readers to edifying discourses on the virtues of indolence. Even so, he amuses us by his ingenious stubbornness in avoiding the ordinarily obvious, and, more seriously, by raising the question why a man should do anything at all if he doesn't have to work for a living. As Oblomov dozes through the morning hours, parasitically sustained by creature comforts, the fascination of his sanctuary grows irresistible. Obsessed with keeping busy every minute of the day, unmindful of possible self-deception, don't most of us add to the already sizeable burden of boredom in the world?

Whereas the Superfluous Man in Russian fiction usually is bored with himself, as well as with his environment, Oblomov enjoys a remarkable freedom from internal boredom. His apathetic orientation toward the world can be interpreted as an inversion of the capitalist ethic. The exact connection of this world-view with Protestantism remains a matter of historical dispute, but there can be little question that in the nineteenth century the sanctification of work proved a major factor in the rapid rise of Western technology and wealth. The "gospel of work" as promulgated by Carlyle is tantamount to a declaration of leisure as inauthentic. The possibility that a man might find his life devoid of meaningful content in spite of having attained the goals he set for himself seems to transcend the psychological purview of the frenetic concern with tangible achievement.

Although Oblomov is undoubtedly guilty of one of the cardinal Christian sins, he is, on the other hand, closer to the composure which Jesus favored when he expressed a decided preference for Mary over Martha. Unlike most men of affairs, Oblomov takes time out to converse with his friends not merely to kill an idle hour, but because he enjoys their company as an end in itself. Instead of projecting himself into an indefinite future with its uncertain prospects of growth and enrichment, Oblomov relishes each moment of his passivity as intrinsically delightful and hence valuable. This positive relationship to immediacy which contrasts so strikingly with the bourgeois capitalistic orientation toward bigger and better things to come, must at the same time be distinguished from the Kierkegaardian conception according to which the individual attempts to overcome perpetual despair by plunging into a whirlpool of debauchery. Where Goethe's Faust must always project himself into yet uncharted paths in order to get through each present moment, and where Kierkegaard's Seducer must lose consciousness of himself in unending fantasies of voluptuous gratification, Oblomov is content to take life as it naturally opens up to him in cyclical routines of eating and dozing. One cannot claim for him the title of sage, but his refusal to entertain false expectations about the value of worldly achievements is a relevant corrective to the demythologized sense of vocation which has prompted so many ideologues to confound abstractions with the immediate requirements of life. In this connection it is worth recalling a passage from Dostoevsky's *Raw Youth* in which he tells of a professional writer who, after thirty years of productivity, has awakened to the appalling fact that he never had anything to say.[15]

Industry is no substitute for thought. Not only would our dialectical hero from Oblomovka subscribe to the truth of this proposition, but in his own behavior he gives the lie to its antinomy, which states that inefficiency is incompatible with mental acuity. Oblomov is no fool, and his friends know it. By a technique akin to Freudian transference he envisages the world as a vast "boratorium" which he, for one, manages to circumvent by staying at home in bed. Like a latter-day Job in the comic mode he is visited by a number of friends who in vain try to persuade him to go out in society and play its conventional roles. Oblomov replies reasonably enough that these activities are either cruel or inane and hence not worth his while. In his own personal style he reiterates Pascal's admonitions against mistaking diversion from routine for a cure of *tedium vitae*. Not that he has the slightest impulse to meditate on higher things in Spartan quarters dressed in a hair shirt, but making due allowance for the attraction of gentry comforts, his commitment not to budge from his couch commands respect in the context of our perpetual escape from ourselves in varied pursuits of no significance. As Socrates professed his ignorance to those who deemed themselves learned, Oblomov professes unworldliness to those who regard themselves as genuinely sophisticated. Existential communication, we might well recall at this juncture, tends to be oblique, through evocative metaphors, rather than through direct statements.

The enthronement of independence does not always supersede solicitude. In his Dream, which Goncharov originally published separately from the novel as a whole, Oblomov relives his idyllic childhood among the simple-minded but goodhearted folk of Oblomovka. Dreary as their lives must appear to the hustlers of modernity, they take care of instead of analyzing one another and know how to appreciate the commonplaces of uneventful days. Doubtless Oblomov idealizes the simple beginnings of his strange career, yet this idealization is consistent with his philosophy of sustained concord and innocuous joys. On one level Oblomov's childhood is an object lesson against overattentiveness in raising the young. Had not his parents and the rest of the community indulged his whims and zealously protected him from the fickleness and turbulence of the larger world, Oblomov might well have been induced to learn to fend for himself, irrespective of disappointments or seemingly insuperable obstacles. Instead, everyone went out of his way to ease Oblomov's path and spare him unnecessary inconveniences, even to the length of smothering any self-assertive impulses present in the boy. (Without Mephistopheles, Faust would never have bestirred himself from his study, where, prompted by intellectual satiety, he was contemplating suicide.) But on the other hand, although singularly devoid of initiative, Oblomov has managed to retain a sensitivity to the needs of others, strikingly at odds with the dictates of competitive striving so characteristic of the modern sensibility.

In a subsequent conversation with Stolz, Oblomov projects his Rousseauesque vision of his past into a refined future existence. Short of relinquishing altogether his fantasies of archaic innocence, he is nevertheless prepared to adapt them to a more civilized atmosphere, where letters are answered, books are read, and the existence of strangers-in-distress acknowledged. In this spirit he ruminates on the delights of matrimony, which include quiet walks in the garden, enjoyable conversation, and Zakhar dressed up in splendid livery befitting a majordomo. His burden of constitutional weariness has not grown lighter with maturity, but the legacy of Oblomovka shines as brightly as ever for him in more genteel surroundings. In the last analysis, Oblomovitis represents not merely a critique of Promethean striving and struggle but also an anachronistic reaffirmation of *laissez-aller*.

Dobrolyubov's classic critique of Oblomovitis, predicated on political rather than literary assumptions about the Superfluous Man in nineteenth-century Russian life, was largely negative.

For Dobrolyubov, intent on transforming imperial Russia into a modern state, Oblomov was the culmination of a line of heroes whose lack of concern for the ills of society was their closest bond. In fairness to Dobrolyubov, his putting Onegin, Rudin, Pechorin, and Oblomov indiscriminately into the same boat can be ascribed to his use of polemical hyperbole as a proselytizer for the cause of the radical reformers. Even so, he cannot conceal his admiration for Goncharov's novel, nor can he bring himself to contemplate Oblomov as a pure villain, however typical his most endearing qualities might be of aristocratic superciliousness and insensitivity to the plight of the wretched. Dobrolyubov saw no deliberate malice in Oblomov's spectator view of reality. If it was not enough for him to be true to himself, at least he did not go out of his way to inflict miseries on others. His acquiescence to the *status quo* may have been simple-minded and inadvertently damaging to society, but even Dobrolyubov sees in it occasional flashes of charm or expressions of an exceedingly individualistic temperament.

In any event, even granting Dobrolyubov's condemnation of a whole society for having made Oblomovitis such an enticing option for the affluent, this scarcely exhausts our contemporary interest in certain aspects of the pathological condition, whatever Goncharov's conscious intentions may have been in creating his remarkable character. Neither literary nor political analysis can do much to explain the interest in Oblomovitis among readers in our nihilistic times. It is the existential context of twentieth-century living that the spectrum of boredom (as previously discussed) puts Oblomov's somewhat frivolous inertia in a serious light. For now we can take his measure not only as an archetypal Superfluous Man with a strong streak of eccentricity, but as a precursor of Beckett's characters in his play *Endgame*: immobile, deformed, and bored as much with eternity as with time. By virtue of repetition *in medias res* the fantasies of the nineteenth century became the nightmares of the twentieth. Our psyches today are so disturbed by the uselessness of all conceivable goals, as well as by our incapacity to reach some common agreement on that disquieting condition, that we are overwhelmed by a seemingly irreducible despair about the future.

Indeed Oblomov was fortunate not to be a twentieth-century

character. Under the penal code of the Soviet Union he would surely have been convicted as a parasite and sent into exile. This fate befell Andrei Amalrik, who, in his remarkable autobiography, *Involuntary Journey to Siberia*, devotes considerable space to expounding the Soviet conception of parasitical existence.[16] While Amalrik, in contrast to Oblomov, did not live off the proceeds of others, both men could be accused of failing to do useful work for the state. By that criterion in contemporary Russia all drunkards, malcontents, and nonconformists are subject to arrest and imprisonment. The Marxist kingdom on earth has no room for those who love to dabble in the arts and who enjoy themselves carrying out pursuits whose utility to the authorities cannot be unambiguously established. Historically, Oblomovitis is dead in the Soviet Union, but, ironically enough, certain aspects of it live on precisely among those Russian citizens who refuse to conform to the new System by upholding at the cost of their lives the virtues of intellectual leisure and disinterested repose. In this sense, it may even be said that Oblomov has become a hero of our time.

CHAPTER 4

Tolstoy and the Varieties of the Inauthentic

"I once tried to read 'Resurrection' but couldn't. You see, when Tolstoy just tells a story he impresses me infinitely more than when he addresses the reader. When he turns his back to the reader then he seems to me *most* impressive . . . It seems to me his philosophy is most true when it's *Latent* in the story."

LUDWIG WITTGENSTEIN
letter to Norman Malcolm

Introduction

I

IN RECENT YEARS, due largely to the impact of existential philosophy, the terms "authentic" and "inauthentic" have gained wide currency in Western thought and literature. For the most part, the usage of "inauthenticity" has been derived from and certainly associated with Heidegger's discussion in *Sein und Zeit*, where he contrasts the inauthentic conformity of the masses to public opinion and conventional wisdom with the autonomy of individual self-determination and self-expression. Following in the footsteps of Rousseau, Heidegger seems convinced that the achievements of technological man, however democratically based, are no less dishonest than the inherited roles once performed by the privileged classes of Europe.

Another existential writer, Sartre, in his *L'Être et le néant* addresses himself to the problem of inauthenticity in a different manner. His concept of *mauvaise foi* is an attempt to separate the quintessential and basically indescribable character of each individual from the roles society imposes upon him or he chooses for himself to hide his freedom. Without having recourse to the dogma of original sin or similar preconceptions, Heidegger and Sartre view man as primordially disposed to hypocrisy in his innermost being. Their main contention is not the familiar one to the effect that much of the time we lie to ourselves and to others but rather that the social environment which shapes modern man has peculiar affinities for the cultivation of play-acting which threatens to tear us psychically apart. Like repression in Freud, inauthenticity in Heidegger and *mauvaise foi* in Sartre symbolize the depths of our self-alienation.

In the discussion to follow the terms "inauthentic" and "insincere" (and their antonyms) are used loosely as equivalent. While from a literary-historical point of view it may be very convenient to distinguish sincerity from authenticity, such a distinction becomes meaningless unless the usage of specific manifestations of either one is spelled out in detail. The widespread use of "authentic" is rooted in the stress placed by most philosophers of *Existenz* on the importance of each individual's being "inner-directed." But there is really no compelling reason why a man who resists the lure of the crowd could not as justifiably be called "sincere" as "authentic."

So far as ordinary usage is concerned we distinguish between an insincere Christian mass composed in the nineteenth century and, for the sake of example, an inauthentic performance of this composition today. By insincere in this context we may mean that the frivolity of certain parts of the score is incongruous with the setting of the text: that, in other words, the composer did not believe in the words which he set to music. By inauthentic in relation to performance, on the other hand, we have in mind some technical failure on the part of the performer to realize the discernible intentions of the composer with respect to such matters as the use of certain instruments, faithfulness to the score, the size of the musical forces employed, and so forth. Although the difficulties of establishing either of these two judgments with respect to a given example, are skirted here, it is clear that the former is a moral judgment of a negative kind, while the latter points to a deficiency in competence, more than one of conscience. To be sure, this need not be a hard and fast distinction. An inauthentic performance of a Bach fugue may be due as much to a lack of "soul" on the performer's part as to his lack of skill in approximating the genuine. Conversely, Wagner's failure to write a convincing Christian opera (see Nietzsche's critique of *Parsifal*) could be ascribed by a musical scribbler to flaws in his technique for composing for human voice.

II

Concomitant with the cry for revolution which has swept the world since the events of 1789 has been a passionate insistence on sincerity and candor. If the permanent desirability of revolution is, among other things, a reflection of the breakdown of traditional social-political-economic modes of society, the avowal of sincerity for its own sake often betokens a loss of faith in substantive convictions—a void to be filled by relentless candor even at the price of relapsing into barbarism or, as far as many intellectuals are concerned, hovering without any illusion or hope over a bottomless abyss. While the young of each generation feel justified in accusing their elders of cynicism and hypocrisy, they invariably overlook the thorny questions of how sincerity on a wide scale is to be achieved and, should this be attainable, whether it would prove an unmixed blessing. Just as Voltaire's dream of the un-Christian society has been compatible with manifestations of unprecedented stupidity, brutality, and insensitivity, absolute sincerity, far from being a guarantor of pervasive decency, all too easily degenerates into or is accompanied by total heartlessness and anomie. As an erstwhile Berlin judge was fond of observing, should subway riders in a modern city suddenly learn of the suspension of all laws, they would display their sincerity by being at each other's throats in a trice. Unless we assume the good will of most men (an assumption made by many of the *philosophes* and the Romantics, though profoundly challenged by Kant's notion of "radical evil in human nature") an unqualified affirmation of sincerity proves as much an invitation to egoism as does insistence on single-mindedness.[1] To be true to oneself is morally ambiguous apart from other variables, cultural as well as personal.

The avowal of faith in rapport with intellectual integrity is dramatized by Kierkegaard's vacillation as to whether it is preferable to try to become a Christian or to try to become honest in Christendom, a position compatible with Nietzsche's Anti-Christ. In this regard his situation is typical of a large number of modern writers and thinkers who, in the wake of repetitive disenchantment with highly questionable symbols of meaning, are tempted to take refuge in the bitter delights of free-floating open-mindedness. Particularly the existentialists, given their emphasis on the spirit in which an action is undertaken rather than on the substance of that action, are vulnerable to drifting precariously, if ingenuously, amid innumerable options—experimental, explored, struck from intimacy, or refuted with the keenest logic, but still vividly recalled. Where ordinary men are seduced by outrageous distortions of worthwhile Utopian longing, the existential intellectual enjoys playing the hazardous game of retreating from "objective correlatives" of inner states of certainty. His idolatry of Becoming can be as daemonic as the more familiar one of Being. Only with these issues in mind—the peculiar lure of sincerity in the nineteenth century and today, the frequently underestimated obstacles to its realization, and the ambiguities inherent in realizing it—can we set out to clarify Tolstoy's personal quest in the context of the Inauthentic in general and Rousseau's critique of civilization in particular.

When in 1749 Rousseau published his subversive observations[2] on the vices of civilization, it was widely assumed, not least by some of his celebrated compatriots, that Europe stood on the threshold of a new era—a technological Utopia accompanied by moral and aesthetic progress. Nor was such an assumption as absurd as we in the twentieth century with the benefit of hindsight might be led to believe. In fact, even today one is compelled to acknowledge a vast momentum of humanitarian reform implicit in the agnostic humanism of the *philosophes*. The validity of their protest against feudal institutions as well as their positive efforts on behalf of enlightened causes have in large measure been accepted even by their most severe critics. But this scarcely diminished the prophetic power of Rousseau's attack, nor can it obscure the sense in which the Utopianism of the Enlightenment proved to be incorrect. If historical hindsight should only be used sparingly and cautiously, it is also the case that we must remain open-minded enough to learn from previous misjudgments. Clearly the increasing "amendments of nature" by ego have not proven an unqualified success: the separation of church from state has failed to realize the millennium; and the evangelical fervor with which culture has been disseminated has ironically enough proved an occasional handmaiden to outbreaks of mass savagery. This by itself confirms Rousseau's thesis of a chasm dividing the fruits of civilization from the attainment of personal integrity.[3]

Like Rousseau, Tolstoy became convinced that only individuals relating to themselves honestly could seek salvation. A further striking resemblance between these two intellectual giants is their pessimism about the human condition in general, punctuated by half-hearted espousals of the power of reason to deliver us from the tragic contradictions of our perennial predicament.[4] Hence it is hardly surprising that one of Tolstoy's principal themes both before and after his "conversion," is the modes of insincerity generated and abetted by the refinements of civilization. For both Rousseau and Tolstoy the well-being brought about by the increasing control of elemental threats to human existence exacts its terrible price. Although both these writers tried to remain rationalists in spite of themselves, the thrust of their ideas on the subject of what Freud later called the "uneasiness of civilization" constitutes an unambiguous departure from the *philosophes'* view of human autonomy rooted in rational self-scrutiny. As a Christian heretic, Tolstoy early reached the conclusion that the kind of righteousness most entrenched in the world is self-righteousness and proceeded to spell out the implications of this momentous discovery throughout his career, from the evocation of adolescence in *Youth* to the lamentations of saintliness in *Father Sergius.*

Tolstoy found an irreducible element of hypocrisy no less in the purity of the heart embodied in childhood than in the capriciousness of rules governing our conduct in society. Much as he professed to despise all cunning worldliness, he was scarcely prepared to opt for the visible brutality of the peasant as against the devious sanctimoniousness of the bourgeois. From time to time he was driven close to madness by his failure to find a viable compromise between Rousseau's noble savage and a Russian *intelligent*.

The lies men live by, in any event, are far more severe than the lies they tell. Moreover, as Tolstoy knew only too well by acquaintance, one can tell the truth without being truthful in doing so. Thus one may advise another with impeccable logic, yet the truths one describes to others "with infinite passion" may mean nothing personally to the speaker himself. Truth-telling is perfectly compatible with dishonesty where speculative possibilities are spelled out in terms of dead options, as if, to cite William James's example, the seemingly plausible prospect of becoming a Mohammedan could relieve the spiritual crisis of a nineteenth-century New England farmer. This type of inauthenticity grounded in a confusion of theoretical purity with personal relevance seems particularly common among intellectuals. False arrogance, by permitting them to treat existential urgencies as mere exercises in thought, blinds them to the "disorder and sorrow" within which we actually make our choices.

Tolstoy was especially appalled by insincerity in high society, which at one and the same time worshiped at the shrines of vibrant narcissism and hardness of heart. He could never forget those glittering balls at which radiant beings expended a great deal of energy and time saying nothing with many words or feeling nothing with a multitude of disarming gestures. This jarring discrepancy between apparent abandon and genuine hollowness shocked his social conscience, which could not abide the presence of suffering or pomposity amid the wonders of spontaneous expression. Aristocrats in his time, like functionaries in ours, can perhaps be singled out for rarely saying what they mean, or meaning what they say. Tolstoy preferred "honor among thieves" to the underhandedness characteristic of C. P. Snow's Masters, whose respectability might lead one to believe that the ordeal of being human could once and for all be resolved at High Table. Again and again Tolstoy holds up to shame human beings who have traded their capacity for instinctive response for a set of frigid gestures. Anna Karenina, for all her "sinfulness," remains a sympathetic figure by virtue of her unflagging warmth and affection. This cannot be said of Karenin whose devotion to

propriety and legality reinforces his role as a monstrous, tyrannical husband.

From salon socialists, leading a bourgeois existence while presumably dedicated to the overthrow of the bourgeoisie, to debu-
tantes, vacuously smiling into their escorts' faces, civilization
presents a spectacle of innumerable shadings of deception and
self-deception. Some of these, no doubt, are essential for the
survival of morals and manners which help distinguish man from
the brutes; others, as Rousseau perspicaciously saw, are symptomatic of the dehumanization accompanying the overrefine-
ment of culture. It follows, in Freudian language, that the
total requirements of the ego and superego must in part be
redressed by eruptions of the id; the Indispensable Man is com-
plemented by the Superfluous Man, the logician by the dabbler or
putterer. After 1870 industrialization had become a *fait accompli*
not only for Russia and the West but, as Tolstoy sensed correctly,
for the world at large. He feared that the ever-increasing complexity of human relationships in a technological age would more
than fulfill Rousseau's prophecy. In the ambiguous name of virtue, Tolstoy laid bare the depths of inauthenticity in modern life,
dwelling most perceptively on those forms of "other-directed-
ness" which give the appearance of reasonable choice. The
timeless question remains: how can scrupulosity and spontaneity
coexist with intellectual and moral concessions to the requirements of civilization?

The Structure of Inauthenticity

The discrepancy between word and deed pervades the entire
dilemma of being human. Voluntarily or inadvertently, man is
wedded to inauthenticity in all his undertakings. The Kierkegaardian chasm between the possible and the actual portrays our
dangling condition, be it construed in terms of artistic, moral, or
political unpreparedness to realize our intentions. Throughout
history man has gone on record against being himself in every
conceivable manner. Whether it be inauthentic piety (sanctimoniousness) in religion or inauthentic joy (*Schadenfreude*) in
rejoicing in the misfortunes of others, he has displayed a seem-

ingly inexhaustible genius for inventing variations on the theme of deceit. From offering apologies meant basically as insults, to masking the worst news under euphemisms, his genius for evasion never deserts him. Yet there is a tragically ironic paradox: though we can only be authentic when we are happy being who we are and doing as we please, all too frequently we act more inauthentically when those very conditions hold true. (An individual carried away by unrestrained impulses is acting inauthentically when these impulses undermine his notions of his own responsible conduct.) Just as frequently, when we do the right thing we did not intend to do it, and our unhappiness, however thickly veiled, makes us inauthentic.

Just as Kierkegaard's "stages on life's way" at once overlap and collide with one another in dominating the self, so the spectrum of inauthenticity is contiguous, yet not without curious twists and turns, making for considerable internal tension. For Kierkegaard a seducer has more in common with an apostle than with a complacent bourgeois Christian, even though a wide gulf separates the aesthetic from the religious mode of existence. Analogously, the double-mindedness of a deceiver is more akin to the flighty moods of an unhappy girl than to the coyness of a debutante, even though a "leap" is required to get from ambivalence to two-facedness. In other words, the affinity of opposites can supersede the proximity of intermediate positions. From a moral point of view, the great Gatsby and Anna Karenina stand out as paragons of virtue compared to Iago, but Tolstoy's unstable heroine shares with Shakespeare's calculating villain a passionate flair for intrigue which links them much more strongly than common good-naturedness does Anna and Gatsby. The deeper reaches of inauthenticity attract the impulsive and compulsive alike.

A) INSTABILITY OR FLIGHTINESS

Man is disposed to inauthenticity by virtue of his emotional volatility. This is best seen in the ambiguous innocence of childhood. Children laugh one moment and weep the next for no discernible reason. They also love to be contrary for the pleasure of asserting their individual wills. Nor, ordinarily, can one be sure whether they are serious or frivolous when, for instance, they tell a parent, "I wish you were dead." Our basic temperamental instability, however well covered up in later years by eloquence and sophistication, always remains with us. To the extent that we are creatures of impulse we will love and hate the same object at the same time; our moods will fluctuate; our emotions waver; and our minds change. Without making any special effort we shall live up to the existential requirement of being always on the way—whether or not toward a specific goal is another matter. Not only philosophers contradict themselves much of the time. Often we cannot help but give the appearance of being inauthentic; even our self-conscious single-mindedness strikes us as not being beyond dispute. The stupid man who does not realize what he is doing may be unjustly accused of hypocrisy. Clearly, on the other hand, we can as adults make a virtue of our fickleness by using it to deceive others.

B) PRETENSE OR AFFECTATION

Children like to pretend; with the greatest of ease they assume roles and proceed to take them in deadly earnest. Unlike them, pretentious fools and cunning opportunists no longer acknowledge a dividing line between a sincere masquerade and witting self-deception. But the issue is less clear-cut than this. Playing politics, being diplomatic, impressing people, speaking rhetorically, etc., often turn out to be legitimate claims made on fundamentally honest individuals. Insofar as the workings of society depend on self-exhibition, a willingness to compromise with principles—flexibility—becomes a necessary condition for coping with its problems. Without masks communities as well as theaters could not function. Yet in the realm of personal relations there are few things as disturbing as the pretentiousness of frauds and charlatans. Although such characters may amuse us, by providing diversion from our own lack of authenticity and by bearing consoling witness to the vanity of most finite concerns, they invariably end up as insufferable bores. At the same time, it behooves us to make a careful distinction between one person's spontaneous showmanship, unconsciously ingrained in his very being, and another's sham exposure of ego, consciously contrived to serve as a vehicle for manipulating others. Perhaps the most loathsome form of affectation reveals a chronic rift between a man's "character" and his "nature."[5]

c) INSCRUTABILITY OR DEVIOUSNESS

Next to being constitutionally unreliable, man belies the canons of analytic philosophizing in his penchant for obscurity. He delights in not thinking out loud and in covering his tracks. Even John Locke invented a private language, in part, no doubt, to confuse his future biographers; Kierkegaard communicated indirectly; and there is considerable evidence that a major tradition of ancient and Renaissance wisdom-philosophy (the Platonic-Pythagorean) was deliberately esoteric.[6] More ordinary mortals, too, will go out of their way to disguise their innermost feelings and thoughts. The staunchest champions of utter frankness are often precisely the ones who will talk about any conceivable topic save that which touches them directly. The capacity to cover up successfully resembles inconstancy in being morally ambiguous. Obviously, a great deal can be said in favor of both spontaneity and discretion. On the other hand, their analogues, capriciousness and evasion, invariably threaten the integrity of human relationships. When we don't know what a person is driving at because he is determined to lead us astray, his efforts to justify his inscrutability become problematical. The man who cannot confide in anyone may be described either as silent as the grave (meaning that he can be trusted) or as being incapable of opening himself up to others (meaning that he repudiates love).[7]

d) THE DIVIDED SELF OR DUPLICITY

Most ethicists would not be overly bothered by the aforementioned instances of inauthenticity. How innocuous, they would be prone to exclaim, is the inconstancy of lovers, the showmanship of politicians and diplomats, or the hidden *Geist* of intellectuals in comparison with the malevolence of determined evil-doers. Since the levels of the inauthentic self interact, it would be misleading to separate its elementary from its more pronounced manifestations. At the same time, the "magnificent sinners" are endowed with a finesse for duplicity which might well be the envy of ordinary deceivers. Anna Karenina's adultery, Hamlet's self-acknowledged crocodile tears shed over Hecuba, and Gatsby's poses as an important "sport" may be regarded as "stages on life's way" toward the concentrated malice of an Iago.[8]

Duplicity usually entails indifference qualified by dissimulation. "Giving with a cold hand" amounts to indifference masquerading as scientific objectivity; "being cruel in order to be kind" may suggest indifference concealing intense resentment; not caring about the meaning of what one says or, its corollary, not saying what one means, translates into indifference regarding the desirability of communication. For the sake of becoming furious in order not to be bored, the deeply double-minded individual is prepared to provoke any sort of controversy. Even at the risk of being humiliated he will feign friendship, love, and concern. His talk will be double-talk, in action he will play a double role, and, if he is an intellectual keeping a journal, his private diaries are apt to be inconsistent with his published work.

Whereas hypocrites as ordinarily understood do not live up to what they profess to believe, villains like Iago or Claggart exemplify in their actions their outspoken estimate of themselves. While the duplicity of the typical hypocrite is rooted in a disjunction between his avowed beliefs and practice, the duplicity inherent in malice exploits the illusions of its intended victims by justifying their tenability as viable truths.

E) DECEPTION AND SELF-DECEPTION [9]

Man's susceptibility to deception, especially through the machinations and manipulations of fellow human beings, is in no need of being established as a living truth from generation to generation. Our senses frequently deceive us or we misjudge their reports and formulate false propositions about what we seem to perceive. Beyond these lapses of correct judgment we are, most of us, to some degree Machiavellian entrepreneurs, utilizing our reasoning faculties to pull the wool over our neighbors' eyes. The varieties of deception practiced by us invariably involve moral and intellectual facets. On the one hand, these types of deception point up our mental gullibility, that is, our inability to evaluate evidence with sufficient foresight; on the other, they expose the weakness of our will in its substitution of wish-fulfilling fantasies for reality or of self-enhancing vanities for the truth about our condition.

A man who deliberately deceives himself is no longer self-deceived, since he is aware of what he is doing. He may, of course, acquiesce in his self-deception as if he were ignorant of his true state of mind, but whatever others may think of his mood and actions, in relation to himself he cannot blot out his recognition of "bad faith" vis-à-vis himself, whether or not he makes a virtue of this double-edged insight. His situation must be clearly distinguished from that of a woman who continues to cling to her belief that her husband is alive in spite of the fact that he has officially been reported killed in action. Sincerely and compulsively she harbors this illusion which, however, from her point of view, is no illusion at all but an unshakable certainty. The severest kind of self-deception is akin to madness, where the self-deceived individual himself does not understand his departure from reality. There results a chasm between what he is in the eyes of others and what he is in his own. Just as a schizophrenic cannot legitimately be accused of hypocrisy, his split personality lying outside his control, a pathologically self-deceived person can scarcely be accused of a lack of self-examination. If, as it were, the acknowledgment of deception represents an insult to the intelligence, since no one likes to find himself in the wrong, the acknowledgment of self-deception invariably arouses feelings of guilt and resentment. It is embarrassing enough to be fooled by the world, either through its malicious manipulations or through one's stupidity, but to be fooled by oneself points up, among other things, one's inability or unwillingness to bring motives into proper rapport with cognition. Hence many men who knowingly deceive themselves will prefer to pose as deceived by a wicked world rather than adjust their actions to their refined understanding of themselves.

A monumental historical episode which dramatizes this distinction is the case of former Nazis, who much prefer to blame Hitler for the woes settled on Germany by the defeat of the *Wehrmacht* in World War II than to allow for the possibility that they themselves were all the time susceptible to persuading themselves of the rightness of the Führer's cause. Similarly, our failure to resign ourselves to unhappiness as a concomitant of being humanly alive is due in considerable measure to our inveterate habit of identifying a change in time and space with the wishful thought of a change in mood, even though experience has taught us that the predicament is rooted in our timeless perversity. But were some of us to admit this to ourselves, we might crack under the burden of such a truth consistently maintained and acted upon. Not that taking the bull by the horns here is necessarily better. Iago for all his perspicacity about himself did not contribute much to the happiness of humanity. The cruelty of the clairvoyant can turn out to be as destructive as the guile of unthinking majorities.[10]

The Inauthentic and the Existential Tradition

Philosophers of *Existenz* have a marked preoccupation for Authenticity and Inauthenticity. Kierkegaard's ahistoricity, his desire to leap over two thousand years of the past into contemporaneity with Ur-Christianity; Nietzsche's adulation of pre-Socratic and Dionysian modes of thought and feeling; Heidegger's undisguised contempt for technology and his nostalgic hankering after Hölderlin, Parmenides, and the Greek deities manifest, each in its own way, a rejection of the Industrial Revolution and its aesthetic as well as practical consequences for the new styles of life that emerged in the nineteenth century and came to fruition in the twentieth. What Ortega y Gasset came to call the dehumanization of art is synchronous with the dehumanization of man as attributed by Marx to the demeaning power of money, by Kierkegaard to sanctimoniousness in Christendom, by Nietzsche to the varieties of cultural philistinism (which for him is not exclusive of Platonic and Kantian moralism, didactic art, and an uncritical admiration for scientific truth), and with Sartre's *mauvaise foi*, his attack on role-playing as imposed upon us by the exigencies of making a living in a deadly world of mechnical contrivances, conspicuous consumption, and nauseous ennui. However inconsistent and unjust these thinkers may be, especially in advancing their own panaceas, their agreement on the galloping vulgarity of life since the French Revolution is compelling. At one with the Romantics in their yearning for organic simplicity of one sort or another, a simplicity incongruous with the demands of faceless efficiency and anonymous citizenry, they themselves are far from simple in their diverse insistence on returning to the things themselves.

Just as many outstanding members of the first generation of the Russian intelligentsia were mesmerized in turn by the organic philosophy of Hegel, Fichte, and Schelling and the poetry of Byron and Schiller, then by the amorphous ideal of the Russian commune, and last, but not least, by a special halo presumably attaching to the undifferentiated masses, so the existentialists, for all their psychological acuity, have frequently allowed themselves to be carried away by phantoms of Authenticity with which they hoped to overcome the Inauthenticity of their benighted contemporaries. There is, in short, a strange mixture of truth and pretension in their respective cries for honesty above all. Disillusioned Romantics to the core, they, like Gogol, Dostoevsky, and Tolstoy, have been tormented by a civilization they found increasingly devoid of spiritual meaning and genuine sociability. While their diagnosis rings as true for us today (still incorrigibly genteel or stupidly liberal), the evidence they gathered to justify it and, more important, the cures they proposed for the disease are without exception strikingly inadequate.

Without the benefits of any residence in Victorian England, Kierkegaard crushingly exposed the sanctimoniousness of middle-class Christians in the nineteenth century. At the same time his call for a return to Biblical Christianity with denigration of our historical experience, rings factitious and hollow. Kierkegaard was tortured by doubts akin to Darwin's, nor could he rid himself of these by rejoining Father Abraham in the Sinai desert. His favorite philosopher of Essence, Hegel, had justly described the consciousness of the post-Humean thinking man as inherently divided. Kierkegaard knew too much and knew it too well to espouse Jehovah in the manner of a pagan ready for his first conversion to theism and Christ.

Similarly, Nietzsche's preference for authentic history—i.e., the use of the past to illuminate the present and the future over antiquarianism, an uncritical absorption in what has been for its own sake—could scarcely be faulted as untimely, especially in Germany, where the confusion of scholarship with wisdom has repeatedly plagued its better citizens in their pursuit of truth. Nietzsche, moreover, correctly saw the authenticity of the Dionysian uttering his truth with concealment and disguise as against the overvaunted Apollonian with his simple directness. In this connection it is worth noting how Kierkegaard's pseudonymous authorship complements Nietzsche's love of play-acting, of deliberately breaking whatever continuity there might be between the "dancer and his dance." The "indirect communication" of truth is far more authentic, notably in Kierkegaard's aesthetic writings, than his or Nietzsche's "philosophizing with a hammer," as in Kierkegaard's *Attack upon Christendom*, the weakest of his religious writings, or in Nietzsche's *Anti-Christ*, the most inflated example of his straightforward polemical style. Their personal point of view comes across most effectively when, with irony, hyperbole, and the like, they mask their role of dogmatic advocate. Nietzsche was as much misled in his glorification of the Ancients as the source of all Authenticity as Kierkegaard was in his fixation on Jesus and His disciples. However justifiable his disgust with the bourgeois ethos may have been, the latter has not been unilaterally evil nor has any other age been unilaterally good. His colleague and friend, Jacob Burckhardt, saw this with far sharper clarity. According to Burckhardt, every era pays a price for its distinctive achievements.[11] Nietzsche's celebrated candor has its own inauthentic moments in the rhetoric of Zarathustra, in his narcissism and in an intermittent tone of hysteria which is out of kilter with his remarkable powers of discrimination.

Although Heidegger himself claims to present us with a "value-free" description rather than a moral judgment of Inauthenticity, his association of *Gerede* (idle chatter) with not being oneself represents a critique of society as subjective as Kierkegaard's or Nietzsche's. For Heidegger the inane chatter of talk-show hosts and other men of our day, who refuse to assume any personal responsibility for their utterances, is a quintessential form of self-betrayal. Heidegger's distinctive notion of Inauthenticity may be understood as the culmination of an existential dichotomy between "moral man and immoral society" which found its classic formulation in the writings of Rousseau. Contrary to Plato and Aristotle, who defined man as a social animal, Rousseau and his disciples discern the corruption of human nature in the role-playing demanded of the individual as the price of survival in society. Since they regard modern society as peculiarly artificial and demeaning in the sense of running counter to what each of us really is or ought to become, they connect salvation with apartness and separateness. Heideggerian Inauthenticity as *Gerede* mirrors a widespread contempt in modern times for politicians, propagandists, public relations men, commissars, and related spokesmen for the general welfare of humanity. What they have in common with the masses to which they address themselves is a penchant for platitudinous sayings so ingeniously parodied by the dramatists of the Absurd.

Yet Heidegger's conception of the Authentic is as unreliable as his analysis of the Inauthentic is trenchant. Like Kierkegaard he proposes a leap away from the complexities and admitted banalities in the industrial West to some "fairy land forlorn" about which Hölderlin sang so beautifully and which German classicists have been wont to praise to the sky with uncritical admiration not untouched by envy. Even granting Heidegger's contention that the unmediated experience of Poseidon by Thales was more authentic than the molecular formulation H_2O, the Greeks had their own varieties of the Inauthentic of which the figure of Alcibiades might serve as a fitting example. Furthermore, it is puzzling how Heidegger would set about reconciling the autonomy of an Athenian citizen with the institution of slavery on which it was based. Such quibbles aside, it is historically misleading if not downright false to hypostatize any ideal of Authenticity detached from its embodiment in mixed rights and wrongs. Heideggerian *Gerede* is at least as old as the Socratic irony devised to expose its vacuity. On the other hand, it is undeniable that democracy and the mass media have had a way of spreading and accentuating certain manifestations of Inauthenticity even while giving more people than ever a chance to get out from under the clutches of heteronomy in its multiple shapes and guises.

Tolstoy and the Inauthentic

With respect to his critique of Inauthenticity, Tolstoy is squarely in the existential tradition outlined in the preceding section. His resemblance to Kierkegaard proves uncanny in many ways, not least in their shared detestation of Christian hypocrisy and their break with their respective orthodox Establishments. His ideal Christian community is as anachronistic an alternative of authentic living for the oppressed Russian masses as Kierkegaard's *Urchristentum* for the sophisticated intelligentsia of western Europe after the Enlightenment. In the epilogue to *War and Peace* he mocks the pretentiousness of those historians who confuse an explanation with an invocation, not unlike Nietzsche in his *Use and Abuse of History* exposing the inauthenticity of the past as merely studied in contradistinction to the past as lived. Both Tolstoy and Nietzsche, it is worth observing here, were fatalists; hypersensitive to the inevitabilities in human destiny, yet at the same time perspicaciously attuned to individual differentiation. Above all, as already suggested, Tolstoy entertained a Heideggerian antipathy to society and its rules. Tolstoy's greatness as an unmasker of the Inauthentic surpasses similar efforts of all but Pascal because he was unsparing of himself in probing the depths of his own deceit. It is fair to say that the writings of the philosophers of *Existenz* on this subject are propaedeutic to Tolstoy's testimony both in his fiction and in his autobiographical writings.

The life of the master of Yasnaya Polyana began to inspire torrents of words even while he was still very much alive. His conversion, for example, not unlike Heidegger's *Kehre* or Wordsworth's premature decay, has provided his biographers with seemingly inexhaustible material for educated guesses, bizarre speculations, and just plain drivel. The long-held opinion that there is a sharp chronological cleavage between the artist who created *War and Peace* and *Anna Karenina* and the moralist who wrote *Resurrection* and *What Is Art?*, though thoroughly discredited by the best scholarship on the subject, still lingers on. Such an interpretation not only cannot account for *Hadji Murad*, written in the style of *War and Peace* and published posthumously, but fails to do minimal justice to the continuities which run throughout Tolstoy's checkered career.

To put the matter another way: far more puzzling than any discrepancies between his pre- and post-conversion outlooks are the internal inconsistencies at any juncture in Tolstoy's development. From a formal point of view, the hold of the Gospel-oriented system of values on the late Tolstoy is not too dissimilar from Count Leo's earlier attempts to find a master key to all the loose ends of the contingent. In one of his earlier stories, "Lucerne," a scathing attack on social callousness, Tolstoy, for all his disillusionment with the improvement of morals through civilization, nevertheless discerns the hand of some higher power in man's apparent inhumanity to man.[12] Although Nekhlyudov (Tolstoy) is unashamedly appalled by the hotel guests' utter disregard for the plight of the singer to whom they had listened with such enjoyment, after condemning them for their lack of compassion and after mercilessly analyzing the fusion of sophistication and heartlessness in human events, he turns around and, in the manner of Alexander Pope, reaffirms that "partial evil" is "universal good." Similarly, in his essay "The Meaning of the Russian Revolution," Tolstoy, after elaborating in great detail the evils of modern nationalism and chauvinism and suggesting the most dire possibilities for the future of Europe, startles the reader with intimations of a Christian rebirth. In each case it is difficult to reconcile Tolstoy's analytic acumen with his professions of faith.[13]

Tolstoy, the fervent rationalist in his educational experiments at Yasnaya Polyana, not only anticipated many of Freud's insights into man's unconscious motivation but became an advocate of anarchism in politics. A consummate literary stylist, he condemned Shakespeare's works, as well as his own, as detrimental to the growth of character. And just as his Schopenhauerian death-wish was belied by the fathering of numerous children, his pacifism did not suppress his enthusiasm for the chase and the hunt. It might be said that where Peter Verkhovensky found beauty in nihilism, Tolstoy discerned exultation in controversy and pointed contrariness. Moreover, Gorky was probably correct in pointing out in his *Reminiscences* that Tolstoy's brand of Christianity was superimposed in a strained manner on his natural paganism.[14] What helps make these incongruities so intriguing is Tolstoy's lifelong quest for authenticity and sincerity. Indeed it is hard to think of another writer who has so doggedly pursued the truth both about himself and society. His exposures of society, with its anti-values of prestige, likableness, power affection, and daemonic insensitivity to human suffering, retain an inescapable vividness. Nothing along these lines seems to escape Tolstoy's merciless eye as he probes deeper and deeper into our self-created hells on earth. At the same time there is something pathetic about the aging writer duly garbed in peasant attire, desperately trying to toil on an equal basis with his peasants, many of whom are quoted as saying that their master probably had more important work to do. His failure to come to terms with his own uniqueness is no less striking than his inability to combine sainthood with libertinism. Turgenev on his deathbed pleaded with him (in vain as it turned out) to be content with remaining a great writer, just as Belinsky, at an earlier time, tried to dissuade Gogol from his own kind of Orthodox fanaticism. In many ways like Dostoevsky, Tolstoy was one of those rare tormented souls in whom the gifts of a genius and the calling of an apostle fruitfully if uneasily commingled.

In his *Confession*, written in the course of his conversion, Tolstoy recounts with Augustinian hindsight and self-laceration the story of his restless quest for a meaningful mode of existence. Very much in the manner of his semi-autobiographical heroes, Levin and Pierre, he moves from one possible answer to the next, only to discover the latest solution failing him in its turn. Neither life, knowledge, art, nor institutional religion can assuage his terror of death and emptiness. What seems to trouble him most about the futile stages of his spiritual journey, a characteristic Tolstoyan objection by the way, is the disagreement he finds among the experts on the issue of life and death. This is odd, because in his fiction Tolstoy displays an uncanny awareness of the individuality of this ultimate struggle. He must have realized that expectations of expertise in coping with the perplexities of life are as incongruous as formulas for the composition of symphonies. Yet, apparently distraught over his own instability in the realm of the spirit, he postulates various sets of rules for self-improvement, designed to insure his eventual redemption. Naturally they cannot do so, not only because Tolstoy was a somewhat more complicated person than Benjamin Franklin but, above all, because there cannot be any guaranteed invulnerability to the trials and tribulations any man may have to confront in the course of his career.

Perhaps the climax of *The Confession* is Tolstoy's chapter on the knowledge of death, in which he berates himself for lacking the courage to commit suicide, as he was frequently tempted to do. With respect to death he classifies himself among the weak who are unable to follow through on their Schopenhauerian insight into the vanity of concrete personal existence. Whereas the stupid, Tolstoy argues, are unaware of the treacherous character of finitude, and the rich and privileged too unimaginative to perceive this truth beyond their indulgence in fleeting pleasure, only the strong are prepared to act in accordance with their convictions. Considering that Schopenhauer himself rejected suicide as inconsistent with one of his supreme virtues, equanimity, and that orthodox Christianity has regarded it as a mortal sin, Tolstoy's apparent regrets about his powerlessness to take his own life are highly idiosyncratic. This lover of the hunt, of sexual intercourse, novel writing and reading, teaching and farming, knowledge and sensuousness, was subject to a recurring horror of existence compared to which Dostoevsky's epileptic fits may well have been mild, at least as far as their repercussions on his will to live were concerned.

The Diary of a Lunatic recapitulates a number of scenes from Tolstoy's life in which he felt the earth disappearing beneath his feet. In one of these he overheard an angry exchange of words between his nurse and a housekeeper. His sensibility was so bruised by this occurrence that he broke out into uncontrollable sobs. For that matter, there can be no doubt about Tolstoy's genuineness of feeling, rationalist *malgré lui* that he often professed to be. Subsequently, he relates an incident from his life where a friend of his was cruelly beaten for some minor misdemeanor. Once more the abyss opened up beneath him. He was similarly affected, he tells us, by reading about the Crucifixion, with its senseless cruelty. But following a lengthy period of respite from these attacks, the most severe occurred while he was on a business trip to purchase some new piece of property. Suddenly the whole enterprise struck him as hopelessly ludicrous and pointless. Transposing this terror to the entire sphere of life, especially as lived by members of his class, he broke out in a cold sweat which forced him to return home before completing his business. Unlike Gogol's Madman, who was correctly if brutally certified as insane, Tolstoy makes a point of telling us that the authorities judged him responsible for his actions, though he himself entertained serious fears that his self might be divided.

Another crucial sphere of life in which Tolstoy was cast in the role of *Doppelgänger* is that of sexuality. Yielding again and again to what he regarded as his sinful lust for his own wife after thirty years of marriage, the author of "The Kreutzer Sonata" publicly came to advocate the extinction of the human race as a preferable option to any deviation from celibacy. Prior to his marriage Tolstoy, like the majority of his class had, by his own account, indulged himself with women socially inferior to him. His description of his lechery may in fact be exaggerated, just as St. Augustine's, Pascal's, and Kierkegaard's reminiscences of this kind appear at times inflated with the wisdom of spiritual hindsight. In any case, by his own admission, even in his seventies Tolstoy was unable to control his sensuous impulses and thus gravitated back and forth between public declarations of total abstinence and private compulsiveness, which proved so humiliating to his wife. For her part, she insisted on reading his private diaries whose entries, particularly on sex, so glaringly contradicted his profession of ascetic Christianity. If religion consoled Tolstoy for the hopelessness of the human predicament, sexuality provided an outlet for his enormous spontaneity, whose daemonic shadows he wished to exorcise from the world.

When the young Wanda Landowska played the harpsichord for the aging master of Yasnaya Polyana, he reputedly burst into tears, though the author of *What Is Art?* had no use for absolute music or any other expression of art which did not ostensibly serve to build human character along strict Christian lines. But although Tolstoy could deceive himself into thinking that physicians, judges, and women were singled out to compound our sins on earth, he was too fundamentally sincere a man to conceal his tears of joy or pain when some experience, however inconsistent with his avowed principles, went straight to his heart. In this light one may question Prince Andrey's single-mindedness in telling Natasha from his deathbed that he loved her too much as a particular person, meaning that each of us should love everyone else with perfect equality. Tolstoy himself was given to this sort of pontification on solemn occasions, but almost everything in his life testifies to a contrary impetus in these matters. With St. Augustine he could well have said: Lord, give me chastity, but not yet.

The Deviousness of Self-Realization

In the closing decades of his remarkable career, Tolstoy, the embattled polemicist, continued to display his genius as a novelist in a sequence of stories acidly dissecting the quintessential manifestations of human misery and inauthenticity. Of these works of art, "The Death of Ivan Ilyich," with its interweaving themes of self-deception, death, heartlessness, and social duplicity, stands out as an unsurpassed exploration of inauthentic behavior. From Heidegger, who in a footnote to *Sein und Zeit* somewhat grudgingly acknowledges his debt to Tolstoy's narrative, we learn that each man must die for himself, and that it is impossible to hide from our most crushing boundary situation by taking refuge amid the generalities of *Das Man* (the editorial "we") and interminable ice-breaking small-talk (*Gerede*). What Tolstoy shows us, in concrete detail, is the physical and moral decomposition of an individual, whose "normal" mode of existence has poisoned his life with treacherous falsehoods. Only as he comes to see these in the hypocritical behavior of his family and friends during his final ordeal does he find the strength to save himself. In "The Death of Ivan Ilyich," Tolstoy confronts us with three inseparable dimensions of inauthenticity; first, the horrendous emptiness of society masquerading as respectability; second, the frightening power of a man to deceive himself; and third, our adamant desire to conceal from ourselves what we abstractly admit to be indubitable truths.

If Ivan Ilyich had been allowed to die alone on some desert island, his physical sufferings and even some of his moral torments might well have been the same, but at least he would have been spared the experience of society holding up his now discarded views to him in cruel mockery of his former robust self. It is quite likely that the responses evinced at his death and funeral tallied substantially with his own when, as must have been the case, he attended the last rites of deceased colleagues during his official career. Fortunately, men are prevented from witnessing their own funerals. Nevertheless, the overall behavior of Ivan Ilyich's immediate family and friends would in fact have prepared him for the display of bad faith occasioned by his demise.

Tolstoy begins his narrative not with an account of his hero's existential anguish in dying or with the "normal terror" of his living days, but rather with a careful analysis of comfortable mediocrity in relation to our *terminus ad quem*. The news of the irreparable loss of Ivan Ilyich first appears to his colleagues in the innocuous guise of a newspaper obituary. Tolstoy tells us that their thoughts at once turn to the vacancies and promotions opened up by the departure from the world of the living of yet another official.

Quite apart from the vanity and self-seeking of people in such special circumstances, a qualitative chasm divides the immediate experience of dying from its presentation in an obituary column. Newspapers are notorious for throwing together facts of the most indiscriminate kind, so that after reading them awhile, one's senses become dulled to the moral difference between, say, the senseless slaughter of millions and the trivial lunacy of an exhibitionist. Only on rare occasions does the tone in which an event is presented in day-to-day journalism mirror anything resembling its true relative significance in the wider course of human affairs. More specifically, an obituary notice, far from leading the reader to dwell self-referentially on his own death, often provides him with therapeutic relief in the form of nostalgia from the pressing dictates of personal choice. Reading in the comfort of our living rooms about somebody else's death, we are more than usually apt to be deceived by our "animal faith" in immortality. Even though we may be fleetingly saddened by the report of someone's permanent absence whom we may have genuinely cared about, the contrast between our aesthetic stance as conscious absorbers of such information and the quality of that information is almost irresistibly ego-inflating. A veritable gulf divides the usual newspaper description of someone's death from the reader's awareness of his own inevitable demise. In the light of Ivan Ilyich's terrible end it is doubly inauthentic that his cold-hearted friends are apprised of it in this manner.

Having taken note of Ivan Ilyich's death, his mourners must now pay their respects to their colleague's wife, whose capacity for affectation is an extraordinary phenomenon in itself. The irony of the whole situation is heightened further by the possibility of hazardous eruptions of genuine emotion in this precarious setting of contrived grief. However insincere men act in society, they rarely attain the stature of utterly reliable performers whose every move is properly calculated and executed to achieve a specific effect. Ivan Ilyich himself had a singular talent for moving back and forth between coldly professional and personal modes of behavior, not only because he had carefully trained himself to perform this juggling act in the interest of impartial justice, but also at times because of an irrepressible element of his basic humanity partially immune to the dictates of mere expediency. Similarly his friends, who have come to give him their final farewell, are not invulnerable to giving themselves away, even while living up to the highest demands of deception and self-deception as practiced by Ivan Ilyich's widow.

Peter Ivanovich, Ivan Ilyich's colleague, exemplifies with particular vividness the Heideggerian syndrome of Inauthenticity. While he remarks that the widow will never get over the death of her husband his thoughts are fixed on being able to do his brother-in-law in Kaluga a favor (now that a vacancy has opened up). The element of insincerity between his thought and speech might well be unconscious on this occasion. There is no blatant contradiction between lending a helping hand and the expression of sorrow. Yet in subsequent incidents the impression is reinforced that Peter Ivanovich has been conditioned to relate himself opportunistically to experience even where other more spontaneous impulses cry out to be heard. In contrast to the widow, whom Tolstoy presents as a veritable monster of contrived two-facedness under ironclad control, Peter Ivanovich perhaps is to a larger degree the victim of the circles in which he learned to struggle for success and popularity. His second reaction to Ivan Ilyich's death is one of relief that he himself was spared. With the possible exception of saints this feeling is common to all men who can take a detached view of human disasters. On the assumption that the terror of death is indeed even greater than that of life, Peter Ivanovich's self-congratulatoriness under the circumstances is perfectly intelligible. Our capacity for placing ourselves in another person's shoes when the chips are down is narrowly circumscribed by our visceral imperatives.

When Peter Ivanovich views the corpse he is made uncomfortable by what he takes to be a reproof of the living on the part of the dead. Unlike Schwartz, another mourner, who in Peter Ivanovich's eyes is above such morbid responses which may go so far as to interfere with the pursuit of everyday business and pleasure, he, Peter Ivanovich, is strangely if only fleetingly unnerved by the sight of the dead Ivan Ilyich, whose appearance is at odds with the last agonies leading up to his demise. Peter Ivanovich is among the living, for most of whom the presence of the dead is far from diminished by their objective soullessness. On the contrary, a lifeless body, a face no longer capable of radiating animation can bear uncanny witness to the meaning of life and death.

Compared to Praskovya Fyodorovna, to whom he must presently convey his personal condolences, Peter Ivanovich turns out to be a superior specimen of humanity. As was noted already, for all his craftiness in staying ahead in society, he has been unable to root out every vestige of his Rousseauean self, whereas Ivan Ilyich's widow has managed to appropriate *mauvaise foi* as a coherent life style to the point where whatever innermost being she once possessed has for all practical purposes vanished from view. Where Peter Ivanovich has been swept along by a vast tide of social hypocrisy, so that he is frequently unaware of his personal implications in imitating poses of the successful, Praskovya Fyodorovna knows only too well what she is doing. No wonder that in the course of their encounters she clearly outclasses Peter Ivanovich in the finesse of her deception.

The initial ice-breaking encounter between Peter Ivanovich and Praskovya Fyodorovna is carried off without a hitch. Both parties know precisely what the situation requires of them and since nothing unusual happens to disrupt the carefully anticipated routine of showing crocodile tears, success is a foregone conclusion. Just as Peter Ivanovich had remembered, Tolstoy tells us, to cross himself at an earlier stage of the proceedings, now the time had come for him to sigh as part of the overall effect which, we learn with cutting irony, society expected of both of them. For once the morality of marionettes has received its vindication. The next situation, however, is already somewhat more problematic. Peter Ivanovich and Praskovya Fyodorovna go to the drawing room. He sits on a low ottoman, while she sits on the sofa. When she catches her lace and he jumps up to undo her, the springs, recoiling, almost throw him off. Then the identical sequence of events happens all over again.

> When this was over she took out a white batiste handkerchief and began to weep. But Pyotr Ivanovich's spirits had been chilled by the episode with the lace and the struggle with the ottoman, and so he just sat and scowled.[15]

From a Freudian point of view his scowl represents a devious trick played by his libido on his rigidly held ego, whereas Praskovya Fyodorovna retained her composure as she played to perfection her role of a widow grieving over her loss.

She proceeds to explain to Peter Ivanovich that her undiminished capacity for carrying out practical tasks in her present circumstances is really for her husband's sake. For his part, Peter Ivanovich, despite his awareness of his own and the widow's hypocrisy, remains shaken by the death of a man whom he had known as a carefree schoolboy. Just as his spirits were cast down by the lace episode, his soul is touched by this recollection of youth. It is the tyranny of inclination which makes consistent insincerity of the sort projected by Ivan Ilyich's widow a closed option for Peter Ivanovich.

Nevertheless, by continuing to regard Ivan Ilyich's death as a mishap rather than something that will happen to him as well, he too cuts himself off from any adequate understanding of man's most crucial *Grenze* situation. This abstract nonchalance, Tolstoy observes with his customary psychological perspicacity, enables Peter Ivanovich to take a genuine interest in the details of Ivan's final hours. Only those who don't get too depressed by the fleet-

ingness and pain of personal existence can investigate it with
scientific curiosity, which of course Tolstoy himself shared. But
the rare genius of the novelist that on sundry occasions drove
him to the brink of insanity was to combine existential insight
into the subjective condition of his own self with the powers of
scrutiny of a mortician preparing a corpse for burial.

Tolstoy wants us to believe that Ivan Ilyich's life, with the
possible exceptions of his childhood and concluding mystical
experience, was consistently false and worthless. This unflattering
estimate is scarcely borne out by the kind of evidence normally
adduced to judge failure or success. In those "commonsense"
terms Ivan Ilyich had worked hard and conscientiously to become
an efficient examining magistrate with a recognized capacity for
fairness and responsible judgment. Though there were some
typical indiscretions before his marriage, these cannot be said to
cast any blemish on his deserved respectability as a citizen or on
his standing as a family man, considering the double-standard
morality widely accepted in his day.

It is worth noting how Ivan Ilyich's very virtues underscore
his moral vulnerability. In a characteristic passage we learn that
on being appointed examining magistrate he used his power
graciously, if self-consciously; scrupulously assessed all relevant
facts in a particular case; and, observing the formalities to the
letter, divested his opinions of every trace of personal slant.
What could not be formalized, in other words, the elusive circumstances differentiating one concrete particular from another,
ceased to exist for him. Yet as the proposition "All men are
mortal" failed to console him in his last days, so he himself
previously failed his petitioners in completely overlooking the
idiosyncratic elements which are so much a part of individual
experience. Abstruse philosophical arguments, however coherently formulated, may well be inauthentic in relation to the
facts of life, as witness the theodicy of Leibnitz. Similarly, the
very purity of Ivan Ilyich's legal judgments casts doubt on their
intended relevance. In facing the accused on trial before him as
in facing his own death Ivan Ilyich tries to apply Occam's
Razor, only to find himself deceived by the unyielding dogmas of
brute empiricism.

Ivan Ilyich's gift for accommodating himself to the whims of
others or for being himself only insofar as he projected a flatter-

ing image in the eyes of his audience is emphasized in this superb passage.

As secretary on special commissions, Ivan Ilyich had danced as a rule; as examining magistrate he danced as an exception. He danced to show that, although he was an executor of the new legal code and a lawyer of the fifth rank, in matters of dancing, too, he was above the average.[16]

Putting up a brave front was also the key to the apparent success of his marriage. After a few months of conjugal bliss a disturbing element which he did not quite know how to cope with entered into his relationship to his wife. Instead of facing the inevitable irritations of family happiness even at its best, he threw himself frenetically into work, as if this could serve as a substitute for domestic tranquility. In fact, the same sort of inauthenticity which marred his humanity as a judge now destroyed his solace at home. On the one hand, he reduced justice to mere legality; on the other, he came to conceive of marriage as nothing but decent meals, a comfortable bed, and, at any costs, the maintenance of correct appearances. In both cases he deceived himself into thinking that everything was as it should be. "As a matter of fact," Tolstoy comments on Ivan's new house, "it was just what is achieved by all people who are not really rich, but wish to resemble the rich, and end up by only resembling one another: hangings, ebony, flowers, carpets, and bronzes, everything dark and highly polished—precisely what a certain class of people create so as to make themselves like all other people of this particular class."[17] His house was so much like other people's that it made no impression, but he felt it to be very exceptional. Thus Ivan Ilyich misunderstands himself in all his activities, from the weightiness of the law courts to the ultimacy of family happiness. This pervasive act of misunderstanding in his life is tantamount to a false assessment of sustained graciousness and formal flawlessness as equivalent to substantive self-fulfillment. If society expected and required his all too willing wife to practice deception with consummate skill, Ivan Ilyich himself, more in the manner of his colleague Peter Ivanovich, was half-unconsciously seduced into living a lie in relation to himself.[18]

In the light of the foregoing it scarcely comes as a surprise that Ivan Ilyich is as self-deceived in the face of death as he was amid his affairs in life. As the narrator in Dostoevsky's *Notes from Underground* must descend into the basement to expose the Victorian illusions of man's perfectibility, Ivan Ilyich must be laid low by terminal illness before, now ailing and miserable, he can comprehend his self-deception in better times. At first, as long as things in general continue to go well for him, Ivan Ilyich deceives himself into thinking that the pain in his stomach is just a temporary setback, like bad luck at cards. This attitude is consistent with his deep-rooted unwillingness to accept intractable dilemmas. Even when recognized as a blessing in disguise death does not offer opportunities for a fresh start or, as Ivan might have put it, for recouping one's losses. Indeed, only a streak of bad luck in trivial matters prompts him to despair over his constant discomfort. Ironically enough, just at the point where Ivan Ilyich begins to understand, those around him pretend obnoxiously that everything is all right. The focal point of his awareness shifts from self-deception to the chicaneries of ceremonial deception. "Ivan Ilyich suffered most of all from the lie, the lie adopted by everyone for some reason, which said that he was only ill and not dying, and that everything would be all right if he just kept quiet and did what the doctors told him to."[19]

Tolstoy, whose dislike of physicians was second only to his contempt for judges, presents Ivan Ilyich's doctors as exploitative deceivers in league with society at large to conceal truth for the sake of decorum and selfish gain. Like the Sartrean waiter in *L'Être et le néant*, they put on such a good show at Ivan's bedside that it becomes impossible to distinguish their studied role as professionals from their honest selves. On this point Tolstoy has been regarded as unfair. No less a Christian than Dietrich Bonhoeffer observed in his *Letters and Papers from Prison* that the fallen nature of man necessitates a certain degree of camouflage out of respect for its fragility. Quite aside from their falsely comforting bedside manner Ivan Ilyich's doctors may have been charlatans, though on this score too Tolstoy had a way of confusing partial knowledge with total ignorance, not allowing for genuine helplessness in the face of unsolved problems.

If one grants the absurd position which Tolstoy's fanatical logic sometimes led him to entertain, his insistence on absolute candor in "The Death of Ivan Ilyich" is essentially consistent with his recurring attack on pretense and false consciousness as the core of human folly. From an existential point of view, a dying man who wants to know the truth about his condition is entitled to receive it, if only so that his relationship to himself and his family will not be poisoned by the resulting disingenuousness. If, as Plato maintained in the *Phaedo*, true philosophy is preparation for death, each individual should be given the opportunity to meditate on the meaning of his life in the face of the cessation of consciousness. Had Ivan Ilyich been content to die without asking embarrassing questions about his illness, his physicians might well have been under humane obligation to keep the truth from him. But since he insisted on knowing it, their evasive answers to his questions and their fatuous smiles merely served to reinforce his family's hypocrisy and insensitivity to his spiritual needs. In sum, it is easy enough to accuse Tolstoy of being prejudiced against physicians and fanatical on telling the literal truth at all times and under any circumstances. Nevertheless, in spite of these faults, his genius for applying philosophy to life was as great as ever in portraying the dying Ivan Ilyich as tormented not only by pain but by an apparent conspiracy on the part of the living to ruin his last days on earth with intolerable deceptions which make a mockery of one of life's rare redeeming features: a reciprocal attitude of openness toward one's family and friends.

An interesting contrast to the plausibly benign deception practiced on Ivan Ilyich by his attending physicians is the cold-hearted hypocrisy of his wife. In a characteristic manner of speaking she informs her protesting husband that she has decided to call in a specialist for *her* sake, she claims disingenuously in order to appease him, rather than for *his*. The truth of the matter is that everything she undertakes is done for no one else's sake but hers, thus robbing her half-hearted gesture of concern of all potential authenticity. Praskovya Fyodorovna's bad faith is so deeply engrained in her nature that, unlike his physicians, she becomes incapable of even pretending in her husband's behalf.

Intimidated by his own family, deceived by his doctors, self-deceived by confounding social success with personal happiness, Ivan Ilyich lies dying. The ruffled decorum around him merely exacerbates his realization of bottomless anguish. Memories of childhood soothingly recall a vanished state of single-mindedness.[20] Ivan Ilyich is further consoled by his servant, Gerasim, who hopes that someone will do the same for him when his turn to die arrives. Gerasim's intuitive understanding of his master's agony as well as his willingness to carry out the most disagreeable tasks of nursing is, as Tolstoy would have us believe, indissolubly tied to his lack of formal education and his lowly social standing.

Like Dostoevsky in this respect, the intellectual Tolstoy did not believe that intellectuals were likely to act in accord with their superior powers of moral discrimination. On the other hand, far more than Dostoevsky, Tolstoy at times succumbed to a demonstrably false correlation between a state of ignorance and "purity of heart." Just as historical evidence does not support the liberal's contention that being cultured furnishes any guarantee of behaving well towards one's fellows, the obverse has scarcely been borne out by the brutes who ran Hitler's and Stalin's liquidation camps. Only in the context of a pronounced Germanic idolatry of men of learning as paragons of virtue, which reached its zenith in the half century before World War I, does Tolstoy's uneasy veneration of ignorant peasants serve as a justifiable corrective to this kind of *kultur*idolatry.

Gerasim's loving care of his dying master thus exemplifies Tolstoy's dominant philosophy of death.[21] Accordingly, it is only by helping one another, by putting ourselves in the place of the closest victim, that we become undeceived about the realities of finitude. Authentic dying always presupposed an insight into the frailty and precariousness of one's grip on happiness. In "The Death of Ivan Ilyich" Tolstoy incriminates society as a major purveyor of falsehood and self-deception, but he also shows how authenticity surfaces amid this quagmire of conceit and boastfulness.

What, had he lived authentically, would Ivan Ilyich's life have been like? It is of course impossible to consider such a contrary-to-fact state of affairs without lapsing into questionable speculation. One might suppose Ivan Ilyich working away diligently but not overambitiously to see that justice tempered by compassion is implemented wherever the decision lies within his control. Instead of giving himself airs of superiority, he would address himself to court cases as a fellow human being, as vulnerable to pain and suffering as those appearing before him. His attitude toward his good fortune, whether in family or professional affairs, would not be divorced from a feeling of gratitude for having been spared those blows of fate which frustrate, embitter, or lay low the large majority of mortals. Within limits of self-concern he would turn his back on the ways of hypocritical society save where his taking a forthright stand might lead to the amelioration of the human lot. He would rejoice in or grieve over the experiences of his friends and acquaintances pretty much (in kind if not in degree) as he would over his own. He would substitute openness and humility for stuffiness and vanity in relating both to himself and to other selves. This transfigured Ivan Ilyich, almost beyond good and evil in the Kantian sense, would approximate saintliness. Quite obviously the tormented Tolstoy would never have made such a character the hero of this study of death. Just as Plato, in the *Symposium*, defined man's condition as chronically semi-ignorant (unlike the gods in knowing so little and unlike other animals in wanting to know anything at all) and Pascal saw him occupying a position halfway between the angels and the beasts, Tolstoy's existential hero can enter his kingdom of heaven only after having suffered the trials and tribulations of deception and self-deception to which all of us are constantly exposed.

The Unnaturalness of Sex

Perhaps the most crucial statement about man made by Tolstoy in his later fiction centers on the fact that men take refuge in a false security which sooner or later will come crumbling down over their heads. They take things for granted which are anything but self-evidently true, especially in assessing their particular ego as outstanding precisely when they should be appalled by its mediocre normalcy. While Ivan Ilyich misses the self-referential import of the proposition that all men are mortal, Pozdnyshev fails to see that the emotion elicited by sublime works of art is an inadequate bond for a happy marriage, that, in fact, coldness of heart in the closest interpersonal relationships is perfectly compatible with passionate intensity in the realm of spiritedness, desire, and mood.

In "The Kreutzer Sonata" Tolstoy focuses on sexuality and deception. Once more he confronts his readers with the idolatry of the exceptional, blistering attacks on physicians, and the corruption of the upper middle class by a veneer of decorum and pseudo-respectability. Moreover, just as Ivan Ilyich's self-esteem is irreparably undermined by the shaky foundations of capricious fortune, Pozdnyshev's *amour propre* is shattered, although he is exonerated of the murder of his wife. But there are also significant differences. The substance of "The Kreutzer Sonata" is narrated in the first person by a man broken in spirit, whose "glittering" eyes, Tolstoy suggests, express a touch of madness which is also reflected in the extremity of his views. While Pozdynshev voices some of Tolstoy's teachings on sexuality and marriage, his presentation of these is colored by frenetic restlessness. Tolstoy stresses Pozdnyshev's distraughtness by repeatedly referring to an eerie noise he involuntarily makes (like a hiccup) whenever he clears his throat.

In the manner of Dostoevsky's Underground Man, Pozdnyshev is pathologically burdened by his experiences. Certainly Tolstoy's famous statement in "The Death of Ivan Ilyich" to the effect that Ivan's life was so terrible precisely because it was so normal does not apply (without numerous qualifications) to a man who murders his wife in a fit of jealous rage. At the same time, Tolstoy would want to insist on the normalcy of the social conditions which made Pozdnyshev into a partly deranged criminal. Pozdnyshev's compulsive tea drinking, his walking up and down the aisle of the train and the station platform, his unsparing self-debasement, and his gruffness toward his listener do not help to make him a dispassionate witness of the events he describes nor of the theoretical reflections he has based upon them. Unlike Ivan Ilyich (until, half dead, he screams with pain), Pozdnyshev, still very much alive, has lost his composure and is beside himself with fury and grief. His confessional statement of his experiences gives them an air of terror and urgency surpassing in existential pathos the second-hand description of events in "The Death of Ivan Ilyich."

Before Pozdnyshev narrates the incidents leading up to the murder of his wife, Tolstoy initiates us into a discussion of sexuality which is in progress in the railroad-carriage taking Pozdnyshev to his voluntary exile from society in the south of Russia. The tone of the discussion is at times anticipatory of Women's Liberation talk in our own day.

"Vice, you say?" I put in. "But you are speaking of the most natural human function."

"Natural?" said he, "Natural? No, I must say that I have come to the opposite conclusion—that it is against nature, that it is highly unnatural. Ask children. Ask innocent young girls. When my sister was very young she married a dissolute man twice her age. I remember how surprised we were on the night of her wedding to have her come running out, pale and in tears, crying that she wouldn't—not for anything, not for anything! That she could not even find words to describe what he wanted of her!

"And you call it natural! There are things that are natural. There are things that are pleasant and delightful and without shame from the very beginning. But not this. This is loathsome and shameful and painful. No it is not natural! And I am convinced that an innocent girl always hates it."[22]

Tolstoy, who, Nietzsche-like, made no bones about his dislike of women, in "The Kreutzer Sonata" would appear to take their side against the double-standard morality of those upper classes that he despised utterly. In his polemical writings on sex and marriage there is to be found many a tirade against the perpetuation of the human race and the sexual act in particular. But in "The Kreutzer Sonata," while seriously playing with the same ideas, Tolstoy's argumentation is far subtler than that. What disturbs him above all is the discrepancy between the profession of Victorian puritanism and the incongruous actualities of sexual practice. Or, translated into the terms of the narrative of "The Kreutzer Sonata," he is bothered by the glaring non-reciprocity between Pozdnyshev's insistence on virginal purity from the woman he is going to marry and his seduction of girls from the lower classes. The bachelor Pozdnyshev, Tolstoy observes with his customary relish for exposing man's infinite capacity to veil selfishness in the guise of correct behavior, at one and the same time worshiped the Madonna in whoever might qualify for his middle-class bride, while deflowering maidens of humbler origin with smug gratification. Don Giovanni himself had not made such distinctions.

Tolstoy, furthermore, is worried about another aspect of this double-standard sexual practice. Not only, he claims, does it destroy Pozdnyshev's self-respect in negotiating with himself and others in society but it also has the effect of ruining the integrity of those carefully nurtured upper-class virgins whose advantages in the world are supposed to set them on a pedestal infinitely removed from the experience of coquettes and prostitutes. As Jane Austen had already observed in her correspondence, young women of the upper classes ostentatiously display their shoulders at balls first in order to be noticed and then in order to be conquered. Tolstoy, who, incidentally, regarded the English as models of insincerity,[23] takes up the same theme in "The Kreutzer Sonata."

Pozdnyshev's wife is portrayed as a representative woman of her class, which is to say, spoiled, decorative, flighty, and educated solely to become a desirable matrimonial object. Her fickleness, which leads directly to her doom, embodies one kind of inauthenticity with peculiar vividness. Her excitability having been divorced from any genuine warmth of feeling, except where accident may bring them together for a brief while, she is in Tolstoy's view typically incapable of autonomous devotion and self-sacrifice. Shaped by the hypocrisy of the salon, her character responds capriciously to the most serious choices of her life. Whatever philosophy she might come to adopt, the juvenile education of her sentiments will end up reducing it to yet another example of juvenilia. She allows herself to be seduced by the violinist not because he means substantially more to her than her husband but rather because the supposed spirituality of his music-making engenders in her a passing sense, however unacknowledged, of carnal fulfillment. Trukhachevsky thrills her with his elegant attire and manner, his proximity as a duo partner for piano-violin music, and his dignified bearing under social stress.

Like Natasha Rostova and Anna Karenina, the undeniable beauty of Pozdnyshev's wife easily plays tricks on her virtue and encourages deception as well as self-deception: the former on account of radiating a sparkle behind which lurks emptiness; the latter by inducing excessive states of self-intoxication. It is one thing for the young Natasha to captivate a beau's heart merely by being her mercurial self, but the wife of Pozdnyshev should have outgrown this hazardous virtuosity. Granted that in the role of Pierre's wife, Natasha is transformed by Tolstoy into a puritanical caricature of her former spontaneous overflowing self; but this possibly may have been the price she had to pay for assuming responsibility for the well-being of her family. Pozdnyshev's wife, on the other hand, neither assumed such responsibility nor gave up her craving for living in daydreams. Although Pozdnyshev vilifies himself as her murderer, the fact that he cannot forgive her until she is dead, added to her own machinations and insensitivity while she was alive, speaks for a revision of the guilt assessed. Anna Karenina, a far more lovable person by nature, also conspired to bring about her own fate, if only by misjudging the character of Vronsky. If Pozdnyshev was consumed by jealousy, and Karenin by overweening arrogance and coldness, their respective wives were too unstable, too deficient in authentic selfhood, to withstand the lures life cast their way.

A second mode of inauthenticity Tolstoy associates with Pozdnyshev's relationship to his wife is their mutual confusion of spiritual and carnal love. Tolstoy's views on this, as on so many other subjects, are not consistent. In the novella *Father Sergius* he comments favorably on the Romantic Idealism of the forties by which the betrothed was elevated to inaccessible heights as against the crude materialism of the eighties and nineties by virtue of which every bride-to-be is immediately reduced by her husband to a mere object of carnal desire.[24] At least so far as a woman's view of herself is concerned, Tolstoy argues here somewhat surprisingly, her etherealization by the disciples of European Romanticism helped her to preserve a dignified image of herself, however alien and artificial in other respects. In "The Kreutzer Sonata" Pozdnyshev's account of his tragedy ruthlessly mocks all incantations and intimations of spiritual love as resting on a flagrant lie. Thus he maintains that conjugal bliss is rooted in sexual rather than ideological compatibility. Any talk to the contrary, in Pozdnyshev's estimation, is sheer stupidity. His wife, however, and perhaps even he prior to his conversion, took such talk quite seriously. One could maintain that she succumbed to such "high arguments of love" precisely because she was disposed to confuse sensuality with the cerebral excitement induced by classical music. Only after his downfall does Pozdnyshev fully realize that a coquette's seductiveness is to be discerned in the shape and texture of her frock rather than in any of her mental acts or habits.

Clearly Tolstoy means to tell us something about the error of

John Stuart Mill's implicit separation of the so-called higher and lower pleasures. Just as intellectuals can become as bored as "satisfied pigs," musical duets have a definite "family resemblance" to mutual affinities in the bedroom. Pozdnyshev's wife and the violinist innocently enough, it might seem, want to play violin sonatas together. Blameless or not, such "higher pleasure" incites Pozdnyshev to uncontrollable fits of jealousy and rage. Nevertheless his almost irrational suspicions that the musicians' primary desire is to sleep with each other prove ironically sound. While Pozdnyshev would never choose to be "Socrates dissatisfied," his grasp of sexuality as permeating the entire core of our being is integral to his obsessional frame of mind.

A further aspect of Tolstoy's critique of music as a spiritual delight above reproach is also revealed in "The Kreutzer Sonata." As did that other great libertine-saint of the nineteenth century, Kierkegaard, Tolstoy passionately loved music. Yet in the manner of the Danish thinker's *Either/Or*, he too postulated an exclusive disjunction between aesthetic receptivity and ethical religious seriousness. The very title, "The Kreutzer Sonata," underscores the import of music in Tolstoy's narrative of pathological jealousy and the unnaturalness of sexuality. Here he takes great care to make the kind of distinctions that endow his views with an undeniable degree of intellectual respectability. First, doubtless guided by his favorite philosopher, Schopenhauer, he affirms music to be the most noble of the arts. Yet how is it possible, he asks rhetorically, that precisely this refined monument to human creativity can serve as such a powerful corrupting influence on human relations? Both Pozdnyshev and his wife are transported into a state of ecstasy by the ravishing sounds of Beethoven's composition. This is also true of the violinist with whom she performs the work. If there is one thing on which these three are sincerely agreed upon, it is the irresistible beauty conveyed by the sonata for violin and piano. Pozdnyshev does not care for the more frivolous pieces played in the course of the musical *soirée*, a typical Tolstoyan touch to stress the incomparable vividness of excellence in the arts as well as in life. In theory Tolstoy may condemn Shakespearean tragedy and his own epic novels, but *de facto* he is only too cognizant of their irresistible beauty and of the aesthetic irrelevance of what he might enthrone as supreme in the sphere of morality.

It is worth recalling that Tolstoy like Dostoevsky repeatedly rejected the utilitarian view of art as solely ancillary to political and social ends. As Solzhenitsyn makes plain enough in *The Cancer Ward* and *The First Circle*, Tolstoy would have been the last person in the world to produce the kind of literature sanctioned by writers whom Dostoevsky had labeled "officials in a department." To be sure, Tolstoy adopted the role of a Christian apologist, without, however, surrendering his autonomy as a creative artist. His attacks on autocracy and Orthodoxy are at least as unsparing and, even more important, as unmistakably composed in his own voice as his tirades against the materialism of his age. The writer as ideological hack was an abomination to Tolstoy simply on the ground that in this position he could not be himself.

To return to Pozdnyshev's love of the Kreutzer Sonata: aside from helping to accomplish his wife's seduction by Trukhachevsky, the composition excites Pozdnyshev in ways which he finds painfully hazardous. It is in this connection that Tolstoy astutely comments on the difference between liturgical, military, and dance music vis-à-vis the absolute music of the masters. Whereas the former, he observes, leads directly to some form of action through which the inner agitation generated by the sound finds external discharge, the latter stores up a superabundance of nervous tension in the psyche of the listener which is put to no use whatever. On the contrary, such lovers of the best music as Pozdnyshev tend to wallow vicariously in high-keyed emotions they themselves never felt directly nor make any effort to translate into discernible events.[25] Beethoven at least, Tolstoy assumes, experienced firsthand whatever he evokes in his own compositions, while we listeners indulge ourselves in abstract pathos basically unrelated to direct intuitions. For us, in brief, music is *Erfahrung* (sense perception) rather than *Erlebnis* (internalized experience), or what Nietzsche described as the emotions delighting in themselves, undisciplined by any self-referential demands upon ourselves.

Tolstoy's reflections on the inauthenticity of music appreciation are full of undeniable existential insight. The least to be said for them is the cultivation of a well-founded mistrust of passionate music lovers as warm-hearted individuals. In fact, Tolstoy is probably correct in suggesting the opposite to be the case. The most refined taste in music is apt to appear hand in hand with the most rarefied intellectuality which spurns the imperfection of everyday mediocrity. Conversely, those who profess to like Tchaikovsky as much as Bach, for example, could well prove more dependable friends than those who prefer silence to the *1812* Overture. Aside from the experiential accuracy of these speculations, Tolstoy in "The Kreutzer Sonata" exposes the paradox of the sublime inviting evil. Counter-intuitively he forces us to associate genuine concern for others with musical sobriety, if not musical indifference. As generalizations about these matters go, this is far from a poor conjecture. Historically it must be seen in the context of an age which worshiped at the shrine of art and was prepared to commit the worst crimes, presumably in its behalf. Nietzsche, Rimbaud, Verlaine, Baudelaire, Maeterlinck, Oscar Wilde, and many other outstanding contemporaries often talked and acted irresponsibly in precisely this way. Tolstoy exposed their illusion with his unsparing self-criticism. When, as mentioned earlier, he was deeply touched by music in spite of his theoretical objections to its ill effects, the overpowering experience was accompanied by a degree of self-knowledge only a handful of creative artists since Plato have attained.

Tolstoy's focus on deception and self-deception in "The Kreutzer Sonata" as well as the subtlety of his argumentation is clearly evidenced throughout the narrative. In the train compartment, during the abstract discussion of the advantages and liabilities of modern marriage (a discussion carried on in innocence of Pozdnyshev's existential nightmare), Tolstoy observes that the shopkeeper was looking at the merchant for a clue as to how he should react to what was being said. This instance of outer-directedness contrasts glaringly with the passionate intensity evoked by the debate in progress. The narrator of these preliminaries, who must be distinguished from Pozdnyshev, the narrator of his own tragedy, proceeds to inform us that the advocates of orthodox puritan marriage catch themselves in a contradiction, having previously acknowledged extramarital adventures. Tolstoy, like Dostoevsky, spares no one from self-incrimination, not excluding those who might be supposed to agree with his publicly stated views. Pozdnyshev alone here speaks in an authentic voice. "Whoever heard of unity of ideas leading people to sleep together?" he asks rhetorically. If spiritual affinity and unity of ideas really prevailed, he shrewdly discerns, sleeping together would become unnecessary. (Surely this must be reckoned as one of the better arguments advanced against Hegel's claim to mediate all conflicts through the instrumentality of pure Spirit.) Neither the lawyer and the young woman with their advanced views, nor the shopkeeper and the merchant with their conservative ones are able to bridge the gap between "knowledge by acquaintance" and "knowledge by description." Only Pozdnyshev, who has been through hell, knows what it is all about, and he, significantly enough, does not join in the conversation except when addressing himself in a confessional tone to the first narrator. Though he is most qualified to perform the role of a discussion leader on the subject, he refuses to do so, going so far in the opposite direction as to stop speaking entirely when the conductor enters the compartment to check the tickets. His whole mode of communication, far from being that of a tolerant bystander, is in turn self-demeaning, frenzied, and unconsciously sincere.

Although passages advocating the renunciation of the sexual act as such can be found in Tolstoy's literary output, this is not the position Pozdnyshev embraces. What he decries is not the moral depravity of the sexual act but the irresponsibility of a man of the upper classes who exploits lower-class women solely for his pleasure—as if what they offered him could be paid for in coin or simply taken for granted. In a dramatic outburst he turns to the narrator:

> "Do not shake your head as if you agreed with me," he suddenly shouted. "I know better. You, you, all of you—you are all the same, unless you are some rare exception. At your best you hold the same views as I held. But what of it? Forgive me," he said. "I cannot help it; it is so dreadful, dreadful, dreadful."[26]

Note Pozdnyshev's existential consistency in rejecting abstract agreement from his travel companion whose nod of the head, like all gestures of this kind, is dishonest. Pozdnyshev hates himself not for having had sexual relations but for having attempted in vain to make restitution payments to his partner and, moreover, for taking special pride in being so generous. This particular manifestation of self-deception is centered in that bottomless vanity, which has prevented Pozdnyshev from coming to terms with his guilt feelings. Tolstoy, incidentally, makes some far-sighted statements about modern man's failure to practice birth control in contrast to the so-called lower animals whose breeding habits are, he asserts, apt to be more in accord with their prospects of survival. On the other hand, however unnatural the sexual instinct may be in Tolstoy's eyes, what drives Pozdnyshev to a nervous breakdown is, above all else, his gross violation of the I-Thou relationship in making love to his wife (as he had violated it in similar relationships with other women prior to his marriage).[27] His refusal to acknowledge his male chauvinism in this regard brings him to despair.

"Yes, I was a loathsome pig who fancied himself a saint," Pozdnyshev asserts with abrasive candor. He had not married for money or connections like so many members of his class, but what bothered him was his hypocritical insistence on his wife's purity when he himself had wallowed in the mud. Once again, as in his disparaging contrast of Napoleon and Alexander I in the epilogue to *War and Peace*, Tolstoy is basically concerned with exposing a man's excessive love of his own virtue. Nothing which Pozdnyshev had done up to the murder of his wife would have been conspicuously wicked, had it not been falsely authenticated by a misunderstanding of himself as unfailingly self-righteous. Possibly Pozdnyshev's most radical manifestation of inauthenticity consists in his living up to Dostoevsky's prophetic pronouncement that without God man can do as he pleases, if only because he no longer acknowledges a power greater than himself which gives weight to his affairs and aspirations.

Like the double-minded monk in the posthumously published novella *Father Sergius*, Pozdnyshev casts himself in the role of a Nietzschean *Übermensch* pitilessly at odds with his ineradicable inclinations. So enormous is man's vanity that he will worship himself regardless of what he may think or do. This was Tolstoy's dilemma, and one, ironically enough, which he, the relentless truth-seeker, could never satisfactorily overcome. Just as Pozdnyshev betrays himself in putting his future wife on a pedestal of rarefied beauty, proud in the knowledge that henceforth he will be monogamous and that he is not impelled by gross considerations to link her fortunes with his, Tolstoy himself came to exalt in suffering non-Christians to come unto him for spiritual counsel, terribly conscious of the compromising position in which this placed him as an incorrigible lover of life. Whereas inauthenticity for Dostoevsky lay primarily in his spiritual identification with the Underground Man while he, his creator, preached a gospel of obedience and humility, Tolstoy's inauthenticity above all took the form of disguising his pagan nature in the interest of gospel truth rationalized beyond credibility. On the other hand, Dostoevsky's unmatched expression of our most authentic moments of dread and hope corresponds to Tolstoy's remarkable gift for being faithful in his fiction to the widest range of our normal and abnormal experiences in life. Simply consider this incidental observation from "The Kreutzer Sonata": an innocent young girl knows intuitively what a coquette figures out with cunning—namely, as already noted, that men will forgive her her sins, but never an ugly, ill-fitting gown.

CHAPTER 5

Solzhenitsyn and the Inconsequence of Politics

"In our time the destiny of man presents its meaning in political terms."

THOMAS MANN

How can I, that girl standing there,
My attention fix
On Roman or on Russian
Or on Spanish politics?
Yet here's a travelled man that knows
What he talks about,
And there's a politician
That has read and thought,
And maybe what they say is true
Of war and war's alarms,
But O that I were young again
And held her in my arms!

W. B. YEATS
"Politics"

Introduction

AMONG THE NUMEROUS heart-rending passages in the fiction of
Solzhenitsyn, none lingers more vividly in the memory than those
which suggest an invidious comparison between exile in Siberia
under the tsars and the same fate suffered by millions of Soviet
citizens under Stalin. Indeed, even given the excessive grotesqueries of twentieth-century history, with the possible exception of
Hitlerian genocide, it is hard to think of a tragedy as staggering as
the fate of the Russian people at the hands of their new rulers,

notably Stalin, who always claimed to have their best interest at heart. Where the exiled Decembrists were joined by their families[1] and at least provided with those basic amenities which could serve to preserve their self-respect, Stalin's prisoners are systematically brutalized and deprived of any possible hope of redeeming themselves in society. Arrested in the middle of the night, beaten into confession and submission, shoved from one transit prison to the next in a merry-go-round of horror piled upon indignity, arbitrarily resentenced, they present a picture of the damned whose distinctive irony is its location: the official paradise of the people supposedly governed by socialist ideology. Eugenia Ginzburg, whose account of her own sufferings before World War II reinforces Solzhenitsyn's, reveals how above all, after two years of solitary confinement, she feared being cast to the sharks as she lay dying from starvation and incredibly inhuman treatment on a steamer transporting her to the northernmost reaches of the Soviet prison system.[2] Like Solzhenitsyn himself, she had been judged one of the enemies of the people, more criminal in the eyes of the state than murderers and rapists who presumably had remained faithful to the unshakable principles of Stalinist Marxism.

The agonizing analogy which Solzhenitsyn evokes again and again between nineteenth- and twentieth-century Russia, to the unmistakable advantage of the former, extends beyond the features of their respective prison systems to such seemingly indestructible institutions as censorship of literature.[3] However much he may have had to conceal or veil thinly, no novelist of the nineteenth century was compelled to glorify the Imperial regime. If his accentuation of the negative was restricted in some ways, at least he was spared the humiliation of having to sanctify the *status quo*.[4] This alone makes Solzhenitsyn's achievement doubly remarkable. Not only do his underground novels fly in the face of socialist realism but in doing so they challenge the rules of the game of surviving as a writer in the Soviet Union. An uncompromising foe of professional optimism, Solzhenitsyn, speaking from within his own country, goes out of his way to expose the shallow faith of the party bosses (quite apart from scrutinizing their misuse of power).

The major theme of Solzhenitsyn's fiction is the inconsequence of politics. This judgment may at first strike the reader as perverse, considering Solzhenitsyn's repeated and impassioned preoccupation with the theory and practice of Communism in the Soviet Union. Nevertheless, not unlike Turgenev in his chronicles of events in Russia, from serfdom in *Sportsman's Sketches* to the analysis of the "back to the people" movement in *Virgin Soil*, Solzhenitsyn, though intensely absorbed with the Soviet political scene in general and Stalin's machinations in particular, focuses his attention on the perennial dilemmas of human existence. Just as Turgenev's *Poems in Prose*, with their Schopenhauerian motifs, are far more representative of his writings in general than his critics have supposed, Solzhenitsyn's religious musings in his short prose fragments exhibit his central preoccupation with man's metaphysical plight, whether or not this be experienced in the context of a camp for political prisoners. Though this is impossible to demonstrate, a close reading of Solzhenitsyn's fiction reinforces Turgenev's conclusion in *Smoke*, where the hero, Litvinov, returning to Russia after his active involvement with revolutionary exiles in Baden-Baden, puffs on his cigarette and adds the resulting smoke to the smoke blowing into the compartment from the locomotive. To be sure, Solzhenitsyn's attitude toward our predicament is far more religious and at the same time less aesthetic than Turgenev's, but what both writers have in common is a hankering for the transcendental (in the Kantian sense) overriding their immediate concerns with Russia's dilemmas of historical progress.

From any point of view the existential credentials of Solzhenitsyn are beyond dispute. As a man he survived eight years of concentration camps without compromising his integrity either then or subsequently when tempted by any *rapprochement* that might make life easier for him. His work is essentially a testimony to his dreadful experiences. This element of Kierkegaardian "duplication" between art and life is especially brought home by the scene in *The First Circle* in which a prisoner divorces his wife in order to spare her the wrath of the regime for having married an enemy of the people. It was under similar circumstances that Solzhenitsyn, first arrested for mocking Stalin's command of the Russian tongue, was separated from his own wife. *The Cancer Ward* is based on his battle with cancer shortly following his release from exile in 1953. In short, the unusual degree of persuasiveness in his work stems directly from first-hand knowledge of his subject.

Beyond this personal testimonial of courage which is conjoined with literary inspiration, Solzhenitsyn's work parallels that of his predecessors, who were similarly tested by life. Like the author of *Notes from the House of the Dead*, Solzhenitsyn is particularly interested in unusual human types whose unrepresentativeness would make them poor subjects for a value-free account of their shared predicament. In a characteristic passage, the complexity of Stavrogin is juxtaposed with the insistence of the socialist realist on simplicity and transparency.

"Well, for example, how ought one to interpret Stavrogin?"
"There are already a dozen critical essays—"
"They're not worth a kopeck! I've read them. Stavrogin! Svidrigailov! Kirilov! Can one really understand them? They are as complex and incomprehensible as people in real life! How seldom do we understand another human being right from the start, and we never do completely! Something unexpected always turns up. That's why Dostoevsky is so great. And literary scholars imagine they can illuminate a human being fully. It's amusing."[5]

Dostoevsky's mockery of the idea of progress in *Notes from Underground* consciously or unconsciously achieves its tragic denouement in Solzhenitsyn's encounter with the Soviet paradise. Like Tolstoy in *War and Peace*, Solzhenitsyn, especially in *The First Circle*, mixes historical and fictional characters in the construction of his narrative. More important, however, than the correspondences between Stalin and Napoleon or Platon Karataev and Spiridon, is the spiritual kinship of the two writers as exemplified in their common belief in the small indestructible inner voice.[6]

As has already been noted, Solzhenitsyn shares with Turgenev a basic preoccupation with metaphysical issues. But if one were to select a single adjective to fit Solzhenitsyn's quintessential conception of things, it would be *Gogolesque*. Nothing absurd is alien to his imagination, whether it be a confusion of Leo Tolstoy with the Stalin Prize winner Alexey Tolstoy in *The Cancer Ward*,[7] the visit of Eleanor Roosevelt to a prison cell transformed into a Potemkin village (*The First Circle*), or Stalin's order to change the hour of noon to 1 P.M. in *One Day*. The distortions and perversions of reason in the *sharashka* by virtue of Stalin's paranoid megalomania give rise, as we shall see, to grotesqueries which would have made the author of that other hell, *Dead Souls*, wince in recognition.

In calling attention to these resemblances between Solzhenitsyn's art and that of his predecessors, it is impossible to say with any certitude what is a traceable influence and what possibly an inadvertent affinity. In any case, this is a more suitable task for future literary historians than one pertinent to the present discussion. Suffice it here to say in summary that existential elements in Solzhenitsyn's fiction rest more immediately on the duplication of his lived experiences; beyond that they may be associated with Gogol's genius for depicting a topsy-turvy world, Dostoevsky's for annihilating the more bizarre illusions of the radicals about the future happiness of mankind under socialism, and Tolstoy's preoccupation with inauthentic features of modern life.

Solzhenitsyn is thoroughly existential and thoroughly Russian in the sense of its generations of intelligentsia, in taking all he writes about personally as well as in assuming a gloomy and censorious stance toward the experiences he records both as observer and as victim. His work belongs to the dominant tradition of the Russian novel which, we see again and again, is meant to shock us out of our complacency rather than to amuse us. However intense at times, the aesthetic pleasure we derive from reading these works is incidental to their Socratic effect of subversion of our most cherished beliefs and preoccupations.

Nevertheless, in contrast to the unrelieved pessimism of Beckett, Solzhenitsyn does not despair, however much he focuses on the brutishness of man. Rejecting, with Chekhov and Turgenev, all consolations of abstract philosophizing, especially those of histrionic stoicism, unable to partake to any degree in Gogol's, Dostoevsky's, and Tolstoy's fanatic notions of Christian belief, he nevertheless will not renounce his faith in that small segment drawn from all classes of the people who do not deceive themselves or others. These are not Stendhal's "happy few" who while full of sympathy for the humiliated and offended would rather spend two weeks in prison than listen to the man on the street, nor Stalin's "friends of the people," who denounce each other for the sake of maintaining the appearances of ideological purity, but such noble souls as Spiridon, Nerzhin, and Kostoglotov, whose authenticity has deeper roots than education and environment can distort. None of us, according to Solzhenitsyn, can be sure that he belongs to this group. Possibly the element of irreducible doubt on this score is the most disturbing, the most existential note struck in Solzhenitsyn's fiction. Short of experiencing camp life or something akin to it we are not safe in our own hearts and minds.

Existential Elements in Solzhenitsyn

As one turns to the existential *per se* in Solzhenitsyn's fiction, it may be helpful to call attention to certain recurring concerns salient to his particular representation of reality. These concerns are: the primacy of self-referential knowledge, the inescapable dread of individual non-being, and the avowal of consciousness as partly sovereign over and independent of circumstance.

In *The Cancer Ward*, we learn that "the surest test of a doctor is to suffer an illness in his own specialty," an observation dramatizing the difference between fulfilling clinical duties toward others and relating them to one's own predicament, thus necessarily transcending the merely clinical perspective. Dontsova, the heroic physician of *The Cancer Ward*, suddenly finds herself changed from someone wisely controlling the destinies of her cancer patients to someone reduced to a helpless victim of a killer raging within herself.

Now she found the course of her own illness and its place in the treatment just as unrecognizable. Now she was not to be the wise, guiding force of the treatment, but the unreasoning, inert object of this force. Her first admission of the ailment's existence crushed her as if she were an ant. Her first adjustment to the illness was unbearable: The whole world was topsy-turvy, the whole order of things was capsized. Not yet dead, she had to take leave of her husband, her son, her daughter, her grandson and her work—although this work would now thunder over her and through her. In one day she had to put aside everything that constituted life, and then, as a pale-green shadow, still endure many torments, without knowing for a long time whether she would go on to a complete death or return to life.[8]

In a similar passage from his play *The Love-Girl and the Innocent*, Solzhenitsyn describes a haunting scene in one of the transit camps, where a new batch of prisoners is being rounded up for transportation to the Arctic—a fate which entails certain death or at best extreme mutilation. Kostya, a teenager, proudly helps to round up the prisoners, firmly but good-naturedly shoving them into an open lorry on an ice-cold wintry night. Just before the truck is to depart, the commanding officer reads the names of three additional prisoners to be transported. Included among them is Kostya. In the twinkling of an eye he is transformed, like the cancer specialist, from a proud ego to a humiliated victim. His screams of betrayal and his threats to cut himself open with a knife are of no avail. Eventually, bound head to foot, he himself is thrown on the truck, which in an unforgettable scene moves away while he screams intentions of revenge toward his former associates (one of whom, the camp doctor, stole his boots in the bargain). "How can anyone say from the outside," Solzhenitsyn remarks elsewhere, "whose life is the hardest or the worst?" Our understanding of others and ourselves as objects is hazardously undercut if not refuted by our experience as subjects. By virtue of confronting the individual with his own infinite vulnerability, this Kierkegaardian "truth as subjectivity" has the most unnerving implications for contemporary man's faith in value-free rationality. Rather obviously it is the kind of truth which cuts close to the bone in hospital wards, concentration camps, and such institutions where Solzhenitsyn's characters bear awesome witness to this fact twenty-four hours a day.

One of Solzhenitsyn's finest achievements is his creation of Rusanov, the undauntable party member in *The Cancer Ward*, whose loyalty to every facet of socialist realism, in literature as much as in life, seems unshakable. In a passage already mentioned, it is he who unhesitatingly answers Count Leo Tolstoy's question, "What do men live by?": "By ideology, of course," and proceeds to sing the praises of Alexey Tolstoy, who did not waste his time on such abstruse musings. A fastidious Soviet bureaucrat, he begs Kostoglotov not to think or talk of death. Kostoglotov responds by pointing out to Rusanov that if people are not going to think of death in a cancer ward they fall into a contradiction with themselves.

"I beg you! Please!" warned Pavel Nikolaevich [Rusanov], no longer out of civic duty, no longer as a subject but as an object of history. "Let's not talk about death! Let's not even think about it!" "There's no use begging me." Kostoglotov waved him off with his shovel-sized hand. "If *this* is not the place to talk about death, where are you going to talk about it? 'Ah, we're going to live forever!' "[9]

Here is a supreme existential moment in modern literature. Nevertheless, Rusanov remains anxious about the prospects of his personal non-existence. Ivan Ilyich-like, it is not death in general that unsettles him but his personal extinction at some still indefinite moment in time. For all his disciplined party thinking he cannot bring himself to conceive of the world without his presence in it. Just as Dontsova could not regard herself as a mere object of clinical study when diagnosing the causes of her disease, no man can maintain unqualified optimism about the future in the face of his own non-being. Thus the timelessness of man's radical contingency acts as a foil against the Form of Good as proclaimed by the official ideologues. Whether or not Solzhenitsyn's typical existential suggestion that modern man has extraordinary difficulties in meeting death is correct, what can scarcely be disputed is the continued urgency of the problem even in a climate of opinion freed from the fires of hell in an afterlife and from other related opiates of supernatural religion.[10]

A further existential theme is the affirmation of consciousness as superior to environment in determining human destiny. Sartre's futile attempt to reconcile Marxism and existentialism in his *Critique de la raison dialectique* points up again a deep rift between those who ultimately place their faith in behavioral conditioning and their adversaries, like Solzhenitsyn, who opt for the triumph of character over circumstance.[11] This is not the place to demonstrate, if such a demonstration be at all possible, the inherent failure of sociological analysis to do justice to the complexities of *Existenz*, but merely to corroborate the contention that Solzhenitsyn in his fiction has placed himself squarely in the camp of the anti-ideologues for whom consciousness is anything but epiphenomenal. In *The Cancer Ward* we are told that it is not the standard of living which makes a man happy, but rather the way he feels, the attitude he takes toward what he experiences. One is reminded afresh of Tolstoy's epilogue to *War and Peace*, especially of those sentences in which the would-be determinist contrasts Napoleon's vanity with Alexander I's presumed self-abnegation toward the same body of evidence, that is, the campaigns of 1812. However inevitable the outcome may have been in Tolstoy's eyes, the role of the individual in history is never merely one of being a vehicle of material forces. On this score Tolstoy would have been more consistent with his own practice had he followed Kant in suppressing counter-intuitively the iron-clad chain of necessity for the sake of responsible conduct, rather than adopting the opposite course.[12] In any event, (however inconsistently in Tolstoy's case), both Count Leo and Solzhenitsyn indict some individuals for relating improperly to themselves and praise others for acting conscientiously in circumstances where they might have done otherwise and where, in fact, others did otherwise.

Solzhenitsyn's position on the dichotomy between consciousness and society is, in any case, relatively well defined. Kostoglotov in *The Cancer Ward* remarks that "there was greed before the bourgeoisie and there will be greed after it," a proposition Sartre, for one, would still find very difficult to accept, because it places the blame for human inadequacy not on any collective class consciousness but rather on the failure of individuals to live up to their highest notion of themselves. It is precisely in this vein that Kondrashev-Ivanov, the artist in the *sharashka* in *The First Circle*, replies to Nerzhin's insinuation that in the camps life forms the man rather than vice versa. Nerzhin, to be sure, has seen this happen again and again, but Kondrashev-Ivanov is at no loss to provide counter-instances. Why, he asks, given identical conditions, does sustained hardship transform some decent men into traitors while others maintain their integrity? Solzhenitsyn refers to the artist as an "ageless idealist" who invokes something akin to Plato's Form of the Good as decisive for our moral mode of existence. These mystical overtones have an uncanny ring of authenticity amid the utilitarian splendors and personal indignities of Stalin's Mavrino Institute, where the perfection of voice prints is the daily assignment of selected members of the Soviet intelligentsia temporarily brought together here from the death-camps farther east. There can be little question that Solzhenitsyn himself sides with the ageless idealist whom, in the passage just cited, Nerzhin, for all his doubts, hears out with sympathetic interest.

The existential *per se* in Solzhenitsyn[13] is further illustrated by the following reflections:

> Can man be so constructed that you cannot cure him of being surprised?[14]
>
> The stories themselves were not so terrible except that she had acquired the trick of picking up every *untypical* experience.[15]
>
> Just as the essence of food cannot be conveyed in calories, the essence of life cannot be conveyed by even the greatest formulas.[16]

The first quotation pinpoints our refusal to accept the radical contingency of experience. We stubbornly cling to notions of the Natural in human affairs, though we know full well that nothing is incredible in this realm. This is crucially borne out by the example of the contrast between Hitler's and Stalin's rule by terror. In general, Hitler's terror could be called directed, while Stalin's liquidations and purges were on the whole capricious.

Whereas any Jew, Social-Democrat, Gypsy, or Slav was, sooner or later, destined for the German gas chambers, it was characteristic of Stalin's bestiality to be almost utterly unpredictable. Old Bolsheviks as well as Social Revolutionaries, for example, who had served the Communist Party in Russia faithfully even before the Revolution, were included among the victims. On the other hand, even more oddly, certain fence-sitters, not to mention opponents of the regime, were spared. The somber mood suggested by Gogol in some of his tales by the inversion of reasonableness and the intrusion of the fortuitous into a seemingly established order of events receives in the writings of Solzhenitsyn expression as a perennial truth about our condition. Kafka's celebrated assertion in the opening sentence of *The Trial*, that one morning after having his breakfast, Joseph K. was arrested without apparent cause, has been amplified by the Russian novelist into a crucial key for comprehending some singular aspects of our lot in general and our misfortunes under totalitarian bureaucrats in particular.

In *The First Circle* the girl Clara has a fondness for dwelling on untypical occurrences. Tolstoy ("the fox" rather than "the hedgehog") was at his best in describing actual families which were unhappy each in its own way rather than hypothetical happy families, which, by definition, are all alike. *Mutatis mutandis*, the existentialists have always focused their attention on the unrepresentative departure from the norm, whatever that norm might be. As noted above,[17] Dostoevsky maintains that the best clue to what is often referred to as normal behavior may well be found in such pathologies as that of his hero.[18] Not surprisingly, perhaps, the Soviet government has frowned on Dostoevsky's fiction, not least on account of the atypicality of its tormented characters. In the Soviet paradise, as in *Walden Two*, everyone is thought to be cheerful and predictably accommodated to the *status quo*. Hence Clara represents an existential threat to the Zion of the Rusanovs and their bureaucratic fellow travellers.[19]

Objections raised by existentialists to the cult of scientific objectivity rest precisely on what Solzhenitsyn calls the attempt to convey the essence of life through formulas; he finds this analogous to dieticians trying to convey the essence of food through calories. Some sociologists construe such a critique as a nihilistic break with the traditional goals of understanding in the West. Yet in the name of similar humanistic values adduced to sustain the eventual rationalization of every facet of our lives, it can be argued with equal plausibility that the consequences of this reductionist procedure, unlimited by any overriding criteria, may well prove fatal to all our enterprises, not excluding the scientific itself. Not only, as Nietzsche observed with unsurpassed acuity, does life resist total analytic comprehension but, even assuming the contrary, man the subject rather than the object of history could not get along without illusions, if only to keep up the spirit of systematic inquiry, not to mention an indispensable degree of immunity from the destructive paradoxes of experience. Unless it give us pleasure and consolation, knowledge for knowledge's sake is an empty ideal destined to collapse from its own unchecked momentum. Truth divorced from goodness and beauty represents an enthronement of meaninglessness threatening our very survival. At issue in Solzhenitsyn's quarrel with formulas, the correlative of his insistence of spiritual awareness against which we measure our empirical being, is the negative or positive value of cognitive enterprises which fail to lead to an enhancement of the knower, or, to put it differently, which dehumanize him for the sake of the known. Whatever else it may be, scientific objectivity is not impartial. On the contrary, Solzhenitsyn and the existentialists would argue, it is full of dis-values for our personal existence, granting the obvious advantages of statistical purity by which alone, however, man cannot live.

Because death for him is an even more important reality than the classless society, because he affirms the moral priority of consciousness over circumstance, because he acknowledges the cognitive significance of the untypical, because he agrees with Dostoevsky that suffering is not identical with sickness but can be a symptom of spiritual health, and because he insists on the decisiveness of the personal point of view, Solzhenitsyn is an existential novelist *par excellence.* The meaning of his work extends from his unminced indictment of Soviet theory and practice under Stalin to personal testimony of grotesqueries and epiphanies of timeless weightiness.

The Grotesqueries

A striking feature of totalitarian societies is the misuse of reason, control, and organization, all of which are made to serve inversions of sanity and decency. The barbarism of earlier ages could have matched ours only if, say, someone like Nicholas I had had at his disposal the technological apparatus available to the secret police of his successors. The relative humaneness with which Solzhenitsyn credits the Romanovs as opposed to Stalin may somewhat cynically be ascribed to the indigenous incompetence and inefficiency of a pre-industrialized society, which made the thorough implementation of terror and cruelty an unattainable achievement at that time. Thus Gogol, who was on intimate terms with the grotesque of his day, nevertheless gives the figures in his fiction a breathing spell from the hor-rendous aspect of experience by virtue of ordinary human corruption, indolence, and sheer lackadaisicality (not to mention the salutary intrusion of the transcendent into the mundane). If anything be unrelievedly grotesque, it is the unexcelled success of modern dictators in translating madness into luminous historical fact. The scale of achievement along these lines is unthinkable apart from the recent triumphs of scientific method.

While it remains fashionable to analyze the cultural crisis of today in terms of a lag between our moral and cognitive growth, a closer approximation of the truth would have to take some account of the inherently destructive tendencies in the primacy of the clinical vision itself. The moral implications of reductionism would seem to be inextricably bound up with its usefulness as an epistemological ideal. Only a thin line of precarious sensibility divides the equality of all atoms in motion from the functional evaluation of men in labor camps as a mere sum of their potential productivity. Economic, social, and other pressures have built up to such a degree in modern society that as a consequence the barrier collapses and human beings find themselves reduced to a condition of slavery—no easier to bear for being ingeniously sophisticated in method and archaically brutal in intent. This is not to pass over the bestiality inherent in murdering Jews *en masse* or sending Soviet war heroes into horrible exile or death for having been taken prisoner by the enemy, but to accentuate the exploitative and manipulative factors involved in these schemes of dehumanization. Eichmann was particularly fond of congratulating himself for making his trains to Auschwitz run on time without unduly interfering with the movement of German troops and supplies to the front, just as the obsessive counting of prisoners by the camp guards assures the Soviet state of no loss of work on the part of half-starved, half-frozen, half-dying men engaged in clearing land or cutting down trees.

These examples point up the almost incredible mixture of cruelty and calculation which is an earmark of the collective grotesque in the twentieth century. Though this mixture is not new, its coexistence with ideals of human solidarity and people's democracy confers upon it an unusual daemonic quality, heightened still further, as it were, by the thoroughness with which it is executed. To be sure, this was less the case in Nazi Germany than in the Soviet Union under Stalin, though it should be recalled that Hitler, too, enveloped his reign of terror in ideological claptrap which differs from the principles of Marxism-Leninism and their countless expositors in being cruder and self-defeating as a secular hope for the world. In any case, the panacea of the Soviet bosses enjoys the authority of Marx, the political triumph of Lenin, and the irrepressible respectability of the Left among most intellectuals of the world. Fortunately, no doubt, Hitler even at the crest of his power could not lay claim to a comparable legacy. Consequently, the horrors described by Solzhenitsyn in *The First Circle* and *One Day* have a unique intensity which derives from their historical roots in splendid promises and seemingly untarnished ideals. Sentenced under Section 58 of the Soviet criminal code, the victims of Stalin's paranoia were more often than not sincere harbingers of the socialist dispensation who had devoted their lives to serving the Party. Gratuitously dubbed enemies of the people, these innocent victims suffer acutely; their wretchedness is often in inverse proportion to their previous ideological zeal. (By contrast, common murderers and thieves receive preferental treatment in the camps.) Again and again Solzhenitsyn plays on the tragic irony that under Stalin it was better to be born a good-for-nothing than a potential hero of the Soviet Union.

The Russian dictator remained crafty enough, even during the purges following World War II, to make use of his ideological enemies. The concept of the *sharashka* which underlies the action in *The First Circle* affords the best illustration of Stalin's innovative powers as a coordinator of malice and efficiency.[20] Gogol himself might have been hard pressed to imagine the reality of Mavrino. Among the various levels of grotesqueness enveloping its inmates, not the least is the nature of their projects (especially the voice-print research).[21] The success of such an undertaking in a dictatorship further diminishes the constantly threatened inviolability of a minimal threshold of privacy for every citizen— a fact not lost on some of the conscience-stricken prisoners. There is nothing value-free about such a technological breakthrough, and the *zeks* (prisoners) thus face the moral dilemma of whether or not to prostitute themselves to Stalin. To repeat, the first level of grotesqueness in *The First Circle* is comprised by the characteristically modern complicity of scientific inquiry in the degradation of humanity. The impartiality of scientific knowledge in relation to life seen whole is as mythical as the innocence of bystanders during a riot. Like many less confining scientific institutes, Mavrino has a way of dazzling its visitors with a seductive presence of antiseptic trappings in the service of truth. How refreshingly down-to-earth and brazenly corrupt appears Chichikov's purchase of dead souls when juxtaposed with the selfless plan and execution of the voice-print project!

Although the *sharashka* is a haven from the transit camps and the horrors of the Arctic, this alone cannot resolve the contradiction of coerced intellectuals performing professional tasks. Moreover, besides being under an irremediable cloud of suspicion, the prisoners do not know from day to day whether or not any specific individual among them will be part of the next scheduled transport to the East. These periodic reversals resemble dying, in being fixed for no ascertainable date, yet certain to occur some time in the future. Thus the privileged *zeks* at Mavrino go about their business with the Sword of Damocles hanging over their heads. Their quarters are halfway comfortable, they have enough to eat and drink, but they remain prisoners: everything they do, utter, insinuate, every move they make within absolute confinement is strictly controlled by their guards and ideological bosses, who in turn would have to pay with their heads if the work at the institute did not measure up to official expectations. The conjunction of *humanisme et terreur* did not have to be invented by Merleau-Ponty. Stalin's refinement of the initial reign of terror when the goddess of Reason was worshiped by the spiritual descendants of the Encyclopedists surpasses all earlier models in finesse as well as in overall design.

The Grotesque is distinguished from the Absurd by an element of moral depravity superimposed on the senselessness of an action or a situation. For Solzhenitsyn the Soviet state under Stalin is vicious as well as mad in its operations, and thus productive of grotesque acts and policies. Whatever the degree of discernible rationality in the System, it is gratuitously put to the use of humiliating and confusing the hard-core sanity of its victims. When in *One Day* a prisoner remarks to a captain of the guard that it must be noon, since the sun is at its height, he is reprimanded and told in no uncertain terms that it is really one o'clock by order of the Soviet government. Whatever—the captain snaps back at him—the laws of nature may have commanded for previous generations in this particular matter, under the new dispensation things are different by fiat. Since no note of irony registers in the captain's speech, his Tolstoyan sincerity of manner being as frightening as the content of his propositions, the prisoner together with the reader feels reduced to the level of an idiot.

Yet this episode is less grotesque than absurd: Stalin might suspend the law of gravitation on paper without thereby being able to effect a significant change in the lives of his countrymen (except for insulting their intelligence). While the preservation of sanity could be threatened by an atmosphere of anguished disbelief, should citizens be required to repeat this and similar nonsense, morning, noon, and night, the issue itself remains invulnerable to human meddling. A historical counterpart to the *reductio ad absurdum* of this episode is the Lysenko affair which, in addition to depriving Soviet laboratories of their finest biologists, may well have been responsible for the avoidable and hence grotesque starvation of millions.

"The regulation did not specifically forbid tears, but under a higher interpretation of the Law there was no place for them."[22] Solzhenitsyn makes this observation in reference to the farewells following the rare privilege of visiting hours for the prisoners by their next-of-kin. The omnipresent moral callousness of the regime is emphasized by this shocking example of wives, already exposed to unbelievable loneliness, discrimination, and harassment, being stripped, metaphorically speaking, of their spontaneous indulgence in retrospective emotion after talking to their husbands in the presence of guards and under the strictest regulations. Chances are that the couples may never see each other again. Those wives who keep the faith are predestined to suffer virtual exclusion from civil society. So far as Solzhenitsyn is concerned, this intended suppression of the last spark of humanity on the part of the totalitarian state is the rule rather than the exception.

As prisoners are herded together for transport to the labor camps, they are first placed in neat-looking colorful trucks made to resemble exemplary food vans, with the words "bread" and "meat" painted on in four languages. A French correspondent from *Libération*, on his way to a hockey match at the Dynamo Stadium, concludes on the basis of having seen several such trucks in the course of one morning that the provisioning of the capital must be excellent. In this case the grotesquerie of men treated like cattle and worse is further heightened by the stupidity of the correspondent, characteristically self-deceived about the human condition in the manner of Crystal Palace progressives since the Enlightenment. Whether it be heat provided for molding cement rather than for the freezing prisoners who must mold it or a particular prisoner not being allowed to go to the hospital because the daily sick quota of two has already been filled,[23] life for those on the wrong side of Soviet justice is always the same: a cruel mockery of every vestige of self-respect. When a former captain in the navy, now a prisoner, protests that such conduct on the part of the authorities is inconsistent with Clause Nine of the Soviet penal code, he is promptly apprised of his error; when he persists in pointing out that it is unworthy of Communists, Pascal's eternal silence echoes in the Siberian landscape of his confinement.[24] For anyone placed in such a situation, an appeal to the Soviet legal code would appear to be an act of grotesque desperation. Yet this Cartesian document (whose clear and precise ordinances lend themselves so readily to applied cruelty and injustice) could on occasion be the instrument of at least partial good.

At the heart of the Grotesque lies the lie, Stalin's malicious distortion of the truth which betrayed not only, say, the idealism of a Plekhanov but the lives of millions of individuals falsely accused, interrogated under torture, and sentenced to prison terms which might never have ended for those who survived the camps had it not been for the death and exposure of the dictator by his successor. Yet for all the distortions and perversions of life in Stalin's Russia, Solzhenitsyn does not allow us to overlook the more hilarious aspects of this shattering experience. Even black humor can have its lighter side, just as irony directed against oneself need not be solely sardonic. In a thumbnail sketch of Russian literature which is in accord with Party principles we learn that secondary source material on such writers as Gogol, Tolstoy, and Dostoevsky may be far more illuminating than the original works.[25]

The very idea of judging the masterpieces of classical Russian fiction by the criteria of socialist realism as interpreted by party hacks has an amusingly grotesque side to it which probably was not altogether lost on the members of the Union of Soviet Writers, who dismissed Solzhenitsyn from their ranks. There is also something irrepressibly farcical about the billboards surrounding the camp in *The Love-Girl and the Innocent*; Carlyle might well have approved of their message, but for the luckless prisoners to have to read "He who does not work, does not eat: Stalin" must indeed have struck them in their circumstances as a sad joke, aesthetically as well as existentially. Similarly, in *The First Circle*, piling detail upon Gogolesque detail about the glory of Stalin during the height of his power, Solzhenitsyn reaches a crescendo of ludicrousness which even more than the somber instances of the Grotesque fixes the madness of the Russian dictator indelibly in the imagination.

Never mind. The simple ordinary people love their leader, understand him and love him—that was true. That much he could see from the newspapers, and from the movies, and from the display of gifts. His birthday had become a national holiday, and that was good to know. How many messages there had been! From institutions, organizations, factories, individual citizens. *Pravda* has asked permission to print two columns of them in every issue. Well, they would have to run for several years, and all right, it wasn't a bad idea . . .

There was a certain sensation in his chest which troubled Stalin, and it had to do with the museum, but he could not quite grasp what it was.

The people loved him, yes, but the people themselves swarmed with shortcomings. How could these be corrected? And how much quicker Communism could be built if it were not for the soulless bureaucrats. If it were not for the conceited big shots. If it were not for the organizational weakness of indoctrination efforts among the masses. For the "drifting" in Party education. For the slackened pace of construction, the delays in production, the output of low-quality goods, the bad planning, the apathy toward the introduction of new technology and equipment, the refusal of young people to pioneer distant areas, the loss of grain in the fields, overexpenditure by bookkeepers, thievery at warehouses, swindling by managers, sabotage by prisoners, liberalism in the police, abuse of public housing, insolent speculators, greedy housewives, spoiled children, chatterboxes on streetcars, petty-minded "criticism" in literature, liberal tendencies in cinematography.

No, the people still had too many shortcomings.[26]

The same spirit of banter near the gallows informs the reenact-
ment of the "Song of Igor's Campaign" in *The First Circle*, where
the events of the twelfth-century narrative are transposed in line
with the World War II policy of considering all defeats of Russian
troops as results of deliberate treachery. It is difficult to think of
any greater testimony to the human spirit than this *tour de force*
which Solzhenitsyn puts in the mouths of his *zek* actors in their
sharashka dormitory.

The Epiphanies

Such incidents in the *sharashka* as the performance of the
parody of "The Song of Igor's Campaign" are of course exceptional, but where they do occur in the lives of the prisoners, they
signify the unbreakable power of epiphany over grotesquerie,
even in the least inviting circumstances. Solzhenitsyn never wal-
lows in unrelieved gloom or black humor, though the lot of his
characters offers no apparent reason for any sort of rejoicing.
While Beckett can be amusing in a twisted way, the overall
impression of the platitudinous chatter of his brilliantly conceived
victims of metaphysical exhaustion is one of impenetrable dejection. Solzhenitsyn, on the other hand, in the tradition of Gogol
and Dostoevsky, sets great store by the compatibility, if not the
psychological affinity, of the worst men can do to each other
with their most ecstatic moments of happiness. No reader of
Dead Souls or the *Notes from the House of the Dead* will forget
those occasions on which the Russian landscape of cruelty, pov-
erty, and corruption is suddenly lit up by daring flashes of obscure
illumination: when, to recall but two examples, the crafty
Chichikov falls Romantically in love with an unknown girl whom
he espies in another carriage or when Dostoevsky regains much of
his health amid the physical and moral horrors of exile in Siberia.
Similarly, Solzhenitsyn discovers epiphanies in confinement which
go far beyond man's irrepressible proclivity for self-mockery.
The mock celebration of the October Revolution in *The Love-
Girl and the Innocent* provides further evidence for the efficacy
of this disposition in the grimmest of settings.

CHEGENYOV: . . . Comrades, your attention! Today's anniversary will be celebrated in our camp with particular solemnity. Items on the agenda. Number one—the superb work and valiant exploits of Munitsa. Number two—the despatch of forty or fifty trouble-makers to the forests to chop down trees.

YAKHIMCHUK: You watch it with your forecasts. They'll come true.

CHEGENYOV: Number three—Old Igor has been transferred to the morgue after being stuck with a bayonet to make sure he was dead. Number four—there will be a general search in all barrack rooms, mattresses turned over and floors taken up. Number five—there will be a personal search at the check-point. Underpants will be removed. Number six—there will be a Stakhanovite rally of the best "drudge" prisoners. Each Stakhanovite will be issued with one millet pasty, which means the rest of the camp have to take a cut in flour and millet next week. Number seven—there will be a free film-show, *Stalin in 1905*. Everyone will fight to get in and will end up sitting on everyone else, to make sure we don't feel we're at home. (He jumps astride some suitable object.) Mount your horses! Sabres at ready! Charge! (He makes a mock cavalry charge, waving an imaginary sabre. His elbows are sticking out of the holes of his sleeves.)[27]

In his "Two Concepts of Liberty," Isaiah Berlin gives us some revealing glimpses into the nature of that "negative" freedom which Solzhenitsyn's prisoners are more apt to possess than those on the outside who think of themselves as free.[28] Solzhenitsyn, to be sure, is no advocate of stoicism, with its contemptuous attitude toward human passion, yet he clearly endorses that "inner citadel" of integrity which permits his chosen prisoners to transcend not only the banalities of their prison existence but of life as such. To start with, the prisoners are no longer subject to the gratuitous terror of arrest and interrogation which hangs over the heads of their compatriots. This is not to say that interrogations cease altogether after sentencing and imprisonment, that the prisons do not have their informers ordered by the authorities to betray their fellows if, for example, they talk too loosely among themselves; on the whole, however, to be incarcerated under Stalin meant to enjoy a relative freedom from capricious intimidation which might well have been the envy of many a K.G.B. official—at least before his own constantly threatened downfall. Certainly in the *sharashka*, and no less in the other camps, where the prisoners are assigned to labor gangs, they say things to each other out of earshot of the guards which would have destroyed them were they back in society. Since they have passed through hell already, whether it be the first circle or a lower one, they have, moreover, gained a freedom from ordinary fear which makes them invulnerable to the thrust of trivial dangers and inconveniences. The dilemma of being damned if you do and damned if you don't loses most of its edge in a situation where men united by a common unjust fate realize that without living up to their sense of solidarity all of them are doomed. What binds them together, save in the case of a few diehards whose belief in Stalin survives their own destruction at his hands, is a link of privileged martyrdom far stronger than honor among thieves or respectability among the toiling masses wrapped up in the pursuit of external gain.[29]

In the light of the foregoing discussion it is not difficult to see how life in a Stalinist prison camp could be an improvement for the human spirit over what it had to contend with in the "open society." Even solitary confinement, with all its horrors, kept one away from the state's propaganda machine unceasingly grinding out its slogans. Doubtless Solzhenitsyn is correct in his suggestion that precisely in these unlikely surroundings many Soviet citizens got their first opportunity to think and speak in their own voices —a possibility scarcely reckoned with by any tradition of Marxist dialectics.

Beyond this therapeutic "cunning of Reason" in a totalitarian dictatorship, other, more general, redemptive features of imprisonment are worth mentioning in passing. Inasmuch as social rot is not confined to the Soviet paradise, escape from society through imprisonment has a universal appeal. For those who suffer from no longer wanting anything consumer goods have to offer, prison may serve to reactivate the craving for what they had previously taken too much for granted or satiated themselves with beyond further endurance. Deprivation frequently induces us to gain a sharper perspective on the viability of our values. Along these lines Nerzhin admits to his wife a fondness for prison routine which, one may assume, contrasts agreeably with his former proclivity for drifting when he enjoyed the dreadful freedom of being perennially distracted.[30] The discipline demanded by Bach of a performer on the composer's favorite keyboard instrument, the clavichord, requires of the latter an enormous degree of concentration and in turn rewards him with a creative freedom which the grand piano cannot match; the very narrowness of prison life may open up to an inmate hitherto undreamt-of reaches of inner growth and maturity. If Gorky, as Solzhenitsyn remarks with irony, declared that the way we live is the way we think, the experience of Stalin's prisoners teaches a lesson quite distinct from its intended moral. The thinking of the *zeks* inside the *sharashka* is conspicuously sharper than that of their fellow citizens on the outside. Together with Tolstoy and Dostoevsky, Solzhenitsyn holds that it is the way we think which quintessentially determines the quality of our lives. Prison, therefore, by puncturing many of our illusions and self-deceptions, may well prove to the reflective person a catalytic agent to a more authentic life. Consonant with this view, Solzhenitsyn at one point observes that one must suffer for twenty years before commencing to philosophize. He himself never dissociates his experience from his attempts to explicate it. Herein lies the distinctive freedom of thought inspired by daily humiliation.

The strongest vindication of Tolstoyan inwardness in Solzhenitsyn is his account of Nerzhin's retrieval of a collection of Yesenin's poems which the despotic Major Shikin had illegally taken away from him. Nerzhin, a chronic "troublemaker" among the *zeks*, knows that he is about to be sent to a probable death in the Arctic. Nevertheless, also knowing that the book will be removed from him during the final search before his transport from the *sharashka*, he insists that the letter of Section 95 of the Criminal Code of the Soviet Union be duly observed by the major who, as the chief security officer, represents the embodiment of Law and Order in Stalin's state. Fleetingly within his rights in his nightmarish world, Nerzhin stubbornly persists in his quest for justice. The scene deserves to be quoted, if only in part:

Nerzhin stood up angrily, without taking his eyes off the Yesenin. He was remembering how his wife's kind hands had once held the small book and how she had written in it:

And so it will be that everything lost will return to you!

The words shot from his lips without the least effort: "Citizen Major! I hope you haven't forgotten that for two years I demanded from the Ministry of State Security the Polish zlotys which had been

taken from me—they'd cut the sum in half maybe twenty times; it
was down to kopecks—and I got them back through the Supreme
Soviet. I hope you haven't forgotten my demand that the one-fifth
ounce of sifted flour allotted by law should be actually included in my
ration. They laughed at me, but I got it! And there are other cases. I
warn you: I will not give up that book to you. I will die in the Kolyma
—but from the other side of death I'll tear it away from you! I will
fill the mailboxes of all the Central Committee and the Council of
Ministers with complaints against you. Give it back without all that
unpleasantness."

And the Major of State Security yielded to this doomed helpless
zek, being sent to a slow death. He had, in fact, inquired of GLAVLIT,
and been informed, to his surprise, that the book was not formally
prohibited. Formally! His keen sense of smell told Shikin that this
was negligence, that the book ought beyond a doubt to be forbidden.
But it followed that he had to protect himself from the accusations
of this indefatigable troublemaker.

"Very good," agreed the Major. "I will return it to you. But we will
not let you take it with you."

Nerzhin went out to the stairway triumphantly, holding the precious book in its shiny yellow dust jacket. It was a symbol of success
at a moment when everything was in ruins.[31]

The Inconsequence of Politics

There is an unresolved paradox in Tolstoy's avowal of Christian anarchy in the last three decades of his life which should
help us to understand better the sometimes hidden thrust of
Solzhenitsyn's fiction. In fact, this particular paradox, already
alluded to in previous discussion, offers a significant clue to the
existential character of Russian prose in general. While, on the
one hand, it is steeped in historical actuality, with many of its
heroes and heroines drawn unmistakably from the political and
social struggles of the time, it is, on the other, universal in its
preoccupation with such problems as growing old, for which
there is no technological solution. Tolstoy believed that an ultimate revolution can occur only in the human heart, yet maintained at the same time, that an individual's outlook on reality
is unavoidably shaped by the responses demanded of him by the

accoutrements of civilization. The unintelligibility of elitists' art to the masses of humanity he does not ascribe to their failure to become aesthetically responsive individuals, but to the corrupting and degrading emotions he associates with the rich and powerful. Nevertheless, in the realm of conscience, and, *mutatis mutandis*, in every area of a person's being, Tolstoy makes the individual accountable *qua* individual: be it for the translation of precept into decisive deed or some musical experience into compassionate feeling. Tolstoy's faith in the leopard's power to change his spots is the existential correlative of his devastating critique of society as virtually monolithic in imposing evil and falsity upon each of its members. For anyone to seek nirvana under Nicholas II was as sublimely absurd as to discern the coming of the classless society in Lenin's proclamations. Forced to choose between the two, Tolstoy on the whole opted for nirvana. In other words, when it came to a showdown, the influence of Rousseau and Schopenhauer proved more compelling than that exerted by Marx and Plekhanov. It is in this sense that Tolstoy was not a political writer but an *Existenzerheller*, just as Turgenev, the political chronicler of nineteenth-century Russia, plays second fiddle to Turgenev the dissector of vanity, weak will, and all the varieties of *Schwärmerei*.[32] Though the Nechaev Affair inspired *The Devils*, the magnificence of Dostoevsky's achievement completely dwarfs his caricature of the radicals in that novel. Similarly, Gogol's arch-conservatism and Goncharov's indolence, however construed as reflections of social conditioning, are insignificant next to the former's uncanny recognition of the Absurd and the latter's parody of the Protestant work ethic.

Solzhenitsyn, too, can be interpreted as a political novelist both on the basis of his major theme, the politics of Stalinism and their repercussion on Soviet society, and, more specifically, because he shows us the politicization of every aspect of life, not excluding the most personal, in a modern totalitarian dictatorship. Yet this hard-core dimension of his art illegitimately pushes into the background his negative attitude toward this body of experience. We have already seen how the moral survival of the prisoners in *One Day*, *The First Circle*, and *The Love-Girl and the Innocent* as human rather than subhuman beings is linked to their spiritual growth into authentic personalities more or less invulnerable to the perverse cunning of the authorities. The same applies to the institutional setting of *The Cancer Ward*, where those patients who face their death with dignity set out to master its terrors as a personal triumph of the will over the generalized rule of impersonal necessity. But nowhere does Solzhenitsyn sound this note more strongly and clearly than in his portraits of extreme suffering, contrapuntally put against each other; the disintegration of Joseph Stalin in the Kremlin and the indestructible love of life of Spiridon, a simple peasant unjustly condemned to an endless cycle of physical and spiritual punishment.

Solzhenitsyn's characterization of Stalin fits in squarely with the tradition of the Russian novel as unmasking the falsity of society by means of showing in depth a highly idiosyncratic individual, who stands out even in the context of the madness and corruption which helped to form his personality, or for which he himself may be largely responsible. It is the peculiar quality of Russia's great novelists not to focus directly on one of their main concerns, the social ills of their times, but to concentrate instead on what Tolstoy called "the terror of normalcy" as embodied in a unique manifestation. Nicholas I in *Hadji Murad* rather than Napoleon in *War and Peace* is far likelier to have served Solzhenitsyn as a model for his portrayal of the brutal Stalin. Whereas Tolstoy's Napoleon is in the end little more than a cog through which the inevitabilities of history are made known, his Nicholas strikingly resembles Solzhenitsyn's Stalin in their shared trait of mindless malice and, above all, in their acknowledged power to be willful causes rather than mere catalysts of destruction. Tolstoy presents the Russian Emperor as the source of both his own dehumanization and of that endured by his subjects. The power of his personal vindictiveness is strikingly revealed in a memorable passage, in which a medical student who drew a knife on his professor under the strain of taking an examination is sentenced to run a gauntlet of twelve thousand blows. Five thousand, Tolstoy adds, would suffice to kill the sturdiest of men, but Nicholas, who, we are also told, takes great pride in not wishing to re-introduce the death penalty, insists on the number twelve. Like Number One in *The First Circle* he revels at once in the self-intoxication of megalomania as well as in its dire effects on his victims.

The case was as follows: A young man who had twice failed in his examination was being examined a third time, and when the examiner again would not pass him the young man whose nerves were deranged, considering this to be an injustice, seized a penknife from the table in a paroxysm of fury, and rushing at the professor inflicted on him several trifling wounds.

"What's his name?" asked Nicholas.

"Bzhevoski."

"A Pole?"

"Of Polish descent and a Roman Catholic," answered Chernyshov.

Nicholas frowned. He had done much evil to the Poles. To justify that evil he had to feel certain that all Poles were rascals, and he considered them to be such and hated them in proportion to the evil he had done them.

"Wait a little," he said, closing his eyes and bowing his head.

Chernyshov, having more than once heard Nicholas say so, knew that when the Emperor had to take a decision it was only necessary for him to concentrate his attention for a few moments and the spirit moved him, and the best possible decision presented itself as though an inner voice had told him what to do. He was now thinking how most fully to satisfy the feeling of hatred against the Poles which this incident had stirred up within him, and the inner voice suggested the following decision. He took the report and in his large handwriting wrote on its margin with three orthographic mistakes:

"Diserves deth, but, thank God, we have no capitle punishment, and it is not for me to introduce it. Make him run the gauntlet of a thousand men twelve times.—Nicholas."

He signed, adding his unnaturally huge flourish.

Nicholas knew that twelve thousand strikes with the regulation rods were not only certain death with torture, but were a superfluous cruelty, for five thousand strokes were sufficient to kill the strongest man. But it pleased him to be ruthlessly cruel and it also pleased him to think that we have abolished capital punishment in Russia.[33]

Kostov! How that name irked Stalin! Rage flooded his head, and he kicked out hard with his boot—into Tracho's bloody snout! And Stalin's gray eyelids trembled from a satisfied feeling of justice.

That accursed Kostov, the dirty bastard!

Surprising how, in retrospect, the intrigues of these scoundrels became clear! How cleverly they had disguised themselves! At least he had slammed down on Bela Kun in 1937; but just ten days ago Kostov had defamed a Socialist court. How many successful trials Stalin had conducted, how many enemies he had compelled to abase themselves and confess to any despicable crime—yet he had failed in Kostov's case! A disgrace throughout the world! What black resourcefulness, to deceive the experienced interrogators, to crawl at their feet—and then in the public session, in the presence of foreign correspondents, to repudiate everything! What had become of decency? And the Party conscience? And proletarian solidarity? All right, die, but die so that you're some use to us![34]

Yet the most remarkable facet of Stalin's personality as drawn by Solzhenitsyn is his hardness on himself, his inability to enjoy the fruits of his triumph over his real and imagined foes. We catch glimpses of him suffering from insomnia, loneliness, and paranoia. Food no longer appeals to him. Even the utter subservience of his servant offends him. He had set himself the task of living to ninety, but with old age creeping upon him it no longer holds his interest. During World War II, with the Germans at the gates of Moscow, he punished himself by attending a military parade in the beleaguered capital from which, in a moment of panic, he had thought of fleeing. In order to expiate for this temporary weakness he subjects himself to public exposure which, given his delusions of persecution, proves a tormenting experience. Ironically enough, like the victims of his purge trials who incriminate themselves to excess, he adds to the burden of his guilt as if its actual enormity was not sufficient for one lifetime. Whereas he would have few objections to the return of Nicholas II, whose autocratic ways would pose little threat to his own existence, Stalin abhors the stifling regime he heads, precisely because its untrustworthy supporters fill him with dread of emptiness and mortality. Without friends, faith, or desire, his virtual omnipotence proves a cruel mockery of his cruel nature.

The supreme irony of the entire characterization is the inconsequence of politics in the life of an individual who set out to politicize every conceivable aspect of human existence. Yet when the chips are down, at the height of his power over his compatriots, he is racked by spiritual and physical suffering: a "boundary situation" akin to such intractable states of mind as the boredom of Stavrogin, the double-mindedness of Levin, the spite of the Underground Man, the paralysis of Oblomov, and the tears of laughter of Gogol's uncertified madmen.

On the other hand, there is Spiridon, one of Stalin's victims who, with every reason for despair, does not succumb to it. In fact, had he but known it, the aging Stalin might well have wished to change places with this distant descendant of Platon Karataev. Spiridon was seventeen at the time of the Revolution, over forty at the time of World War II. His wife had married him out of love. He worked in a glass factory; he had a plot of land; during the Civil War he had been drafted into the Red Army, had fought on the side of the "Greens," had been humiliated by the Whites, and in the end had surrendered peacefully to the Bolsheviks. Prospering after the war through intensive farming, he sat on the local council before an accidental blaze destroyed his property. Eventually he became a commissar and participated in forced collectivization. When the capricious policies of Moscow became unintelligible to him, he took to drink and soon became inept as an administrator. As a consequence he received a prison sentence of ten years for economic counter-revolution. After his release, he worked again as a glass-blower. During World War II he had fought with the partisans, leaving them in order to join his family in their deportation to Germany. (At this juncture in this profile Solzhenitsyn states "His instructive actions challenged the most rational pages of Montaigne and Charron.") He became separated from his wife. A slave-laborer in a factory, he raised his axe to a German foreman who had struck his son. Subsequently, he is able to rejoin his wife, finding her by instinct. Blinded by drinking raw alcohol, his sight is partially restored by a German surgeon, but he sacrifices his chance for a complete recovery in order to return to the Soviet Union with his family—yielding to his children's pleas, but against his better judgment. On their return the family is separated again and sent to different camps. (The daughter is sent to a farm where her survival as a human being is almost impossible.) "The wolfhound is right and the cannibal is wrong." This is Spiridon's summation of his unbelievable sufferings.

For him too, as for the aging Stalin, the inconsequence of politics is clearly demonstrated. But in his case, the moral is drawn from a positive rather than from a negative biographical datum. Not allowing himself to be crushed by the System and unafraid of irrational fears and anxieties, this patient intuitive man refuses to yield an ounce of his humanity.[35] It is with him that Nerzhin leaves the volume of poems by Yesenin. In a scene reminiscent in tone of the conclusion of *Crime and Punishment*, Nerzhin and Spiridon bid each other adieu—the lives of both men a spiritual triumph over the claims of politics raised to an idolatrous Absolute.

CHAPTER 6

The Broken Icon

"When Tatiana Pavlovna had cried out 'Let the ikon alone,' she had snatched it out of his hands and was holding it in hers. Suddenly, at his last word, he jumped up impulsively, snatched the ikon in a flash from Tatiana's hands, and with a ferocious swing smashed it with all his might against the corner of the tiled stove. The ikon was broken into two pieces."

DOSTOEVSKY
A Raw Youth

"Now Stavrogin stopped near the desk, picked up a small ivory crucifix, and started twisting it around in his fingers. Suddenly he snapped it in two."

The Devils

Introduction

RANDOM ABSURDITY, overweening intellectuality, crushing boredom, rampant inauthenticity, and the misplaced primacy of politics—these, among the major themes of classical Russian fiction, also add up to the existentialist syndrome of reflection. While it may be premature to formulate a definition of *Existenzphilosophie,* there can be little doubt that writers and thinkers who have interpreted human reality in an existential manner repeatedly stress these motifs in their works.[1] Admittedly, the tragic dimensions of human life are perennial, but given the false promise held out by the *philosophes,* the subsequent letdown has prompted a literature of dark forebodings which is tantamount to an innovative reaffirmation of human vulnerability. One need only think of the incorrigible rationalism of John S uart Mill (whose spiritual rebirth through the poetry of Coleridge was no less an intellectualized *tour de force* than his conception of the general welfare in relation to personal happiness) to realize the gap between such cerebral exercises and the prophetic insights of Dostoevsky's Underground Man.

It would be reckless, of course, to suggest a causal relationship between historical events and the course of literature, just as no set of conditions can serve as an adequate explanation for the emergence of any particular genius. At the same time it would be difficult to deny some correlation between the series of disappointments after the French Revolution and the existential masterpieces of fiction and philosophy which were created in its wake. Whether we focus on Schubert's *Winterreise* or Dostoevsky's *The Double,* or, in our own century, on Solzhenitsyn's *The Cancer Ward* or Berg's *Wozzeck,* in each of these cases the human imagination has grasped an inimitable facet of our dilemma as spiritual nomads. The outstanding Russian writers of the nineteenth century, precariously poised on the edge of Western civilization, yet looking at it "from the other shore," were historically privileged to discern behind the dogmas of sweet reasonableness the abysses which only a handful of exceptional geniuses in the West could perceive at that time. Where today everyone is born an existentialist, if only by virtue of being confronted by every variety of insanity posing as the normal state of affairs, in the nineteenth century it still required considerable effort and insight to pursue rational inquiries into the irrational.

While some historians would object to the identification of such writers as Tolstoy, Dostoevsky, and Gogol with the intelligentsia on the ground that the latter has inevitably been committed to the overthrow of the tsarist regime by radical means, Martin Malia has persuasively argued the alternative thesis that anyone who thought or thinks independently in Russia is thereby a member of the intelligentsia, irrespective of his specific political views.[2] Malia's view is sustained, to mention but one striking example, by the case of the Slavophiles, who were harassed and arrested on occasion by the tsarist regime precisely for maintaining autonomously what the government wanted them to submit to blindly. All too similarly Soviet dictators have repeatedly persecuted Old Bolsheviks, who, in the tradition of previous generations of the intelligentsia, persisted in presenting their own versions of the prevailing party line, instead of conforming unquestioningly to the maxims of Lenin, Stalin, and their successors. To be sure, up to the October Revolution there was a relatively small nucleus of the radical intelligentsia whose commitment to the destruction of the monarchy took precedence over everything else in their ideology and lives. Nonetheless, this particular manifestation of dissident thought and action scarcely contradicts the wider pattern of rebelliousness so characteristic of the Russian intelligentsia as a whole.

It is precisely this power of negative thinking that places the Russian intelligentsia squarely within the existential camp. As this book has tried to show, the major nineteenth-century Russian novelists in many significant ways share with Pascal, Rousseau, Kierkegaard, and Nietzsche seminal existential insights into the ambiguities and paradoxes of modern civilization. However divided on political and religious issues, all these poet-thinkers cast doubt on prevailing modes of apprehending personal relations and cultural values. Thus, despite his reactionary political views and religious fanaticism, the dominant thrust of Gogol's fiction is destructive of bureaucratic cant and madness posing as coherent structure. His celebration of banality is an ironic twist on the Romantic daydreaming of nineteenth-century meliorists. Dostoevsky, in turn, anticipated many of Freud's ideas about the role of dreams and the unconscious, speculated on the death of God, and immortalized the uprootedness of the modern intellectual in search of meaning. Though his intentions in writing *Oblomov* may have been in part to arouse Russia's gentry from their slumbers of superfluity, Goncharov, inadvertently or not, challenged the Protestant ethic of the "advanced" West. Granting, for the sake of argument, that hard work never killed anyone, Goncharov nevertheless raises the question whether there is not something more to life than constant activity for its own sake. Tolstoy condemned virtually every aspect of modern culture as inauthentic and dehumanizing. Although he was opposed to the use of violence, his hatred of the modern state as manipulative and unjust yielded nothing to that of Bakunin and Marx. (In this regard Lev Nikolayevich belongs indisputably in the camp of the intelligentsia.) Finally, Solzhenitsyn decries the worship of the totalitarian Soviet state as a betrayal of the individual conscience.

Historically, the Russian intelligentsia was peculiarly well placed to bear witness to the existential predicament of post-Kantian man. Alienated from the mass of their countrymen by education and from the government by choice of conscience, tormented by ambivalent feelings toward the West, burdened by a feeling of responsibility for Russia's destiny, this ill-defined body was naturally drawn to unorthodox theory and practice. In contrast to Victorian men of letters or German academic intellectuals, the Russian *intelligent* could not take anything for granted as offering him security and recognition. If he did not choose voluntary exile in Europe, he had to reckon with exile in Siberia. His affirmation of life in spite of these circumstances is striking testimony of his faith in a better future. This, moreover, helps to account for the link between the religiously oriented masters of Russian fiction, such as Dostoevsky and Tolstoy, and the atheistic radicalism of Herzen and Bakunin. While these two camps were completely at odds on the nature of religious truth, they believed in common that, in spite of everything, human freedom, spontaneity, and life are sacred. Whatever clandestine affinities these two groups may have had for the Grand Inquisitor's Machiavellian morality, ultimately, however recklessly, they gambled on the eventual downfall of the Torquemadas. It is worth noting in this connection that Solzhenitsyn, who, repudiating Communist practice while remaining sympathetic to Marxist ideals of community, expresses in his novels the same broadly conceived religious faith in vitality and inwardness.

Personality in Existenzerhellung

The preceding discussion has shown that it is little wonder the Russian writer born after the French Revolution, quite apart from personal idiosyncrasies and temperament, was ideally suited to speak in an existential voice. Nevertheless, biographical factors played an important part in strengthening this tendency.

Existential thinkers manifest a striking "family resemblance" in their vulnerability to psychosomatic and physical disorders. Whereas rationalists in the main have enjoyed comparative good health, existentialists have tended to show the strains of being outside the dominant traditions in Western thought. Descartes suffered intensely from the cold, but it would be committing a

"category mistake" to equate his discomforts with the torments
(some self-inflicted) endured by his dialectical adversary, Blaise
Pascal. About a century later Voltaire was wont to remark that
nothing fazed him, while Rousseau, in the grip of paranoia, explored the depths of the Enlightenment Pollyanna cult. Another
classic example is the case of Hegel and Kierkegaard. On the
one hand, we find the venerable German academician rhapsodi-
cally fusing the tautologies of logic with the contradictions of life
in a monumental System expounded under more or less ideal conditions at the University of Berlin. On the other hand, there is the
"melancholy Dane," a hunchback, subject to the most terrible fits
of depression, unable, in his own words, to relate to others in a
normal way, writing his existential dialectics for the edification of
future generations, and dead at the age of forty-two. Nietzsche
was a lifelong sufferer from migraine headaches while William
James, who credited the pathological individual with special insights, knew only too well whereof he spoke. In our own century no one will easily forget Simone de Beauvoir's account of
Jean-Paul Sartre pursued by furious red crabs. The late John
Dewey and Sir Alfred J. Ayer, one assumes, have been spared such
experiences.

It is of course possible to make too much of such connections
between a specific quality of thought and insight and the personal
makeup of the writer who expressed it. Yet insofar as biography
can shed light on ideology, there would appear to be a recurring
correlation between James's "sick soul" and disclosures of the
more problematic aspects of the human condition. Certainly some
conjunction of this sort holds for the classical Russian novelists
vis-à-vis the distinctive traits of the literature they created. Indeed,
it is neither an accident nor mere historical necessity that this literature offers us a stream of confessions, diaries of madmen, and
numerous explorations of abnormal personalities.[3] Sometimes it
seems as if an interpreter of Russian literature and thought must
himself be touched by madness in order to understand his subject
matter. In any case, it is important to distinguish between the extraordinary conditions with which Russian writers and thinkers
have had to cope, and what may best be described as their "psychosomatic" genius for interpreting these conditions in highly
imaginative writing.

Although the Slavophiles may have gone astray in idealizing the religious consciousness of the Russian peasant, they were conspicuously correct in their evaluation of Western Christianity as cerebral, compartmentalized, and, for all practical purposes, dead by the end of the eighteenth century as a life force in European civilization. Cardinal Newman was beating a dead horse in his desperate efforts to revive Roman Catholicism. Had he read Kierkegaard he might have been spared his futile undertaking, for the Danish thinker saw all too clearly that in the nineteenth century only martyrs could become Christians, and that these have been in even shorter supply than geniuses like himself. On this score, Gogol also was capable of misjudging the *Zeitgeist*. He became a religious fanatic, who burned the second part of *Dead Souls* shortly before his death and voiced reactionary sentiments which ill became one of the most radical humorists of all time. There has been a great deal of speculation about Gogol's sexlessness and the lack of convincing female characters in his fiction. Whatever the merits of these views, there can be little doubt that throughout most of his life he was psychically disturbed. Hence it would be odd if his amazing perceptions of the grotesque were not somehow linked with his unbalanced frame of mind. Interestingly enough, one of the outstanding twentieth-century novelists, a devoted student of Gogol's works, Franz Kafka, also requested that his manuscripts be burned prior to his death.

A recent play entitled *Subject to Fits* is intended as a response to Dostoevsky's *The Idiot* and its hero, who, like his creator, suffered from epilepsy. Whether or not Dostoevsky did in fact rape young girls, as some critics have claimed, there is no gainsaying his personal instability nor his obsession with crime—at least in his fiction. Henry James, the master narrator of evil in Anglo-Saxon society, nevertheless felt rebuffed by Dostoevsky's art with its (William Jamesian) stress on the extremes of the human predicament. Had Dostoevsky been welcome guest in Russian country houses it is highly questionable whether he could have left us his remarkable accounts of double-mindedness, self-laceration, spiritual ecstasy, and debasing despondency.

As masters of Russian prose go, the bureaucrat Goncharov was relatively well adjusted, though even he developed paranoia. In a dispute which will probably never be settled to everyone's satisfaction, he accused Turgenev of plagiarizing some of his finest passages. Time only exacerbated Goncharov's persecution complex, until in a memorable park scene, shouting "Thief! Thief!," he ran from his tormentor.

Tolstoy's fear of death and madness is embodied both in his personal diaries and in his fiction. His public pronouncements on Christian optimism notwithstanding, Tolstoy, like Kierkegaard, led a hidden life whose full dimension only became known with the publication of his intimate papers. To the world at large, especially after his conversion, he appeared as an undauntable figure ready to take on the whole questionable legacy of civilization in his quest for sincerity and mutual openness. Yet, in his introspective moments he confided to himself the most gnawing doubts and the gravest suspicions of his own integrity, frequently leading him to the verge of suicide. Tolstoy's rationalism primarily served as a smoke screen for his innermost thoughts and feelings, whose presence in his works even this giant could not wholly control. Inauthenticity, death, and madness are all existential themes which Tolstoy knew by acquaintance and immortalized by description.

Solzhenitsyn's personal acquaintance with suffering needs no special explication. The author of *The Cancer Ward* has himself been on intimate terms with that terrible disease. Thus one sees that the case of the Soviet novelist is another link in a long chain of fiction, closely bound up with a pronounced lack of physical or mental well-being.

An existential approach to this phenomenon might also bring out the uniqueness and exceptionality of the protagonists in this literature. Unlike the role of Plekhanov's individual in history, which is confined to his being a vehicle of inexorable material forces, a Pechorin, Bazarov, Chichikov, or Ivan Karamazov represents a non-repeatable and almost defiantly extraordinary self which goes to the limits of its own volition. These heroes, like their creators, have much in common with Dostoevsky's Underground Man, knocking his head against brick walls to mock the utilitarian hypothesis of utterly predictable human behavior. Burdened by sickness as he generally was, the classical Russian writer can never be confused with a mere "cog in a machine." Hence it is scarcely surprising that the characters he created deviate sharply from the genre characters of Sir Walter Scott, Anthony Trollope, and the norm so typical of Western European literary heroes.

Conclusion: The Broken Icon

In the unrelieved controversy about the world's current predicament, historians are apt to follow one of two major lines of argument. Those steeped in Marxism or persuaded by some related form of socialist doctrine will for the most part attribute our ills and crises to such phenomena as the class struggle, the rapid transition from a basically agrarian to a highly industrial society, or, as C. P. Snow would have it, to the deficient diffusion of advanced technology. On the other hand, there are those who will stress the breakdown of traditional values (Chaadaev argued the decline of Christianity in Russia, and the Slavophiles, its decline in the West.) and waves of disenchantment with one ideology after another: from the god who failed Arthur Koestler and André Gide to the National Socialism of Adolf Hitler. While these interpretations are far from being mutually exclusive, each provides a distinct orientation toward a plausible evaluation of our troubled times.

One must, of course, also reckon with those historians whose understanding empathy for Athenian slaves or Prussian serfs offers them a kind of transcendental perspective on our current difficulties. Yet with all due deference to their vast learning, including their freedom from the tyranny of topicality, they still miss the point. For after we grant them the rather obvious truth that life for man has never been easy on this planet, their task of explaining to us our suicidal dilemma within the context of unprecedented enlightenment and plenty remains woefully unfulfilled. Whatever the exact nature and origins of our crisis may be, we can trust Nietzsche's and Burckhardt's prophecy that it would constitute a unique watershed in man's historical development. Nietzsche's fateful premonitions of nihilistic cataclysms for our century have been borne out by a succession of horrors and futile opposition to senseless events.

The term "nihilism" was popularized in Russia and subsequently throughout Europe by Turgenev's *Fathers and Sons*. It is important to distinguish Russian nihilism in general and Bazarov's in particular from Nietzsche's dark forebodings. At the same time, one should avoid drawing too sharp a separation between the two.[4] Although circumstances in Russia favoring the growth of nihilism in the 1860s and 1870s were historically unique, its emergence then and there, like that of intuitive existentialism among the Russian novelists in the first half of the century, was in many respects prophetic of a spreading malaise in Western civilization everywhere. Whether nihilists do not know or understand anything, whether they have ceased to believe in a supreme Being, whether they question the possibility of justifying any set of values, or whether, Bakunin-like, they are bent on performing acts of creative destruction, their disaffection with the *status quo* is beyond dispute in each of these cases. Contrary to those who argued that Turgenev's hero was a caricature of the real Russian nihilists, Pisarev, the radical polemicist, welcomed him, so to speak, with open arms and a whole generation of Russian youth modeled themselves on this enigmatic hero. The fact is that the nihilists were split among themselves on many issues and that it is simply impossible to associate them with any coherent doctrine. Some of them loved to indulge in innumerable glasses of strong tea while spurning liquor, others were confirmed rationalists whose secular kingdom of heaven was inspired by Bentham's Panopticon or the phalansteries of Fourier, and still others had recourse to outrageous exhibition in attempting to call attention to their crusade. What should always be kept in mind is a precarious balance between positive and negative ideas in the world outlook of these extreme dissenters.[5] Bazarov is certainly closer to Nietzsche's "active" than to his "passive" nihilist. The latter, like Kierkegaard's Christian in Christendom, is willing to pay lip service to beliefs which no longer speak to him from the inside. The active nihilist, on the other hand, is willing to implement his radical convictions in his own life style. Yet it would be erroneous to confuse Turgenev's protagonist with the assassins of Alexander II or the uncritical lovers of the peasants and the workers.

Bazarov, a sort of culmination of the negative existential hero in Russian fiction, is first and foremost an individualist. He does not care for society in general, ultimately not even for his own disciple, Arkady. His fondness for dissecting frogs, a recurrent motif in the novel, symbolizes his contempt for loose talk and Romantic fancy. Nevertheless he cannot help falling madly in love when Madame Odintseva awakens his passionate nature. His rejection of beauty and art is similarly a defense mechanism to protect himself from succumbing to their charm. For what he wants to do above all is to practice medicine, minimally distracted by the hypocrisy and vanity of the world. He is a man of conscience whose repudiation of the "fathers" is matched by his compassion for his needy contemporaries. But he entertains no illusions about the grandeur of the "sons."

Turgenev was very ambiguous toward this creation, alternately rejoicing in Bazarov's candor and bemoaning his anti-Romantic stance. Herein, however, lies not only the genius of this particular character, but, to generalize, of the whole golden age of Russian prose. Again and again, as we have seen, it raises the decisive issues without imposing upon us any dogmatic answers. Fully conscious of dead traditions, it skirts the temptations of sensationalism and blind avant-gardism in its elucidation of modern man's spiritual predicament. Together with the heroes of Gogol, Dostoevsky, Goncharov, Tolstoy, and Solzhenitsyn, Bazarov loves life and lives out his own, until an infection incurred in the course of his medical duties causes his death. In contrast to this, contemporary despair in Western literature even despairs of life. The drama of the Absurd, by piling absurdity upon absurdity, has itself degenerated into meaningless literary *genre*, intent on making a fetish of non-communication and inscrutability. Instead of Dostoevsky's realism, relieved by the poetic fancy of an Ivan Karamazov, we are all too frequently confronted by clinical landscapes of gloom and dreariness, devoid not only of hope but also of thought. Virtually alone today are the dissident authors in the Soviet state who under the most trying conditions help carry on their great tradition of existential realism—broken icons and shattered dreams notwithstanding.

In this line of inquiry, it is worthwhile to consider the fate of the existentialist tradition in contemporary Russia, and, more specifically, the accuracy of Dostoevsky's characterization of the revolutionary intellectual as confirmed or refuted by the latter's historical participation in the October Revolution and its aftermath. As emerges from the trials of Solzhenitsyn, the Soviet government looks with extreme displeasure on those writers who deviate from the canons of socialist realism for the sake of stressing the inner contradictions in man's condition. Insofar as ideological purity demands the identification of all grievances and complaints human beings are wont to have with the evils of bourgeois capitalism, it is blasphemous for a Soviet novelist to suggest, for example, that the gnawing boredom of his protagonist is the result of anything less tangible than the lack of hard work he devotes to his occupation. Nevertheless, Gogol's question "Whither are we going?" has not been suppressed by the most effective Third Section in Russian history nor answered by all the Five Year Plans instituted since the Bolsheviks seized power.

Quite aside from the hard dogmatic line taken by the Soviet authorities against existential realism in prose fiction, it is not a little ironic that, just before and during the Revolution, Russian writers of their own accord turned to aestheticism as their literary ideal. The Silver Age of Russian literature was partly a revolt against the earlier Golden Age, partly a triumph of poetry over prose, of symbolic meaning over meaning emerging from our direct involvement in the struggles of life and history. Thus it can be argued that the Soviet regime unwittingly encouraged the revival of the Old Tradition, first by compartmentalizing literature as an activity normatively devoid of political contents, and subsequently by repressing the creative imagination altogether. In other words, as numerous memoirs of Russian writers caught up in the events since 1917 testify, they were either deceived by Lenin into thinking that aesthetic autonomy would be respected or liquidated by Stalin for raising their voices against the dehumanization imposed upon them and their fellow citizens from above. In creating a climate of opinion favorable to the reverence for and continuation of existential realism, the Soviet government has undercut its own credibility as a judge of sound literature. While many Russian writers became the victims of totalitarian terror, the Russian classics, including Dostoevsky, continued to be read. Not even Stalin succeeded in erasing the Soviet public's great affection for their own literary heritage.[6] A. Anatoli (Kuznetsov) recounts in *Babi Yar* how, during the purges of the thirties, his family destroyed their entire library of Russian literature with the exception of Pushkin's works. Presumably, in spite of Dostoevsky's famous oration praising him, only Pushkin could not be found guilty of violating the Soviet penal code.

Of the classical prose writers frowned upon but grudgingly tolerated by the Soviet regime, none proved more problematic than Fyodor Dostoevsky. Had he not written *The Devils*, his reactionary views could have been trivialized as the inconsequential musings of a towering creative genius. But it is precisely in this most insightful of all political novels that Dostoevsky the poet-thinker rather than the acerbic publicist launches his unsurpassed attack on the revolutionary intellectual as a vehicle of dehumanization. At first glance Dostoevsky's characterizations of Peter Verkhovensky, Stavrogin, Shatov, and the others might indeed be dismissed as caricatures which for all their psychological brilliance did not apply to the flesh-and-blood revolutionaries of the twentieth century. Certainly to the degree that Lenin and Trotsky combined moral fervor with seemingly inexhaustible reserves of determination and amazing powers of intellectual judgment, they supersede Turgenev's dichotomy between Hamlet and Don Quixote, the dreamer and the activist. Moreover, in their personal lives, they show, if anything, not more but less vulnerability to corruption than ordinary men.

As we catch glimpses of the distinguished editor of *Iskra* first planning and then executing the Revolution, we are transported to another world than that of *The Devils*—a world of heroic self-denial, dedicated sobriety, and unremitting single-mindedness in the face of insuperable obstacles. As an analytic philosopher might put it, instead of asking Gogol's wrong question: Whither are we going?, Lenin and Trotsky, supreme pragmatists that they were, asked the right, answerable question: What is to be done?, and, together with their illustrious disciples, triumphed jubilantly over all opposition, not least that of their former allies the Mensheviks. Are we to conclude from these developments that Chernyshevsky was a keen visionary, whereas Dostoevsky, carried away by *ressentiment*, profoundly misjudged the practical role of the revolutionary theorist?

A closer look at *The Devils* shows us that, in his unmasking of the concealed, Dostoevsky's analysis of the state of mind of the radical intellectual was as prophetically sound as Bakunin's condemnation of the Marxists in the early 1870s for seeking to impose the Revolution from above instead of diffusing it from below. What troubled the chauvinistic anarchist, whose *Weltanschauung,* curiously enough, had a great deal in common with Dostoevsky's, was not the dictatorship of the proletariat but the dictatorship of Marx and Engels and that of their successors, burdening the toiling masses with a new tyranny worse than its antecedents for being camouflaged as the genuine expression of the "People's Will." Dostoevsky did not have any illusions about the spiritual unity of the toiling masses, but he did arrive independently at Bakunin's view of the revolutionary intellectual as a potential menace to human dignity and freedom. His Grand Inquisitor, a sort of prototypal Lenin, promises to bear the people's burden in exchange for demythologizing the New Testament, while Peter Verkhovensky promises to redress the balance of too much demystification by introducing Stavrogin as the great Remythologizer who will dazzle his subjects with wonders undreamed of even by Professor Harvey Cox in his secular city. It is precisely in this bit of Dostoevskyan existential dialectic between radical demythologization, on the one hand, and extreme mystification, on the other, that the public personalities of Lenin and Trotsky conform uncannily to the models in *The Devils.*

The countless victims of Stalin's purges must on occasion have raised Alexander Herzen's question: Who Is to Blame? It remains a question whose full moral force lies outside the scope of the ideology espoused by the epigones of Bolshevism. For that matter, even Trotsky in his autobiography, written in Constantinople as an exile from the great Revolution he so assiduously strove to realize, cannot comprehend his own responsibility for the horrors already perpetrated in the twenties in the name of the people's paradise. He loved The Cause abstractly, and, belonging with Lenin to a generation which still had certain principles, his conscience never quite deserted him. Yet this brilliant intellectual-turned-revolutionary fails to see, for example, how his almost blind adoration of Lenin, his unassuageable hatred of those who differed with him, his fascination with power, and his crude anti-religiousness played into the hands of the Party Secretary Stalin, whose biography Trotsky was working on at the time of his murder by the dictator's agents. One can only hope that previously Trotsky had found an opportunity to reread certain passages in

Dostoevsky wherein the Underground Man affirms the insepar-
ability of freedom and unpredictability in contrast to the mechanical operations of a piano key, or wherein Peter Verkhovensky
evokes for Stavrogin an atmosphere of terror and intrigue in
which the spiritless rationality of the Revolution will flourish before
regressing into waves of irrationality that will make tsarism look
sweet and reasonable in retrospect.

Appendices

1. Descartes and Pascal

In every century since the seventeenth (and possibly earlier), two major European thinkers, one representing the dominant rationalism of his age and the other reacting against it with timely "thoughts out of season," have confronted each other in dialectical opposition, whose history coincides with the emergence of existential consciousness as a central facet of modern life and thought. ("Dialectical" in this context signifies an inseparable dependence on, and deviation from, the entrenched point of view.) Thus Rousseau's revolt against his fellow *philosophes* of the Enlightenment is unintelligible apart from his own roots in the "heavenly city" whose shadows he came to trace with such prophetically disturbing power; analogously, Kierkegaard's attack on the Hegelian System presupposes the authenticity of becoming subjective, which is no less a crucial moment in Hegel's speculative *hubris* than in the Dane's preoccupation with passionate intensity. In recent philosophy, moreover, there would appear to be an uncanny connection between Carnap's formalization of meaning and necessity, and Heidegger's systematic exploration of meaninglessness and contingency in *Sein und Zeit*. The most significant encounter of this kind is that between the two seminal mathematician-philosophers of the seventeenth century, René Descartes and Blaise Pascal. A comparison of the views of these two figures on self, doubt, method, and God will show that from its very beginnings modern thought generated its own corrective, like the judge-penitent in Camus's *The Fall*, precariously balancing his vanity against his anguish. Such tangential issues as whether the existentialists merely supplement or explicitly contradict the modern classical philosophers, whether they are anti-philosophical at heart or the counterpart of radical revolutionaries in the domain of reflection, deceptively oblivious to inconsistencies over which they leap in order to get at truths inaccessible to more cautious investigators, all hinge on the clarification of the oddly intertwined perspectives of scientific rationalism and existential illumination.

For Descartes, anything other than Mind is relegated to a subordinate position in his scheme of reality, if not legislated out of existence entirely. Consequently, his concept of the Self is that of a thinking machine, a fleshless computer occasionally disturbed by incidental visceral vibrations, but for the most part a law unto itself in its pursuit of pure knowledge. Even more so than Plato and Aristotle, who in reducing human experience to cognitive activity at least did not find the other parts of the soul wholly superfluous, Descartes postulates a radical dualism between our animal spirits and our intelligence, with the latter, as it were, signifying in splendid isolation our humanity.

Pascal's resurrection of human experience, far from dissociating the dignity of man from his rational powers, reaffirmed it in unmistakable terms, but with the proviso that passion is as integral a part of our being in this world as thought:

All the dignity of man consists in thought. Thought is therefore by its nature a wonderful and incomparable thing. It must have strange defects to be contemptible. But it has such, so that nothing is more ridiculous. How great it is in its nature! How vile it is in its defects!
But what is this thought? How foolish it is! (*Pensées*, #365)

The heart has its reasons, which reason does not know . . . Is it by reason that you love yourself? (*Pensées*, #277)

Feelings permeate even the highest flights of our analytic imagination, not to mention the lives and politics of the greatest philosophers. It is not by reason that we love ourselves, that we find rational explanations flattering to our egos, or that we decide on one set of premises as being *prima facie* superior to an alternative group. On the positive side, intellectual pursuits themselves are inconceivable apart from the intensity accompanying any serious quest undertaken by man. Not only, then, according to Pascal, is there a logic of the heart, which unavoidably intrudes on Aristotelian logic, but that logic itself would never be applied by us to any specific problem unless we felt so inclined in the first place. What men have in common beyond the curiosity to know is the need to be loved. On this point Pascal found Descartes "useless and uncertain."

Along these same lines it is worthwhile to contrast Cartesian and Pascalian doubt. While Descartes worries about such epistemological phenomena as sense deception, the confusion of the waking with the sleeping state, and the possibility that an evil daemon might attempt to deceive us by planting false propositions in our minds, Pascal concerns himself with more practical doubts about the moral uses to which we put our knowledge and opinions, our incorrigible proclivity to treat contingencies as necessities, and our infinite capacity for self-deception. In its profession of "learned ignorance" Cartesian doubt is consistently academic: with the possible exception of some German Romantics most men are able to distinguish their sleeping from their waking moments (even allowing for the mesmerizing effects of nightmares and related somnambulistic phenomena). Interestingly enough, it is the same German Romantics who had severe difficulty in liberating their minds from the influences of evil daemons of the kind Descartes imagined passing off false propositions on us as illuminations of truth. Perhaps the founder of modern philosophy was the first German Romantic—a notion, however frivolous, Marx and Kierkegaard would surely have found amusing. Indeed there are clear indications of egomania, a mood frequently associated with German academic philosophy in its classical period, in Descartes's first doubting everything but then arriving at the conclusion that we exist because we think, as if the consciousness of being alive rather than dead required any demonstration beyond our desire to survive.

Pascal's doubt, on the other hand, was anything but studied, rooted as it was in lived experience rather than in "learned ignorance." He could not share Descartes's confidence in the benevolent dispositions of enlightened minds to make optimal use of what they knew. His emphasis on the indissoluble links between the misery and glory of man contrasts graphically with the Cartesian glorification of ego once it has been purged of all error.

Pascal's fear of the infinite spaces reflects his sensitivity both to hazardous waverings within himself and to the treacherous character of the world at large. This lack of confidence in man's ability to know the whole or any of its parts without first having acquired a consummate knowledge of either, together with his skepticism about our motives in acquiring knowledge, make up two of the existential *Grundmotifs* which appear again and again in subsequent literature. Whereas Cartesian doubt is basically a function of epistemological bafflement carried to a contrived extreme, and hence seemingly resolvable, Pascalian doubt flows from an incurable flaw in the human condition, a perennial state of *Zerrissenheit* that casts aspersions on our most high-minded undertakings.

I blame equally those who choose to praise man, those who choose to blame him, and those who choose to amuse themselves, and I can only approve those who seek with lamentation . . . If he exalt himself, I humble him; if he humble himself, I exalt him; and I always contradict him, *till he understands that he is an incomprehensible monster.* (*Pensées*, #420, 421)

Pascal's image of man walking on a plank his reason assures him is safe, but whose imagination nevertheless causes him to break out in cold sweat over the abyss, recurs in the Kierkegaardian "leap by virtue of the Absurd," in Nietzsche's double-edged treatment of Nature and the death of God—wherever, in brief, there remain persistent doubts regarding the justifiability of our character rather than our acts.[1]

Where Descartes stresses clarity and precision of ideas, Pascal turns his attention to the paradoxes and ambiguities of the human situation. He does not deny the efficacy of the famous "geometric" method in the realm of abstract possibilities, but insists on its supplementation by the "intuitive" method in the human sciences. His argument for the existence of God, directed to freethinkers, is no more valid than the Cartesian warhorses trotted out for this venerable ritual, but at least the Wager has the merit of speaking directly to man's religious needs.[2] Descartes, following in the footsteps of Anselm, wanted to argue that the idea of God entails his existence since lack of such would not be consistent with our having an idea of *a Being no greater than which can be conceived.* But not only, as Hume, Kant, and Schopenhauer pointed out in their different ways, does essence never entail existence: it is also the case, as Freud has suggested, that our very ideas of perfection may well be fantasies we fabricate to mock our disaffection with actuality. The ideal of the perfect woman has a likeness to the idea of God in setting on a pedestal some of our unattainable dreams. So far as the origin of an idea of perfection in an imperfect mind is concerned, today we do not differentiate between the degree of the reality of causes and effects, but rather between their measure of importance within a concrete framework of understanding and activity.

Pascal's beatific calculus makes sense so long as eternal bliss is still a live option for an unbeliever. Militant atheists would hardly be moved by considerations of balancing the prospects of damnation or heavenly bliss against the fleeting moments of earthly joy. Why should anyone cut back on his accumulation of pleasure if the possibility of finite satisfaction is the only one he acknowledges? Though it begs the question for the radical freethinker, the Wager's emphasis on man's stubborn pursuit of genuine happiness in the face of constant disillusionment gives it a relevance strikingly absent from Descartes's scholastic speculations about the deity. Pascal's personal religious experience is recorded in his "Memorial," wherein he contrasts the "God of the philosophers" with the God of the Bible, who addresses himself to man's faith and frailty rather than to his reasoning abilities and metaphysical perfectionism. Here too Pascal exposed a rift in modern experience and thought which has proved irreconcilable. When the existentialists speak of God they do not have in mind the master architect of the intelligible universe, but a broadly based meaning to an individual's existence transcending both his immediate concerns and his longer-range planning in his historical situation.

In conclusion, it should be noted that Descartes more or less confined his philosophizing to the relatively safe areas of epistemology and dogmatic metaphysics.

In passing, I may remark that I do not here treat sin, that is, of error committed in the pursuit of good and evil, but solely of that which arises in deciding between the true and the false. Nor do I dwell on matters bearing on faith or on the conduct of life, but only on those speculative truths which can be known by way of the natural light. (Synopsis to *Meditations*, in *Descartes: Philosophical Writings*, selected and translated by Norman Kemp Smith, New York, 1958)

On the other hand, Pascal, the Jansenist, touched on every aspect of being human. In the course of so doing he did not shrink from adumbrating ethical relativism and related heresies of the modern consciousness in relation to its feudal past.

Who has demonstrated that there will be a tomorrow, and that we shall die? And what is more believed? It is, then, custom which persuades us of it; it is custom that makes so many men Christians; custom that makes them Turks, heathens, artisans, soldiers, etc. (*Pensées*, #252)

Three degrees of latitude reverse all jurisprudence; a meridian decides the truth. (*Pensées*, #294)

Descartes, who is conventionally credited with founding modern philosophy, remained at heart a conservative thinker who, out of fear of the authorities and also out of respect for some of their views, did not find it advisable to descend from his Olympian heights of methodical rigor to the arena of human struggle. Pascal, on the other hand, modernist *malgré lui*, punishing himself in his monastery cell, had the temerity to question all accepted judgments, including the foundations of his own troubled faith. Was it any wonder that next to de Maistre and Schopenhauer he was the most widely read Western European thinker in nineteenth-century Russia?

2. Hegel and the First Generation of the Russian Intelligentsia

In his brilliant study of Alexander Herzen, Martin Malia, after trying to account for the enormous influence of Schelling on the first generation of the Russian intelligentsia along traditional lines of ripeness of thought, *Zeitgeist*, etc., reaches the conclusion that the presence of these and related factors, though undeniable, is not the decisive clue to the Schelling vogue in Russia in the first decades of the nineteenth century.[1] Malia rightly observes that the Russians focused on those of Schelling's abstruse musings which coincided with their own predilections and ignored the rest. Far from undertaking detailed expositions of Schelling's successive systems, whose Absolute reminded Hegel of the night when all cows are black, they seized upon those aspects of the German metaphysician's thought which confirmed their longings or dispelled their fears. The case of Schelling illustrates a generalization about the relationship of the major figures of the intellectual and literary history of nineteenth-century Russia to Western philosophy. The truth here is this: whatever the degree of expertise in the thought of the Western thinkers in question, and this varied from Belinsky's highly tendentious understanding to Khomiakov's thorough knowledge of Hegel, the Russians' concern with any of these figures was existential rather than academic or, in Marxist terms, oriented toward changing the world instead of merely interpreting it.

The appeal of German Idealism has often been explained in terms of a mixture of noble aspirations providing contrapuntal relief from the ills of the day. In the light of the careers of Herzen, Belinsky, Dostoevsky, and Bakunin, such a hypothesis is at best questionable.[2] Whatever else may be said about these men, disengagement from historical actuality was never their aim, save perhaps as a passing mood. In any event, the appeal of post-Kantian metaphysics to this group of writers will always remain something of a puzzle. Herzen and Bakunin hated Germany with a passion only surpassed by their hatred of Karl Marx; Gogol and Dostoevsky ridiculed German character traits at every opportunity, while Belinsky, once he had broken with right-wing Hegelianism, thereafter but rarely resisted the opportunity of poking fun at his intellectual ancestors. Subsequently both Tolstoy and Turgenev settled on Schopenhauer as their favorite German philosopher: Arthur Schopenhauer, who could abide neither Hegel's thought nor his personality, in addition to expressing a lifelong preference for English modes of life. His pessimistic philosophy, to be sure, however anti-academic in tone and content, was expressed in a System as typical of German poetic philosophizing in its own unique way as any he and his renowned Russian disciples rejected. But the fact remains that next to Nietzsche he was the least Hegelian of the German thinkers who were simultaneously inspired and repelled by Hegel's powerful spell.

It was a part of Hegel's genius to put things so ambiguously and nebulously that his propositions could easily be made to serve any conceivable intent. Kierkegaard once remarked that were he trying to become a speculative philosopher he could not think of a better model to emulate than Hegel's System, with its infinite possibilities and its dialectical invitation to unlimited manipulation. As it was, even in his severest polemics against the System, Kierkegaard is unmistakably indebted to Hegel for much of his vocabulary, his existential dialectic, his "stages on life's way," and, above all, his Christian fanaticism. Although Hegel thought that Christianity was simply a stage in man's spiritual evolution which had historically been surpassed by art and philosophy and, not least, by his own System, whereas Kierkegaard regarded what he took to be New Testament Christianity as a unique unsurpassed revelation, both thinkers were incorrigible absolutists in their inconsistent avowal of a single point of view as the only path to salvation. For just as Kierkegaard offers no compelling argument for the identity of candor and Christianity (if "truth be subjectivity" the enthronement of Christian truth as universal salvation is untenable), Hegel, the dialectician of the spirit, is equally unconvincing in assuming an absolute stance, whether it be from the vantage point of the Prussian state (doomed like all other states, according to Hegel himself, to be superseded), or, for that matter, from any Olympian perspective that subverts the inevitable relativity of any *status quo*.

Given these resemblances between the phenomenologist of the
Spirit and the pathfinder "on life's way," it should not be too
startling to find that the first generation of the Russian intelligentsia, while committed to the sovereignty of life over all
abstractions, should still have found a great deal in Hegel consonant with its own aspirations. There was, to begin with, Hegel's
philosophy of history, with its stress on the negation of every
previous manifestation of the World Spirit in favor of hitherto
unfavored nations and peoples. However much Hegel may have
championed the state that bestowed on him his professorship at
the University of Berlin as exceptionally enlightened, his reflections on the goals of history trace a pattern of successive progress
from the Orient to the Occident, with Russia and the United
States perhaps destined, through the Dialect, to inherit the mantle
of their precursors. With England, France, and the German states
having already experienced historical greatness, the Russians, ig-
noring Hegel's reluctance to prophesy the future, felt that their
own "manifest destiny" was about to devolve upon them. It
is obvious why this possibility, so congruent with the thought of
one of the outstanding philosophers of their day, should have
entranced the intelligentsia. Here, at least in theory, was a way
out of the hopelessness disseminated by the reign of Nicholas I
with its reactionary policies. It is worth noting that in many
significant respects both Hegel and his biased Russian readers
were correct. Russia did in fact become the most powerful
European nation (a prospect it took Marx forty years longer to
entertain seriously), and, in his analysis of the Master-Slave relationship in the *Phenomenology*, Hegel put his finger on a major
tragic dilemma of modern times. Up to this time, it was generally
supposed that the Master exercised absolute control over his
Slave, making his position both enviable and seemingly invulnerable. Hegel's analysis not only challenged but significantly refuted
this interpretation. According to it the Slave, by retaining direct
contact with the instruments of survival or the necessities of life,
preserves a relative freedom from excess dependence which, dialectically, enslaves the Master, his apparent sovereignty notwithstanding. For example, the Slave must filch or forge a utensil in
order to eat, thus enabling him to stay in immediate touch with
the exigencies of survival, whereas the Master would be lost like

a babe in the woods without someone to wait on him hand and foot.

In the application of this analysis to that interval of historical time which interested the Russian intelligentsia above all others, it is not difficult to discern how, in Hegel's line of interpretation, the autocracy of Nicholas I could not help but sow the seeds of its own destruction. Nicholas's attempt to prevent everyone but himself from thinking for himself, so characteristic of tyrants, set the stage for the future collapse of imperial Russia. Many an oppressed serf proved far more able to take care of himself than the superfluous landlord, squandering away his estate.

Every proposition in Hegel generates its own negation, thus opening up seemingly inexhausible possibilities of interpretation. Whatever statement we make about anything perforce leaves out of account as much as it includes, giving, as it were, with the right hand what it removes with the left. As in life, nothing in Hegel's philosophy is unqualifiedly true. It is this element of restlessness and constant need of revision which above all fascinated Hegel's ingenious Russian readers. His System in the end proved unacceptable, hopelessly abstruse and out of touch with the tribulations of personal existence, but his vision, however speculative in the Idealistic sense, has a hard-core element of realism which eludes, say, the parody of German Idealism in Dostoevsky's *Notes from Underground*. It is, moreover, a tragic vision, whose apparent rigor and optimistic assumptions about the return of the Absolute unto itself cannot belie a discerning understanding of the partiality and ambiguity of all human developments. As Pascal's "thinking reed" is unthinkable without the Cartesian "transcendental ego," by the same token the intuitive existentialism of a Kierkegaard or Herzen grew out of Hegel's all-consuming Absolute.[3]

3. Alienation

Like "identity crisis," the term "alienation" has become the *cri de coeur* of a whole generation. Aside from its more technical meanings discussed below, it evokes familiar symptoms of emptiness, desertion, and unrelatedness to the world at large. It is as if Horatio Alger's pioneer spirit, undaunted by all the barriers of self-realization, had yielded to that existential vacuum in which one of Samuel Beckett's heroes finds that nothing is happening to him. In this condition, oddly reminiscent of Paradise in the Christian mythology, there is nothing left to talk about, nothing left to do, and nothing left to invest in a future. The alienated individual no longer has any stake in his environment. Worse yet, he experiences himself as pulling no weight and finds that he is superfluous even to himself. If he is a political radical he will be disposed to blame his lack of drive on the prevailing social order, which has made it impossible for him to feel at home in the world he knows. Should he feel more conservatively inclined, he will seek the cause of his disaffection in himself, either as an unhealthy aberration of the species or as a variety of martyrdom chosen by some deity to chastise the world—say, an iconoclast or a misunderstood holy man.

Every form of alienation presupposes a unity from which, under the pressure of events, the individual has become separated. In the theistic tradition the unity in question is the correlation of God's Will with that of man, which the latter's original as well as subsequent acts of disobedience have torn asunder. Hence the religious alienation of the orthodox Christian believer is rooted in his sinfulness, from which God alone can absolve him and which by virtue of faith can be redeemed in the Beyond. Christians have always been strangers in the world. In the New Testament only God is ultimately real; the rest is transient, contingent, precarious, and, so far as human actions are concerned, shot through with cussedness. To be sure, the experience of this mode of alienation is double-edged. On the one hand, the negative aspect of the Fall places man in an inherently tragic situation. On the other, as noted in classical Christian theology, man is given the happy opportunity of experiencing rebirth in the Godhead. In Luke's phrase: "Joy shall be in heaven over one sinner that repenteth, more than over ninety and nine just persons, who need no repentance." Only the complacent bourgeoisie in Christendom, as Kierkegaard never tired of asserting, conceals the paradox of religious alienation from its consciousness. Instead, modern man tries to enjoy the fruits of finitude without qualms: a questionable enterprise, as evidenced by periodic outbursts of discontent and disillusionment. Were the theories of atheistic humanists and humanitarians correct, we should all rejoice in our unprecedented cultivation of worldliness *per se*. If a marked relief of alienation in European society had set in after the Renaissance, the *philosophes* would have been on firmer ground in castigating Rousseau as a madman. As it turned out, the loss of religious transcendence experienced by Western man since the breakdown of theonomous culture, far from reducing his awareness of alienation, merely transposed it into new molds as fragile in their way as the old.

A different type of alienation emerges from the wider human predicament, exhibited in the obverse of Plato's momentous insight to the effect that a rational understanding of the universe requires a similitude of mind and matter, a balanced interplay of the observed and the observer. Greek tragedy invalidates any claim that this ideal state of affairs can be realized. Much of our experience underscores the unbridgeable chasm between our desire to comprehend and arrange things in a definite order and the haphazard way they actually turn out. All too frequently historians as well as philosophers postulate connections between events which, however consistent with their own premises, cannot be empirically validated. It is in this context that the bewilderment of the tragic hero by his fate shows a far greater degree of candor than many pretentious constructions or reconstructions of the professional thinker. An overriding cause of our ignorance may well be the presence of a qualitative difference between the faculties of our mind and the objective correlatives it seeks to embrace in their totality. Kant gave seminal expression to such a notion of epistemological alienation with his postulation of *das Ding an sich*, "the thing in itself"—impervious to being fully understood through any process of knowing, short of becoming distorted as a phenomenon of our limited senses and of the categories of understanding which shape our peculiar modes of apprehension. Interestingly enough, Hegel, while rejecting this Kantian concept (*Grenzbegriff*) as inconsistent with the absolute rationality of the real, nevertheless was compelled to concede in his own System a perennial tension between knower and known, which his keenest dialectical convolutions could not eliminate entirely. The Hegelian Absolute reconstitutes itself only at the end of time. So far as we agents of history are concerned, it is always in a condition of division and self-division, hence incomplete for the beholder. Therefore it seems plausible to conclude that the appearance of the world to us and its actual ontological givenness are at best mediated temporarily in a miraculous act of knowledge, at worst utterly at odds with one another, and for the most part in an uneasy situation of puzzlement. Quite apart from the experience of religious alienation, man gazes upon the world not only with Platonic wonder but also with Sophoclean distress.

No less fundamental than the phenomena of religious and epistemological alienation is the syndrome of self-alienation, a split within human consciousness itself, immortalized by Dostoevsky in *The Double*. Our ability to contemplate ourselves as objects with the subject-knower remaining ignorant of himself, while gaining intimate familiarity with the reified person, leaves us vulnerable to permanent possibilities of schizophrenia. The mystery of the onlooking self is never transparent to us as beholders. What we perceive is rather an objectified replica thereof, which is not coincident with our innermost being. It has become platitudinous to point out the unreliability of Rousseau as an autobiographer. Worth noting, rather, is the fact that even had he told us the "truth" about his illegitimate offspring this would not necessarily represent a closer approximation of what actually went on in his heart and mind, than what he had revealed to us already, however intermingled with falsehoods. Self-alienation is, on the one hand, a triumph of introspection over passive drifting and, on the other, a threatening interrogation of the accused by his prosecutor often disguised as an *amicus curiae*.

More than any other thinker Marx was instrumental in making the concept of alienation in the vocabulary of modern man a near-cliché. The question is often raised what he meant by it, and precisely what role this concept plays in his mature thought. In his early philosophical manuscripts of 1844, notably in his reflections on Feuerbach's critique of Hegel, Marx outlines four meanings of alienation. First he distinguishes man's alienation from his fellow man, as exhibited in warfare, class struggles, and related breakdowns of community throughout history. Second, he speaks of man's alienation from the genesis of the human race, a somewhat obscure notion by which he probably means the divergence of any particular person from the ideal of humanity, much like the status of any particular Kantian moral agent in relation to the embodiment and implementation of pure Practical Reason. Third, there is man's alienation from his labor, which became the familiar notion of the tyranny of technology over humanity, rather than man controlling his own creations. Finally (and this is most germane to an understanding of existentialism), Marx takes up man's alienation from the process of production (self-alienation proper), according to which the natural and free emotions which ordinarily accompany eating, sleeping, and his other sensuous activities are not only absent from his toil but replaced by compulsive sweat and tears—evocative of the curse laid on the labor of the human race in Genesis as a consequence of the Fall. Man alienates himself from himself—argues Marx—when the joyous spontaneity distinctive of his higher faculties becomes nothing but animalistic drudgery more suitable to a team of oxen. The original formulation of this concept is not restricted to any class or, for that matter, to any specifiable constellation of social-economic organization. Man is alienated from himself because from time immemorial he has for the most part not enjoyed fulfilling himself through his work, performing it instead under duress.

Neither here nor elsewhere does Marx probe the underlying causes of this state of affairs. Had he done so, he might conceivably have arrived at a lower estimate of human potential than many of his disciples have all too often entertained. It remains, of course, impossible to measure with any precision whether carpenters are happier at their work than analytic philosophers, or whether the double talk of bureaucrats flows more "naturally" than the *Weltschmerz* of Romantic *Doppelgänger*.

For Marx, everyone at all times is subject to being alienated from himself by virtue of his lackluster employment. Only in his later writings, principally in *Das Kapital*, does he intimate that such reforms as the abolition of the division of labor will result in the total disappearance of self-alienation. Here, Marx's deficient psychology of the problematic in human affairs needs to be supplemented by the insights of a Nietzsche into the irreducible ambiguities of what indeed is "natural" for man.

In the light of Marx's overriding concern, it remains plausible to link his preoccupation with alienation and self-alienation to the exploitation and manipulation of the proletariat by the property-owning classes of nineteenth-century Europe. At the same time it would be unjust to Marx and most certainly to the deeper implications of his thought on this point, were one to associate exclusively his conception of the alienated person with the injustices of the particular social-economic order he set out to unmask and destroy through his writings. In any case, the dubious assumption that property is the root of all evil, including that of alienation, simply does not stand the test of man's historical experiences.

The foregoing discussion falls short of accounting for the intensity with which alienation was experienced by the typical Romantic hero and the generation of writers and poets which created him. Until adequate criteria for the evaluation of revolutions in consciousness are arrived at, the chances are we shall never know, yet one may still make an educated guess. Such a conjecture would focus on a rapidly increasing imbalance between freedom and authority, epitomized historically by the French Revolution and its traumatic aftermath. The long cry for freedom of every variety, which had gathered momentum since the Revolution of 1688, was mocked in the very process of fulfillment by the terrors of vacuity and dreadful choice; much like a strictly raised child thrown into a permissive environment, in which ruthless competition takes the place of warm-hearted but rigid constraint. Again and again the Romantic hero discovers within himself an irreconcilable longing for some tradition to complement his heart's desire for total self-affirmation. Irrefutable, in any case, is the Romantic's regression to extreme conservatism following, and sometimes even simultaneous with, a revolutionary stance toward every facet of existence. If this approach to Romantic alienation be tenable, it should be possible to divulge a recurring pattern of frustrating satiety alternating with deficient self-discipline. What Erich Heller has aptly called the "disinherited mind" circumscribes the paradox of Romantic longing for its own dissolution.

It is still impossible to tell whether enlightened modern man can bear the burden of having cast himself adrift on a perilous sea of endless experimentation to no discernible final goal. In the meantime, he has gained a refined knowledge of madness, which must be the envy of ancient deities.

In our world, the only ingredient of sanity left may be found in the "internal emigré" madman. In him, alienation is conjointly a malady and sign of spiritual health. A demythologized reading of Dante's line that one must pass through hell in order to see the stars would sound as follows: one must become truly alienated to realize that Tillichian talk of reconciliation is at best an oratorical prelude to confronting the real issue in modern times. This real issue is to embrace a life without a demonstrable ultimate concern. Is being "ultimately concerned" without an Ultimate Concern possible? asks the post-Kantian alienated individual.

4. On the Existential Import of Two Philosophical Distinctions

All students of positivism are acquainted with the familiar distinction made by Schlick, Ayer, and Stevenson, among others, between attitude and belief, particularly in the figuration of value judgments bearing on ethical choices. Accordingly, beliefs can be referred to a so-called objective testable referent, whereas attitudes are inherently private and hence non-discussable. We do of course discuss them all the time but, the positivists would insist, without any reasonable prospects of reaching agreement. To offer a simple example: the location of an Italian restaurant and its correct appellation as "Italian" are settled easily enough; on the other hand, the questions whether or not it is worthwhile to eat Italian food, whether it is better or worse than other kinds, or whether what this restaurant serves measures up to the highest standards of Italian cuisine basically defy resolution by rational inquiry. Given the tenets of scientific philosophizing which classical positivists tend to claim for themselves, matters of taste, like all matters involving feeling, are arbitrary and outside the range of confirmability as well as falsifiability.

Obviously this view, like all other philosophical views, generates as many difficulties as it proposes to assuage. Above all, in this regard, it is extremely questionable that the posited dichotomy between attitude and belief corresponds to anything resembling human experience. But it is not my concern here to cover once again well-trodden ground. Instead, it seems fruitful in the context of the present study to explore the crucial role of attitude as an essential component of the world-view of classical Russian fiction.

As the reader must be aware by now, this view was in the main anti-scientific in the sense of rejecting quantitative reductionism, the possibility of value-free appraisals of human action, the crass repudiation of Christianity, and related elements of what William James decried as nineteenth-century scientism. Merely by virtue of their persistent doubts regarding the prospects of human fulfillment, the major Russian novelists set themselves apart from the Voltairean mythology, which came to grip so many of their contemporaries in the West. Even where they did not read it, they had intuitively grasped the somber outlook of Rousseau's *First Discourse*.[1] Men are not free, least of all by virtue of dwelling amid the refinements of technological civilization. This is worth mentioning here, if only to stress the contrast between an emphasis on objectifiable belief over against the human affections and antipathies in the determination of what is right or wrong, beautiful or ugly, just or unjust.

In the latter half of the twentieth century, amazingly enough, many intellectuals continue to talk as if the positions we take in an argument were not, more often than not, veiled rationalizations of our hopes and fears. It is in this state of mental confusion that advocates of permissive and authoritarian child-rearing fool each other into believing that whatever side they may take on this issue makes any practical difference to the child. The fact is that it doesn't. What matters is the attitude expressed in concrete action, irrespective of the ideology evoked to support it. The nanny steeped in Anna Freud will, if she is as cruel as some nannies are, give herself away to the child by her mode of speech, for example, though her talk be of the most elevated kind and her superficial enlightenment beyond reproach. Conversely, a strict parent, however severe with his child, will, if well meaning, reveal himself in this light, though the rhetoric with which he defends his approach as valid may be of the most unimproving kind, if it not border on rubbish. In short, the possible conjunction of every conceivable belief with a self-seeking attitude casts doubt on the most perfect tenets, however lucid and objective they may appear in splendid isolation. Since nastiness appears to outweigh generosity in human affairs, one only deceives oneself in taking formulated beliefs too seriously at the cost of neglecting the attitudes which accompany and in part inspire them. Quite apart from the philosophical difficulties positivists have run into in justifying their splitting off of fact from value, the evidence of lived experience unmistakably points to the primacy of how and what we feel and do over what we say in ceaseless *Gerede*.

The psychological genius of Dostoevsky and Tolstoy thoroughly bears out the Kierkegaardian contention that the manner in which human beings act is inextricably tied to the substantive worth of the action in question. Dostoevsky's characterization of Sonya serves as a case in point. Dante, the Aristotelian, would have placed her in hell for becoming a prostitute, but in *Crime and Punishment* she is given a saintly role both for saving her family from starvation and for rescuing Raskolnikov from the depths of despair. Similarly, Kirilov in *The Devils*, though he espouses deliberate suicide as desirable for himself, is not really a god-man manipulating his fellow creatures, but rather an individual (in Nietzsche's phrase) "beyond good and evil" who, having made his peace with the futilities of life, plays ball with a little girl, gives a helping hand to a neighbor, and even goes so far as to rejoice in the birth of a baby. Herein precisely lies the genius of Dostoevsky's art: that the very character who is portrayed as contemptuous of all human weakness, at the same time sympathizes with the weak and afflicted. Just as Stavrogin's wickedness is ultimately enigmatic, in the sense of being inadequately motivated, Kirilov's acceptance of life flies in the face of his repudiation of his own.

Anna Karenina is undoubtedly an adulteress. But, as numerous critical readers have noted, Tolstoy, deliberately or unintentionally, makes her one of the most sympathetic characters in his novel. Her spontaneity, her special gift for gaining the confidence of children, her efforts to bring peace to unhappy families, and her remarkable sensitivity to the problems of others almost completely overshadow the horrible sin she is supposed to have committed. Compared to Karenin and Vronsky, even to Levin and Kitty, she emerges as a Tolstoyan heroine whose spontaneity liberates her from the artifices of a snobbish and cold-hearted society which maintains its stranglehold on most of her contemporaries, presumably virtuous in their externalized obedience to the appearances of conventional role-playing. Karenin is an insufferable prig; Vronsky, a faithless adventurer; Kitty, an inspired child; Levin, a moody, double-minded, and somewhat stuffy gentleman-farmer. Even if one does not mention the hostesses with their excruciating parties and balls, Anna stands out in this company as a genuinely animated and poised individual. Mistaken as her understanding of her situation undoubtedly was, she is never mean, nasty, or *schadenfroh*. Thus it can be argued that her attitude toward being in the world redeems her most naïve beliefs and vindicates her, if not in the eyes of the God cited by Tolstoy in his famous epigraph, then in those of her creator as well as in ours.

The second distinction I have in mind revolves around the conflicting roles of historicity and ahistoricity in existentialist reflection. So far as the tradition of classical Russian fiction is concerned, no reader can help but observe its recurring roots in the historical experience of the Russian people. In this connection we need only think of Tolstoy's account of the campaign of 1812 in *War and Peace*, of Dostoevsky's "legend of the Grand Inquisitor," of Turgenev's chronicles of the "back to the people" movement and the struggle of the radicals, and of Solzhenitsyn's pivotal concern to bear witness to Stalin's crimes. From Lermontov's Pechorin, the archetypal superfluous man of the alienated gentry class, to Solzhenitsyn's Ivan Denisovich, possibly the archetypal victim of twentieth-century totalitarianism, Russian fiction is steeped in the actualities of historical concreteness.[2] Yet, curiously combined with this focus on everyday reality, is a no less compelling impulse to transcend it. It is worth reiterating here Tolstoy's preoccupation with death and Dostoevsky's with man's wayward psyche. These concerns, far from being bound up with any chosen interval of human experience, must be viewed as timeless features of the human condition. The hindsight of a historian gives way to the indefinite future of any contemporary when a character in Dostoevsky or Tolstoy reflects on the prospects before him or, for that matter, on the destiny of Russia. Whereas, on the one hand, classical Russian fiction is typically existential in its stress on the vagaries of our fortune in history, it is no less so in dwelling on our predicament as being finite rather than "under the aspect of eternity."

What applies to classical Russian fiction in particular also holds for the mainstream of existentialist thought in general. Consider the equivocal usage of "ahistoricity" in this literature. In their emphasis on man's contingent historical situation, Kierkegaard and Sartre assume a position diametrically opposed to that of classical rationalism, whether ancient or modern; we need only think here of Aristotle's subordination of history to poetry in his *Poetics*, or Descartes's contempt for the contingent as unworthy of the really real, or, in our own day, Carnap's attempt to limit existence only to that which yields to formalization.

On the other hand, it is equally accurate to point out that writers like Kierkegaard and Nietzsche are fundamentally ahistorical in their orientation toward the meaning of human existence. Whereas the advocates of progress in the nineteenth and twentieth centuries invariably place every problem of life in some historical perspective, be it directed toward the past or the future, the existential thinkers, by virtue of acknowledging the timelessness of the human predicament, adopt an ahistorical stance toward life. This emphasis on what Kierkegaard called man's inescapable contemporaneity bears a striking resemblance to the Danish philosopher's understanding of Christ as he appeared to his first disciples (giving offense to their reason more than solace to their fears), or Nietzsche's understanding of any historical epoch as autonomous. Seen in this light, the ahistoricity of existentialists signifies a revolt against the overrationalization of human experience by the refined relativism of modern historians, even while these same existentialists never tire of impressing upon us the thrust of fleeting fact or fortuitous circumstance in shaping our respective destinies.

According to Kierkegaard it is no more difficult for us moderns to believe in Christ than it was for His own disciples. Contrary to historians who would stress such factors as a rise of science in bringing about the emergence of latter-day atheism, Kierkegaard, if only as a corrective to such partial explanations, stresses man's enduring capacity for self-glorification and self-delusion. It is in the same sense that the Russian novelists, their involvement in the history of their own times notwithstanding, almost invariably create characters whose thoughts and actions are symbolic of behavior unconfined to the spatial and temporal dimensions in which they happen to find themselves.

Notes

INTRODUCTION

1. The bystander mentality so often criticized by existentialists is brilliantly exposed in Chekhov's *Ward No. 6*. The protagonist, who commends Stoicism to one of his mental patients, ultimately himself becomes an inmate in the ward. Prior to this reversal in his fortunes, his patient had taken him to task for overlooking the context in which the truth or falsity of moral ideals is tested. It was one thing to preach imperturbability and acquiescence from the relative comfort of one's study, quite another to entertain such notions amid the reality of suffering.

2. This theme of radical contingency runs through the corpus of existentialist writings from Pascal's aphorisms to the celebrated incident in Sartre's "The Wall," where a prisoner condemned to death wins a reprieve by directing his would-be executioners to a spot in which, unbeknownst to him, his friend has just taken refuge.

3. See Note 20, p. 213.

4. In their respective ways Gogol, Dostoevsky, and Tolstoy became spokesmen for a Christian belief. Gogol's *Selected Passages from Correspondence with Friends,* Dostoevsky's *Diary of a Writer,* and Tolstoy's polemical works of his last period, show these writers in a light quite distinct from the radical thrust of their flashes of insight in their fiction. As in the case of Kierkegaard and Nietzsche, who combine extreme political conservatism with negative philosophizing, we are confronted here by a striking conjunction of opposites. Some critics have argued that this is not so: that, in brief, Dostoevsky the publicist and Dostoevsky the novelist are one and the same. For my part, I agree with Shestov that one should look for the most authentic expression of these writers' ideas in their destruction of inadequate modes of feeling and thought, however much they may have striven to conceal, if not to distort, this dimension of their writing. In any case, it seems indisputable that the politics of Gogol, Dostoevsky, and Tolstoy shed far less light on their creative genius than their dazzling intuitions of what it means to be human.

CHAPTER I. GOGOL AND THE ABSURD

1. Analysis of this and similar paradoxes (such as "I am lying" or "This sentence is false") can be resolved along lines proposed by Russell and Tarski. Such solutions require the restriction that one cannot apply truth locutions ("true," "false") to sentences that themselves contain truth locutions. Thus one can introduce a hierarchy of truth locutions. But this solution is not wholly satisfactory. According to Quine: "Each resort is desperate; each is an artificial departure from natural and established usage. Such is the way of antinomies" (W. V. O. Quine, "Ways of Paradox," *Ways of Paradox*, p. 11). What is paradoxical in these examples is not simply that they produce contradictions. That can be avoided, as Russell and Tarski have shown. However, to avoid paradoxicality one must resort to counter-intuitive solutions. And this reveals to us the plain unnerving fact that no solution can restore naturalness to these concepts.

2. A revealing counter-instance can be found in Solzhenitsyn's *First Circle*, where the author takes issue with a statement ascribed to Thomas Hobbes, according to which men never become overwrought on account of a mathematical principle such as "the sum of the angles of a triangle equals 180°." The prisoners in their confinement are apt to argue furiously about everything, including the seemingly irrelevant or trivial. Where aesthetes are tempted to formalize matters of taste, victims will existentialize matters of form. Thus the prisoners nearly come to blows over the question whether the middle of the twentieth century should be celebrated on January 1, 1950 or January 1, 1951.

3. "But whether he had failed to notice this ritual or hadn't dared join in observance of it, his cap was still in his lap when we'd finished reciting our prayer. It was a headgear of composite order, containing elements of an ordinary cap, a hussar's busby, a lancer's cap, a sealskin cap, and a nightcap; one of those wretched things whose mute hideousness suggests unplumbed depths, like an idiot's face." *Madame Bovary*, trans. Francis Steegmuller (New York: Modern Library, 1957), p. 4.

4. See Hannah Arendt's discussion of the banality of evil in her *Eichmann in Jerusalem*.

5. See his *Reason in History*.

6. A further suggestive parallel between Gogol and Kierkegaard is their recourse to the power of the extraordinary: as Kierkegaard's Absolutely Other throws into sharpest relief the despair and anxiety characteristic of finitude, Gogol's relentless depiction of mediocrity and pettiness is occasionally superseded by daemonic interventions originating from inexplicable sources. The "teleological suspension of the ethical" in *Fear and Trembling* has a counterpart in the final pages of "The Overcoat," where the ghost of Akakiy Akakievich rips off overcoats from people's shoulders.

7. Hegel and Kierkegaard have much more in common than the latter's bitter diatribes against the great German thinker might lead one to suppose. But on one issue they remain completely at odds: where Hegel regarded Christianity as but one significant link in man's return to the Absolute, Kierkegaard stressed the irreducible uniqueness and unsurpassedness of the New Testament.

8. *Dead Souls*, trans. Bernard Guilbert Guerney (New York, 1948), p. 151.
9. *Dead Souls*, p. 65.
10. *Dead Souls*, p. 166.
11. In *Dead Souls* one of the officials dies as a consequence of the commotion stirred up by Chichikov's strange doings.
12. Many interpreters of "The Overcoat" have emphasized the inhumanity of Akakiy Akakievich's position. Doubtless Gogol wishes us to take exception to the manner in which his hero is treated by his fellow clerks and superiors. But this protest against insensitivity should not obscure the far more interesting point that Akakiy Akakievich does not feel alienated from his work.
13. "The Overcoat," in *The Collected Tales and Plays of Nikolai Gogol*, ed. L. J. Kent, trans. Constance Garnett (New York, 1964), p. 575.
14. "Old-World Landowners," in *The Collected Tales and Plays of Nikolai Gogol* (Kent-Garnett), p. 219.
15. Sidney Monas, *The Third Section, Police and Society in Russia under Nicholas I* (Cambridge: Harvard University Press, 1961).
16. An explanation for the corruption of a private individual by public office clearly lies beyond the intended scope of this discussion. Nonetheless, it is possible to say a few things about this matter which at least have the merit of avoiding needless confusion and obfuscation. To begin with, "moral man" and "immoral society" are never separate entities but distinguishing terms, which emphasize the reciprocal interrelationships between the two. Just as it is impossible to contemplate the self apart from the world or the world apart from the self, the individual even in his most private moments must be viewed in the social context of which he forms a part. Once, however, this obvious truth has been granted, the fact remains that the role ascribed to or achieved by a bureaucrat or technocrat in office may transform a kindly family-man into a monster of insensitivity and unwarranted arrogance or obsequiousness. In her memoirs, *Hope Against Hope*, Nadezhda Mandelstam attributes the behavior of victims and executioners under Stalin not primarily to fear for their lives but to a blind devotion to Marxism-Leninism which in many cases crushed the last spark of life out of the Russian people, submissively doing violence to themselves. In Gogol's day The System was Orthodoxy, Autocracy, and Nationality rather than the inevitable future bliss of a classless society to which an individual would give everything, including his soul. Mme. Mandelstam and Gogol are agreed on another significant point: apart from the arbitrary terror and inhumaneness which characterized the regimes of the tsars and the Soviet dictators, there was always an element of the absurd to set the grotesque in perspective. Thus the Cheka went through the contortions of ludicrousness in relation to its helpless victims: sometimes half a dozen guards accompanied a single prisoner to Siberia or, on one memorable occasion, Lenin himself reportedly was threatened with arrest for having been a member of the old pre-Revolutionary intelligentsia which was now due to be liquidated. The list might be extended indefinitely. What might especially amuse Gogol, were he still alive, was that both under Nicholas I and under Stalin, the lower officials were better off than their superiors because they did not have to counter-sign criminal orders handed down from above. Like the official in "The Overcoat,"

administrators may be as much victims of a System as its willing or unwilling tools. Finally, Mme. Mandelstam notes, in the spirit of Gogol, it was the worship of intelligence as such in the nineteenth century as well as abstract humanism which led to the peculiar distortions and perversions of twentieth-century theory and practice. In conclusion, it cannot be emphasized too strongly that administrative absurdity as a particular instance of absurdity in general exhibits a curious mixture of deliberation and gratuitousness, a kind of methodical madness.

17. Inasmuch as the literature on bureaucracy has become inexhaustible, it may be helpful to set off the existential approach to this familiar theme from other approaches, no less valid in their own way, but less pertinent, in my opinion, to Gogol's preoccupation. The existential approach to bureaucracy is apt to focus on the following: the reduction of the petitioner to nothing more than a vehicle of utility; the notion of the official as blasé—insensitive by profession to human frailty and need; and, finally, the apprehension of the entire bureaucratic structure in terms of methodical madness, i.e., the peculiar fusion of functional incompetence and moral turpitude. Keeping this in mind, one sees it is certainly no mere coincidence that Kierkegaard and Nietzsche went out of their way to address themselves in their works to the solitary individual. A conscientious bureaucrat would never understand, for example, that the psychological makeup of an involved activist differs substantially from that of a cynical spectator, so that the two will comprehend facts of life with totally disparate attitudes and beliefs. The reward for incompetence by being "kicked upstairs" (a standard practice in academic bureaucracies to sweeten the pill of inadmissible failure at a lower level) is a problem for the social phenomenologist, rather than for the existentialist, if only by virtue of the fact that it demands a bracketing of all normal perception.

18. Especially striking in this connection is the following passage from *Dead Souls* in which Gogol muses upon the attitudes of bureaucrats to their inferiors and their superiors:

"Let's suppose, for instance, that there is a certain chancellery in existence—oh, not here, but in some Never-Never Land; and in this chancellery, let's suppose, there exists a Director of the Chancellery. I ask you to have a look at him as he sits there among his subordinates—why, out of awe you simply wouldn't be able to let a peep out of you. Hauteur and noblesse . . . and what else doesn't his face express? Just pick up a brush and paint away: Prometheus, Prometheus to the life! His gaze is that of an eagle; he ambulates with a smooth, measured stride. But that self-same eagle, the moment he has stepped out of his office and nears the study of his superior, a sheaf of papers tucked under his arm, flutters along like any partridge, with all his might and main. In society or at some evening-at-home, provided that all those present are not so very high in rank, Prometheus will even remain Prometheus to the very end; but let there be present someone ever so little above him, such a transformation will take our Prometheus as even Ovid himself could never think of: he's a midge, even smaller than any midge; he has been transmogrified into a grain of sand; 'Why, this just can't be our Ivan Petrovich!' you say to yourself as you look at him. 'Ivan Petrovich is ever so tall, while this is not only such a squat fellow but such a thin one, too; the other one speaks loudly, booming away in his bass and with never a laugh out of him, while the Devil alone knows what this one is up to: he cheeps like a bird and keeps on laughing with never a stop.' You walk up nearer and take a closer look—and sure enough, if it isn't Ivan Petrovich!" *Dead Souls*, p. 51.

19. See the discussion of "The Death of Ivan Ilyich" in chapter 4.
20. See the quotation from "Old-World Landowners" on p. 13 above.
21. A good example of the whimsical-nonsensical is the following:

"Here you meet unique whiskers, drooping with extraordinary and amazing elegance below the necktie, velvety; satiny whiskers, as black as sable or as coal, but alas! Invariably the property of members of the Department of Foreign Affairs. Providence has denied black whiskers to clerks in other departments; they are forced, to their great disgust, to wear red ones. Here you meet marvellous moustaches that no pen, no brush could do justice to, moustaches to which the better part of a life has been devoted, the objects of prolonged care by day and by night; moustaches upon which enchanting perfumes are sprinkled and on which the rarest and most expensive kinds of pomade are lavished; moustaches which are wrapped up at night in the most expensive vellum; moustaches to which their possessors display the most touching devotion and which are the envy of passers-by." "Nevsky Prospect," in *The Collected Tales and Plays of Nikolai Gogol* (Kent-Garnett), p. 424.

22. *Dead Souls*, p. 102.
23. *Dead Souls*, p. 257.
24. *Dead Souls*, pp. 253–4.
25. The irresolvable dilemma revolves around the paradox of verifiability never having been experienced as an empirical fact. In other words, how would a positivist go about verifying his verification principles, short of deviating from the primitive assumptions of his theory of knowledge?
26. *The Inspector General*, in *The Collected Tales and Plays* (Kent-Garnett), p. 601.
27. "The Overcoat," in *The Collected Tales and Plays* (Kent-Garnett), p. 563.
28. *Dead Souls*, p. 31.
29. See the descriptions at the beginning of "The Tale of How Ivan Ivanovich Quarreled with Ivan Nikiforovich."
30. "The Diary of a Madman," in *The Collected Tales and Plays* (Kent-Garnett), p. 470.

CHAPTER 2. DOSTOEVSKY AND THE INTELLECTUALS

1. By "duplication" we mean the embodiment of theory in practice (*praxis*) or, more specificaJly, the Kierkegaardian insistence on bridging the gulf between abstruse possibility and realized actuality.
2. This gulf is nowhere more nobly shown than in the tragic career of Alexander Blok (1880–1921). In his essay "The People and the Intelligentsia" he emphasizes, however sadly and compassionately, the

irreconcilable differences between these two social groups. On the other hand, "The Intelligentsia and the Revolution" is made to serve as an apology for Blok's enthusiastic participation in the Bolshevik experiment. Herein he argues that the burden of guilt deliberately or inadvertently assumed by "the happy few" for the plight of the downtrodden and oppressed is justification enough for making common cause with them, even at the price of sacrificing high individual cultural standards. But, finally, after writing *The Twelve* in 1918, Blok died in agony three years later, when the course of the Revolution expressed some of the nightmarish details of his poetic vision.

3. In this connection it is worth considering John Passmore's argument in his *Perfectibility of Man* (New York, 1970) that, again and again in man's history, human perfection has been found compatible with a lack of flawlessness and sinlessness. Just as no Bach fugue is mechanically beyond reproach as a model of contrapuntal composition, the morality of Kant's moral agent would be meaningless did he not succumb to his phenomenal nature on occasion. In short, an element of disorder would seem to be as indispensable for the creation of the greatest beauty as an element of human cussedness turns out to be a prerequisite for the life of reason in conduct. Benighted academicians, for the most part, are deceived by incorrigible illusions about rational men agreeing on rational governances on soulless quads.

4. For an unorthodox interpretation of Kierkegaard in the role of "devil's advocate" vis-à-vis his purported apology for New Testament Christianity, see Herbert M. Garelick's *The Anti-Christianity of Kierkegaard* (The Hague: Martinus Nijhoff, 1965).

5. Pascal continues to serve as the exemplary model of this type of reasoning. He expressed the profoundest insights into the ambiguities and paradoxes of human experience with uncanny clarity and his thoughts bear striking family resemblance to many of Dostoevsky's own favorite motifs. These largely adventitious overlappings between the author of the *Pensées* and the creator of the Underground Man still await exploration in depth and detail. The following are some of the more striking coincidences:

"A hundred contradictions might be true. If antiquity were the rule of belief, men of ancient time would then be without rule" (#260). [All quotations are from the Everyman edition, trans. W. F. Trotter, London, 1948.]

"Contradiction is a bad sign of truth; several things which are certain are contradicted; several things which are false pass without contradiction. Contradiction is not a sign of falsity, nor the want of contradiction a sign of truth" (#384).

"Each thing here is partly true and partly false . . . Nothing is purely true, and thus nothing is true, meaning by that pure truth. You will say it is true that homicide is wrong. Yes; for we know well the wrong and the false. But what will you say is good? Chastity? I say no; for the world would come to an end. Marriage? No, continence is better. Not to kill? No; for that destroys nature. We possess truth and goodness only in part; and mingled with falsehood and evil" (#385).

"The most unreasonable things in the world become more reasonable, because of the unruliness of men. What is less reasonable than to

choose the eldest son of a queen to rule a State? We do not choose as captain of a ship the passenger who is of the best family" (#320).
6. See p. 40 above.
7. In chapters 9 and 10 of his *Man and People* (trans. Willard R. Trask, New York: W. W. Norton & Co., 1957) entitled respectively "Reflections on the Salutation" and "Reflections on the Salutation. Etymological Man. What is a Usage?", Ortega y Gasset provides a remarkable defense of Dostoevsky's position. Ortega maintains that such interpersonal usages as shaking hands or drinking tea together are indispensable for maintaining the solidarity of social behavior. They exemplify an atmosphere of general trust without which we would be constantly at each other's throats. Developed over hundreds, if not thousands, of years, such usages cannot be repudiated by the refusal of an individual or a small group to comply with them. On the contrary, gestures like the Hitler salute, which are bellicose rather than friendly, arbitrarily imposed from above rather than organically nurtured from below, are doomed to die a rapid death. In his comments on the tea-drinking episode, Dostoevsky once again shows himself an uncanny observer of human action in his discernment of the dangerous breakdown of civility as proudly flaunted by the would-be saviors of mankind. While Pascal was correct in professing the inexplicability of human customs and conventions in purely rational terms, Ortega y Gasset was equally correct in seeing them inextricably intertwined with our humanity.
8. See Lev Shestov, *Dostoevsky, Tolstoy and Nietzsche,* trans. Bernard Martin and Spencer Roberts (Athens: Ohio University Press, 1969).
9. Robert Lord, *Dostoevsky, Essays and Perspectives* (London: Chatto & Windus, 1970).
10. Dostoevsky tells the readers of this confessional narrative that very often the seemingly obvious facts of normality only come to light through a pathological exception. In this view the Underground Man's spite is as much a sickness as a moral fault. This understanding of sickness as a normal condition for man has turned out to be one of his most foresighted perceptions. This contention is borne out not merely in the writings of Freud and Thomas Mann but, even more significantly, in a new approach to mental illness. From this point of view, for example, the world of the schizophrenic is no less real for him than the world of non-schizophrenics is for them simply because his perspective on things is radically different. In brief, a schizophrenic's vision of what is the case is normal so far as he is concerned, however sick he appears in our eyes and, conversely, however sick we may appear in his. If this view of his condition is roughly correct, the starting point of his return to "normalcy" must be an imaginative understanding of his distorted "world-hypothesis" as a possible alternative rather than a mere observation. Moreover, Dostoevsky was uncanny in his anticipation of neurotic behavior as the rule, rather than the exception. What intellectual born since the turn of the century has not been burdened with neuroses? In raising this rhetorical question I definitely do not wish to imply that non-intellectuals have enjoyed superior mental health. Such an implication, frequently drawn from the writings of Dostoevsky and from those of other existentialists, is not only unjustified and false in itself but a dangerous expression of

the sort of anti-intellectualism enthusiastically espoused by the masses and their leaders—especially when the economy threatens to disintegrate.

11. *Notes from Underground* and *The Grand Inquisitor,* ed. and trans. Ralph E. Matlaw (New York, 1960), p. 21.

12. Cf. the discussion in Geoffrey Clive, *The Romantic Enlightenment* (New York, 1960), chapter IV.

13. *The Sewanee Review* (Winter 1961).

14. See Kierkegaard's "Diary of a Seducer" in *Either/Or.*

15. *The Devils,* trans. David Magarshack (Baltimore, 1969), pp. 483–4.

16. In all references to Utilitarianism in nineteenth-century Russian literature and thought, it is necessary to distinguish two distinct meanings of the term: the ethical theory inspired by Bentham and James Mill and subsequently developed by John Stuart Mill, and a materialistic ideology which envisaged man as a machine and his values as functions of purely material causes. Although these meanings overlap, it is fair to say that for writers such as Herzen and Dostoevsky the broader connotations of the primacy of utility in human affairs constituted their principal concern.

17. Aestheticism became a sort of religion in the last three decades of the nineteenth century. It drew its inspiration from such diverse sources as the literary gossip of the Goncourt brothers, certain usually misunderstood texts of Nietzsche, the literary martyrdom of Flaubert, and, far more important, from the void left in the European imagination by the apparent triumph of scientific intelligence (positivism) conjoined with the virtual extinction of the Christian faith. Its adherents vainly strove for redemption through a complete surrender to the agonies and the ecstasies yielded by transient encounters with beauty. It seems fair to suppose that Dostoevsky would have proven himself as severe a critic of this betrayal of Schiller as he had been ruthlessly scornful of the utilitarian dogmas of the Russian nihilists. The worship of art in the twentieth century has, curiously enough, neither been very productive of masterpieces nor conspicuously successful in offering consolations for our tortured awareness that the beautiful, in order not to become counterfeit, has to be rooted in something besides beauty.

18. See *The Romantic Enlightenment,* chapter on Hume.

19. Together with Demea, Philo and Cleanthes make up the three participants in Hume's *Dialogues Concerning Natural Religion,* published posthumously because even the outspokenly skeptical Scottish philosopher feared the wrath of the Establishment which the appearance of his masterpiece would evoke. The main subject of the *Dialogues* is the rational defensibility of the Christian faith, as insisted upon by the deists of the seventeenth and eighteenth centuries who, inspired by Newtonian cosmology and certain pre-Romantic notions of Lord Herbert of Cherbury, maintained that there was no impasse between what today would be called a demythologized Christianity and the mechanical principles of the new science. In his work, Hume once and for all destroyed the intellectual pretensions of the deistic position. Philo plays the part of a philosophical skeptic very much like Hume himself; Cleanthes functions as the apologist for natural religion (deism), whose arguments are ruthlessly shredded by Philo; Demea represents mystical theism, opposed as much to Cleanthes' formalities

of false reasoning as to Philo's irredeemable skepticism. It would be simplistic to equate Hume's own position with Philo's: his radical skepticism, while uncompromisingly incompatible with the faulty logic of Cleanthes, does not thereby necessarily undermine the intellectually unpretentious faith of Demea. By analogy, Ivan Karamazov's transparent contempt for the rationalistic dilution of the problem of evil as common to much of nineteenth-century theology and philosophy does not necessarily call into question the active faith of a spontaneously motivated saint such as Father Zosima.

20. The "argument from design" is one of the weaker classical arguments for rational belief in the existence of God. According to this argument, all evidence of order in the Universe, be it mathematical, aesthetic, moral, etc., entails the existence of a Designer or Architect who put it there. This kind of argumentation is self-defeating, if only by virtue of the fact that the immense amount of disorder and moral perversity in nature and history could similarly be adduced to prove the existence of a daemon. Particularly the modern intellectual (like Ivan Karamazov), with his predisposition for accentuating the negative, will assess the "argument from design" as a mockery of human experience. Here once again the Augustinian formulation *credo ut intelligam* properly reproves the misleading Thomistic dictum *intelligo ut credam.*

Consonant with this proposition would be an interpretation of Ivan Karamazov as a Kierkegaardian ethical man, whose abstract understanding of the religious dimension nonetheless prevents him from appropriating it for himself. While Ivan himself is no model of exemplary conduct, his personal quarrel with the existence of God is clearly based on the incompatibility of such a being with the prevailing irresponsibility and inauthenticity in human affairs.

21. *The Brothers Karamazov*, trans. Constance Garnett (New York, 1950), p. 291.

22. In this connection it is worth bearing in mind a distinction between two types of atheism made by Erich Frank in chapter 2 of his book *Philosophical Understanding and Religious Truth*. Frank maintains that while the ancients argued constantly about the essence of God, it is peculiar to theists to doubt the existence of *any* Deity *per se* when they lose their faith. In other words, while Socrates was charged with atheism for rejecting the gods of the Greek city-states in favor of the religion of reason, subsequently expressed in Plato's Eternal Forms, Nietzsche's declarations of the death of God embraced all conceivable deities in the Universe. Ivan Karamazov, interestingly enough, is in this regard closer to Frank's ancients than to the moderns. His disavowal of God does not explicitly go beyond his rejection of the providential God of the major Christian traditions.

23. "Demythologization" is the term applied by the twentieth-century theologian Rudolf Bultmann to the distillation of primordial Christian truth from the philosophical-theological accretions with which, he argues, they became overlaid through the centuries. The rejoinder of his critics is almost identical with the question raised by the Grand Inquisitor: could Christianity without myth ever have taken hold in the imagination of Christians?

The contemporary Harvard behaviorist B. F. Skinner has attempted to provide scientific reinforcement for the Grand Inquisitor's ideology. Skinner, no less in *Walden Two* than in his recent *Beyond Freedom and Dignity*, maintains that modern man would be far better off if he relied on environmental conditioning for the procurement of happiness and virtue. In brief, both Skinner and the Grand Inquisitor view man's attachment to individual freedom as a burdensome encumbrance squarely at odds with his animality.

24. In fairness to Bakunin it should be observed that the destruction of obsolete modes of life and thought does in fact require far more effort than the complacent acceptance of the *status quo*. Is it not true, for example, that Kant's Copernican revolution, which destroyed traditional metaphysics, proved to be one of the most creative acts of the human spirit?

25. Although there was no love lost between Turgenev and Dostoevsky, it is interesting to note that precisely those features which made Bazarov a parody of genuine nihilists in the eyes of the extreme radicals would have struck the author of *The Devils* as potentially redemptive. In this respect, at least, he agreed with Turgenev on the moral superiority of the erratic individualist over the confirmed party fanatic. Both Dostoevsky and Turgenev, it seems to me, were more concerned in their fiction with analyzing the style in which a man gives himself to a cause, than with the hypostatized contents of the cause itself. This, incidentally, is typical of an existential approach in literature to politics.

26. For a detailed discussion of Stavrogin's boredom, see pp. 75–79 above.

27. Shigalov, another of the revolutionaries, formulates the Utopian model of society which Verkhovensky adopts for his own practical purposes.

28. The notion of the movement from absolute freedom to absolute tyranny is certainly not original with Dostoevsky. It can be found in a source as early as Plato's *Republic*, particularly in those passages in which he traces the decline of the perfect State, whose final forms of decay are anarchy yielding to tyranny. A similar implication, it would appear, is contained in the words of Jesus in which He claimed to have come into the world not to break the Law but rather to fulfill it.

29. *The Devils*, pp. 422–3.

30. See Appendix 2, "Hegel and the First Generation of the Russian Intelligentsia."

31. *The Devils*, p. 328.

32. Edie, Scanlan, Zeldin, Kline, eds., *Russian Philosophy* (Chicago, 1965), vol. I, p. 370.

33. Like Descartes at the dawn of modern philosophy, Dostoevsky, at the zenith of psychological realism in the modern novel, was at once a radical skeptic and a firm believer. Thus, comparable to the first Cartesian *Meditation,* in which the very adequacy of our mental faculties for obtaining reliable knowledge is called into question by an Evil Daemon bent on deceiving us at all times, Ivan Karamazov's reflections represent a devastating critique of Providence. On the other hand, Descartes's circular reasoning, in which the "clarity and distinctness" of his salvation from doubt is presumably guaranteed by what he sets out to prove, is matched in Dostoevsky's writings by a recurring somersault from the depths of metaphysical despair to the joys of religious certainty. While interpreters of Descartes and Dos-

toevsky continue to quarrel over their subjects' "secret position," there can be little doubt that the strongest impact of these two figures on the modern mind has been negative rather than positive. In short, their willingness to doubt everything overrides their nostalgia for a past which on occasion they reconstructed with the greatest ingenuity without themselves being able to live in it any longer.

CHAPTER 3. GONCHAROV AND THE SPECTRUM OF BOREDOM

1. Acedia designates the medieval sin of spiritual sloth and indifference to one's salvation from sin. For an interesting discussion of this state of mind, see William James's *The Varieties of Religious Experience.*
2. In a celebrated passage Sartre longs for the days of the Resistance when, according to him, his fellow countrymen were "truly free." What he means is that under the conditions of German occupation every choice had to be made as if death was its immediate consequence, that the absolute responsibility citizens took for their actions allowed them no time to drift or procrastinate.
3. Doubtless the most striking literary embodiment of contemporary boredom is the immobile anti-hero of Albee, Barth, Beckett, etc.—waist-deep in a sand-pit, unable or unwilling to extricate himself from his paralysis. Consider the predicament of Jake Horner in John Barth's novel *The End of the Road*: finding himself devoid of any reasons for doing anything, he walks up to the ticket window of the Baltimore railroad terminal, incapable of making up his mind about where to go. The agent suggests a variety of destinations which he could reach on $20, but Horner finds it impossible to settle on any of them. Thereupon, in a state of paralytic indifference, he flings himself down on a bench, where he spends the night in aimless terror. If Camus's Sisyphus, like Goncharov's Oblomov, is happy, the immobility of Horner and his kin is usually presented as a nightmare. The main question this condition raises for the student of boredom is the legitimacy, if any, of modern man's insistence on finding reasons for staying alive. Why, it may be asked, will he not be satisfied with Herzen's proposal to the effect that the *telos* of a child is not to grow up, but to play like a child?
4. From Kierkegaard to Heidegger, philosophers of *Existenz* have made a great deal of the distinction between *Furcht* and *Angst* ("fear" and "dread"). According to this distinction, we are afraid of particular specifiable threats to our survival and well-being while, on the other hand, we dread the indefinite condition of being human in this world, especially the temporally uncertain certainty of our death. For Heidegger "dread" is a fundamental dimension of *Dasein* (human existence).
5. Nietzsche's notion of "transvaluation of values" occupies a central place in his mature philosophy. Having reached the conclusion that historical Christianity was dead, as well as basically false, Nietzsche sought to adumbrate an alternative set of values which in his estimation would be more in accord with the radically changed circumstances of modern life. Why continue any talk of various means of saving souls if souls to be saved do not exist? Why speak of justice in heaven, Platonic or otherwise, if heaven is a myth? Finally, why develop a

new theology of hope if the future promises to be no different from the past—in accordance with Nietzsche's correlative doctrine of the cycle of eternal return.

6. Any adequate analysis of the lived experience of boredom would have to consider in detail the various relationships between the self and the world. With notable exceptions, Heidegger being the most outstanding, the existentialists have focused their discussions of boredom on the condition of the self, to the relative neglect of the world.

7. George Steiner has recently attempted to shed some new light on the phenomenon of ennui which affected generations of European intellectuals from the *Stürmer und Dränger* of Goethe's youth to the epigones of Peter Gay's *Fröhliche Wissenschaft* in the Weimar Republic. ("The great Ennui. In Bluebeard's Castle: Some Notes towards the Redefinition of Culture," *The Listener* (March 18, 1971), pp. 327–32.) Mr. Steiner comes up with the startling thesis that men in the nineteenth century became so excruciatingly bored because, after the events of the French Revolution and the death of Napoleon, all experience struck them as anti-climactic. It is difficult to understand how a mind as broad-ranging as Mr. Steiner's surely is can offer such a puerile explanation of a phenomenon which thinkers like Schopenhauer, Nietzsche, and Kierkegaard have explored in depth. Granted that Mr. Steiner is a literary man rather than a philosopher, but it seems odd that the profound analyses of boredom in the novels of Lermontov, Goncharov, and Dostoevsky (to mention but a small sample) should have eluded him completely. Where he does refer to a celebrated incident in *Crime and Punishment,* he is dead wrong: Raskolnikov did not murder the pawnwoman merely because he wanted to be like Napoleon. He killed her in order to relieve a mind overwrought with financial worries, philosophical doubts, and personal anxieties. Then he developed his full-blown version of the "teleological suspension of the ethical" in order to assuage his stricken conscience. Dostoevsky's main point here was to show, in Hume's celebrated phrase, how "reason is the slave of the passions" when man is in need of self-congratulation. For a responsible as well as brilliant analysis of ennui, see *Politische Romantik* (Munich and Leipzig, 1925) by the (later National Socialist) law professor Carl Schmitt.

8. See especially the passage in *Sartor Resartus* in which the eternal Nay is finally superseded. This may be taken as the turning point in Carlyle's own intellectual development, from a kind of Romantic existentialist to a shrill defender of some of the worst features of modern life.

9. In his *Varieties of Religious Experience,* William James discusses the concept of *anhedonia* (pathological depression) in the following terms: "Sometimes it is mere passive joylessness and dreariness, discouragement, dejection, lack of taste and zest and spring" (Modern Library edition, p. 142).

10. For a popular treatment of this idea, see Mary McCarthy's novel *Birds of America.* In the book's final scene, a vision of Kant appears to the hero and tells him: "Nature is dead, *mein Kind*" (*Birds of America,* New York, 1971). Even more intriguing is Miss McCarthy's connection of this theme with a Dostoevskyan position, in her interview with Jean-François Revel (*The New York Times Book Review,* May 16, 1971).

11. Odd as it first appears, the current Soviet practice of placing sane men in insane asylums to cure them of their oppositionist views exhibits a profound psychological insight. Throughout history psychopaths such as Robespierre or Stalin, just as fictional characters like Stravrogin, have demonstrated an uncanny ability to combine valid reasoning with insane behavior. This is only one sense in which the traditional dichotomy between rationalism and irrationality, so beloved by orthodox metaphysicians, will not stand the test of experience. From the point of view of the Soviet government (whose rational credentials are questionable, to say the least), any keen mind which threatens to undermine the officially designated basis of its operations has gone over the edge of self-preservation. Classical Russian fiction from Gogol to Solzhenitsyn has consistently made pathbreaking discoveries about the irrational nature of men of reason and, conversely, the rational prowess of those society chooses to regard as mad.

12. As someone "trying to become a Christian" in bourgeois Christendom, Kierkegaard thought of himself not as a martyr but as an exceptional individual—in perennial opposition to the inauthentic complacency which he attributed to the established Lutheran church of Denmark.

13. The adjectives "teleological" and "deontological" are used by contemporary moral philosophers in referring to two opposing types of ethical theory. Whereas teleological ethics places the value of all human endeavor in the realization of a supreme good at the end of historical time, overriding all the means employed in achieving that end; deontological ethics stresses the inviolability of individuals and their particular rights in the concrete situations in which they find themselves. In his celebrated essay "What is Oblomovitis?" Dobrolyubov condemns Oblomov's "do-nothing" attitude as morally depraved. While his diagnosis of Oblomovitis is consistent with his political radicalism, from a Nietzschean point of view Oblomov's generalized acquiescence represents a kind of perverse Christian saintliness. It is my contention that Oblomov provides a healthy foil to the rash pioneer spirit of all social and religious reformers, be they religious or profane. The ateleological quality in Oblomov's style of life has been found praiseworthy by such unlikely writers as Herzen and Solzhenitsyn, both of whom found in it a compelling antidote to the excesses of future planning so characteristic of totally politicized man.

14. *Oblomov*, trans. Ann Dunnigan (New York, 1963), p. 38.

15. Where Dostoevsky rejects one of the great myths of modern man, namely that there is a necessary correlation between technological progress and spiritual self-improvement, Goncharov (through Oblomov) calls into question the usefulness of any change.

16. Andrei Amalrik, *Involuntary Journey to Siberia*, trans. Manya Harari and Max Hayward (New York: Harcourt Brace Jovanovich, Inc., 1970).

CHAPTER 4. TOLSTOY AND THE VARIETIES OF THE INAUTHENTIC

1. In his *Religion within the Scope of Reason* Kant argues that while man has an indestructible "predisposition" to live up to the dictates of the categorical imperative, by virtue of being a rational creature,

he at the same time has an empirical "propensity" to act according to maxims contrary to his nature; in short, for the most part to prefer wrongdoing to doing his duty. Consistent with this view is Kant's anti-Establishment insistence on man's inability to achieve virtue and happiness on earth. Strangely anticipating the divided consciousness of Hegel, Kant maintained that only the "regulative principle" of immortality will enable the moral agent to square his conscience with the legitimate fulfillment of his desires. In the after-life we shall finally have enough time to perfect ourselves morally by ceaseless effort, and at last to enjoy the fruits of complete self-realization which always elude us in our finitude. This fundamentally tragic vision of the human career was quite alien to Kant's immediate predecessors and contemporaries, bearing fruit only in the dialectical reflections of his great nineteenth-century successors.

2. See the *Discours sur les Sciences et les Arts*. In this work Rousseau, anticipating Tolstoy's point of view, indicts the advanced society of his day for its neglect of naturalness in favor of pervasive pretending: according to Rousseau, the literate intellectual of the eighteenth century was more concerned with saying what others wanted to hear, with making a good impression or cutting a good figure, than with speaking his heart and mind *in and for themselves*. In brief, Rousseau located the corruptibility of civilization in its invitation to the individual to play up to the crowd instead of being himself.

3. For a suggestive discussion of Rousseau's lifelong preoccupation with the problem of inauthenticity see Marshall Berman, *The Politics of Authenticity* (New York, 1970). While I have many reservations about Professor Berman's somewhat forced interpretation of Rousseau in accordance with his own predilections, his book makes an important contribution to the recognized intellectual linkage between Rousseau and Tolstoy with respect to their shared concern over inauthenticity in modern life. Of particular interest in this connection is Professor Berman's contention that Rousseau's idealization of politics in his *Social Contract* is at bottom a cry of despair over his incapacity to envisage personal and interpersonal authenticity beyond the claims of the democratic state.

4. For an illuminating discussion of Rousseau's pessimism see Judith N. Shklar, *Men and Citizens* (Cambridge University Press, 1969).

5. Schopenhauer, whose influence on nineteenth-century Russian writers in general and Tolstoy in particular was enormous, argued that each individual's character is absolutely determined, in the sense of being disposed to respond to its environment in a unique manner. At the same time, Schopenhauer wished to maintain that each of us determines his own values, very much in accord with Sartre's insistence on the fact that existence precedes essence. Clearly Tolstoy grappled with unraveling the relationship between determination and self-determination of human conduct throughout his career. The best-known example of this problem in his fiction is the connection between the determinism elucidated in the epilogue to *War and Peace* and the apparent freedom with which he endows his characters in responding individually, if not autonomously, to similar life situations. Even in the epilogue he calls our attention to a datum such as Napoleon gloating over a military triumph: whereas, according to Tolstoy, the triumph itself can be ex-

plained as inevitable, Napoleon gloating over it was an unmistakable manifestation of self-determined vanity.

6. Kierkegaard attributed many of his works to authors like Johannes Climacus, whose point of view was presumably different from or even opposed to his own. Yet it is almost impossible to tell at times to what extent his pseudonymous authorship did not in effect overlap or coincide with his own point of view.

7. No modern thinker has thrown more light on the connections between inscrutability and deviousness than Sigmund Freud. According to his theories of the mind, we are for the most part unconscious of the true motives prompting our behavior. In order to survive in civilization we sacrifice the dictates of the pleasure principle to the requirements of reason. Thus the conscious part of the ego does violence both to its own unconscious counterpart as well as to those libidinal drives of the id which comprise our basic animal nature. Not only are the intentions behind our acts inscrutable to ourselves but in the process of getting back at its tormentors the id reappears in the consciousness in the guise of devious and self-deceiving masks. According to Freud's analysis, each man is tragically divided against himself by virtue of wishing to live a contradiction between the Hobbesian state of nature and the amenities of civil society. Though we cannot be held to account for our unconscious desires, each of us is subject to neurosis for concealing from himself through repression his destructive impulses. Intelligence here is as much at loggerheads with itself as it is with its traditional adversary the passions. Inauthenticity in the Freudian scheme of things is both externally imposed on the individual by the unbending taskmaster, civilization, in whose interest we pretend to be what we are not, and by ourselves, unwilling to face the truth about ourselves unless painfully helped to do so through psychiatric treatment. Freud teaches us to construe no human gesture as innocent or self-evidently transparent to common sense. Under his scrutiny our most authentic moments are exposed to ceaseless interpretations and demythologization.

8. It is worth noting, in this connection, that the nineteenth century showed a pronounced interest in the image of the Double. Besides being the title of one of Dostoevsky's important short novels, it underlies the following crucial ideas: Kierkegaard's definition of impurity of heart as double-mindedness; Goethe's celebrated metaphor of two souls struggling in the single breast of Faust; Dr. Jekyll's transformations into Mr. Hyde; Dionysus who on occasion becomes Apollo in Nietzsche's reconstruction of Greek cultural history; and love which is concomitant with hate in Freud's epoch-making theory of emotions. Men have always lived according to double standards. In casuistry the scholastic notion of the double-truth came close to being canonized—an undertaking which Pascal annihilated once and for all in his *Provincial Letters*. Still, only in the nineteenth century, the same century which became strikingly self-conscious about inauthenticity as a moral blemish, did the "double" and its implications receive focused attention on the part of philosophers, writers, and psychologists. Schubert's song "Der Doppelgänger," with its unresolved ending, epitomizes the tortured ironies in the fiction of Flaubert, Thomas Mann, and Gide. It makes a good claim to being *the* song of the "disinherited mind." Undoubtedly, the recurring symbolic significance of the Double in Ro-

mantic art and literature forms one of the main links between them and the existentialist consciousness.

9. For an excellent contemporary philosophical discussion of this problem, see Herbert Fingarette, *Self-Deception* (New York, 1969).

10. An unorthodox but provocative treatment of the problem of deception and self-deception is provided by Hannah Arendt in her article "Lying in Politics," *The New York Review of Books* (November 18, 1971), pp. 30–39. Dr. Arendt argues there (in connection with the leakage of the Pentagon papers) that those who deliberately deceive the public by manipulating their opinions are not necessarily deceived themselves, though they may give every appearance of being self-deceived. If I understand Dr. Arendt correctly, she means to assert a contradiction between an elitist minority of high-powered intellectuals creating a public image of falsehood in which their own personal involvement is only minimally present—say to the extent that it accords with the requirements of careerism. For example, the hatred of Hitler's top lieutenants for the Jews was in all likelihood contrived and expedient rather than spontaneous and self-convincing. On the other hand, the German masses with few exceptions were completely deceived by it as an unquestionable truth. In this connection it is also interesting to note Dr. Arendt's conjunction of abstract reasoning with the highest skills of deception as distinctively characteristic of academic intellectuals divorced from the concrete contingencies of life. Certainly Tolstoy and Dostoevsky would have agreed with her that the greatest enemies of human truth are precisely those theorists who, Hegel-like, elevate defactualization and pure logic into a myth of insightfulness concerning our historical situation. Finally, it is interesting to speculate with Dr. Arendt how public madness predicated on deception proves compatible again and again with a lack of ignorance on the part of private individuals merely touched by the opportunistic prospects of apparent self-deception. No wonder, one might observe here, that Tolstoy's hatred of society and the state exceeded even his low opinion of himself as incorrigibly vain.

11. See especially his *Reflections on World History*.

12. Nekhlyudov, the hero of the story, is staying at a fashionable hotel in Lucerne, where the guests are predominantly English. The plot revolves around the reactions of the guests to a wandering singer: they enjoy his performance but, wealthy as they are, remain indifferent to his request for remuneration. The situation arouses Nekhlyudov's indignation: he befriends the singer, tries to bridge the social gap between them, creates a minor scandal at the hotel, and is ultimately unsuccessful.

13. For an elaboration of this contradiction see Sir Isaiah Berlin, *The Hedgehog and the Fox* (New York, 1957).

14. The term "natural" has acquired a multitude of meanings in modern thought and literature. Not infrequently these meanings conflict, leaving the reader's mind in a state of hopeless confusion. For Tolstoy, as for Rousseau, "natural" connotes two principal sets of traits: first, those which refer to man's mere animality and spontaneity, and second, usually in a derogatory sense, those which apply specifically to our style of life as civilized beings in society. Nietzsche hit the nail on the head when he observed that it is as natural for man to compose

symphonies and mathematical treatises as it is for leopards to hunt their prey. Although Tolstoy the thinker could never reconcile himself to this ambiguity of naturalness in human behavior, he was still basically sound in distinguishing our pristine inclinations and impulses from our intellectualizations and complex role-playing. Tolstoy's paganism, in Gorky's sense, was natural in terms of the first definition.

15. "The Death of Ivan Ilyich," in *Six Short Masterpieces by Tolstoy,* trans. Margaret Wettlin (New York, 1963), p. 226.
16. "The Death of Ivan Ilyich," p. 234.
17. "The Death of Ivan Ilyich," p. 242.
18. The inauthenticity of a formalist is centered in his insensitivity to context and personality; the inauthenticity of a juggler, on the other hand, is rooted in his deliberate raising of false hopes, by blowing alternately hot and cold so as to lead others astray. While Tolstoy in the main characterizes Ivan Ilyich as a formalist, who lives up to the letter of each rule without bothering to discern its wider purpose, he allows for Ivan Ilyich's virtuosity, when it so pleases him, in shifting from the official to the human perspective of a particular case as well as doing the reverse.
19. "The Death of Ivan Ilyich," p. 264.
20. Children, as a rule, are unaware of death as a constant threat to their individual survival. Furthermore, they can abandon themselves uncalculatingly to each moment of experience, having no need of a studied self-conscious perspective so inimical to enthusiasm. To paraphrase Herzen, to play like a child is to be unaware of playing.
21. This is borne out by such stories as "Master and Man" and "Three Deaths." In the former a previously arrogant merchant gives his life to save his servant. Trapped at night in an unabating snowstorm, the merchant, first concerned only with his own survival, in the end lies on top of his already half-frozen servant, protecting him with the warmth of his own body. The physical proximity of the two men *in extremis* runs counter to the prevailing alienation in society.

    In "Three Deaths" Tolstoy contrasts the death of a gentlewoman with that of a peasant and a tree: while the gentlewoman is consumed by vanity and egoism during her last hours on earth, the peasant accepts the necessity of death, and the tree, best of all, serves selflessly even in its passing.

    Already in *War and Peace* and *Anna Karenina* Tolstoy indicated his preference for those who die with a minimum of fuss and commotion. As in his philosophy of history he invariably emphasizes the acknowledgment of the inevitable as superior to self-centered protestations, with their accompanying noises of fortuitous mishap or individual injury. In brief: for Tolstoy only those die authentically whose last thoughts are focused on others and, secondly, who view their own death with unexceptional sobriety.
22. "The Kreutzer Sonata," in *Six Short Masterpieces,* p. 310.
23. "At first their elders would have the young ladies believe there is no such thing as the licentiousness making up half the life of our towns and even our villages: later they become so accustomed to this pretense that in the end they themselves, like the English, come to believe sincerely that they are a people of high moral principles living in a highly moral world." "The Kreutzer Sonata," pp. 301–2.

24. Tolstoy's conjunction here of Romantic Idealism and "tough-minded" materialism is reminiscent of the interpretation of Dostoevsky's Underground Man in the previously cited article by Joseph Frank ("Nihilism and *Notes from Underground*," *The Sewanee Review*, Winter 1961).

25. This is yet another example of Tolstoy's intellectual kinship with Rousseau, who in his writings repeatedly protested against modern man's inclinations to display feelings which somehow he could not afford to act upon directly. This point raises a distinction between playing a role in which one believes and playing a role which from the start one views with utter cynicism. Incidentally, this distinction goes beyond Sartre's analysis of *mauvaise foi*.

26. "The Kreutzer Sonata," p. 296.

27. In his *I and Thou* Martin Buber made a classic distinction between two modes of relationship open to the conscious subject vis-à-vis the external world and other human beings. In the I-It relationship the subject regards the object as a manipulable entity, to be used solely in accord with his own satisfaction; on the other hand, in the I-Thou relationship, the subject regards the object as another subject, that is to say, as a Kantian end-in-itself rather than as a mere means. Pozdnyshev in his premarital sex exploited women for his pleasure; after his marriage he confesses to having enjoyed his wife sensually, but unlovingly.

CHAPTER 5. SOLZHENITSYN AND THE INCONSEQUENCE OF POLITICS

1. Recent events in the Soviet Union have brought forth yet another cruel parallel between tsarist and Soviet regimes. The letter Solzhenitsyn wrote in support of the Soviet biologist, Zhores Medvedev, who was sent to an insane asylum for exposing the inanities of Soviet genetics, contains an ironic reference to the nineteenth-century Russian thinker Chaadaev. Chaadaev was declared insane for daring to suggest, in his famous "First Philosophical Letter," that Russian culture was not on a par with Western civilization. According to Solzhenitsyn, Chaadaev was more fortunate than Medvedev, the victim of a totalitarian system, because he was allowed to live at home rather than to be isolated and confined in a mental institution. Medvedev's fate (similar to that of many other outspoken Soviet intellectuals) Solzhenitsyn terms "spiritual murder," akin to, and even worse than the grim work of Hitler's ovens. The provisional release of Medvedev in the wake of embarrassing protest, including that of top-ranking Soviet nuclear physicists, does not in any way detract from Solzhenitsyn's cutting analogy and bears further witness to the latter's stature as a fearless critic of cant and skulduggery. Like Leo Tolstoy, he is not only a great writer but above all a courageous force of conscience, undeterred by tremendous risks to his own personal welfare, if not his very survival. (Since this chapter was written, Solzhenitsyn has authorized the publication in the West of the first volume of his planned trilogy on World War I, *August 1914*. This act scarcely serves to assuage the wrath of the Soviet authorities.)

2. See E. Ginzburg, *Journey into the Whirlwind* (New York, 1967).

3. For a striking example of this theme, see the disparaging comparison made by A. Anatoli (Kuznetsov) in the uncensored version of *Babi*

Yar (New York, 1970) between serfdom and life on a collective farm. "Under serfdom the landowner used to leave peasants whole days free to work for themselves on their own little plots of land. But on a collective farm a man had no such free days, and had no land of his own . . ."

4. I am indebted for this contrast to Sir Isaiah Berlin, who makes this point in his series of articles on the historical development of the Russian intelligentsia.

5. *The First Circle*, trans. Thomas P. Whitney (New York, 1968), p. 381.

6. Solzhenitsyn's literary kinship with Tolstoy is indeed multidimensional. Nowhere does this become more evident than in their shared disgust for modern culture as inauthentic. From the organization of the *sharashka* in *The First Circle* to the dramatization of Stalin's pronouncement in *The Love-Girl and the Innocent*, "Man is what he works" (an ingenious caricature of Feuerbach's famous definition), Solzhenitsyn dwells repeatedly on the falsehoods and distortions of twentieth-century life—from the "Big Bunny" (editor of *Playboy* magazine) "making his own weather" to "The Plowman" (Stalin) authenticating hell on earth, our contemporary style of existence is punctuated again and again by pathological facets of behavior. Possibly the most frightening aspect of Stalin's rule was his sincerity in implementing his inauthentic regime.

7. This incident has taken on special meaning in the light of Solzhenitsyn's condemnation by the Soviet government as a traitor to his country, or worse, for having been awarded the Nobel Prize for Literature in 1970.

8. *The Cancer Ward*, trans. Rebecca Frank (New York, 1968), p. 516.

9. *The Cancer Ward*, p. 160.

10. The existential case made by Heidegger and many other thinkers and writers in the same tradition for the relative unreality of death in modern times, seems in part at least to rest on the availability of drugs and related devices for relieving man's terminal disintegration. Thus the poet Rilke complains in his *Notebooks of Malte Laurids Brigge* about the anonymity of death in a Paris city hospital at the turn of the century, in contrast to its inescapable everyday reality at an earlier time. One finds it extremely difficult to evaluate this type of grievance. While it seems indubitably correct to point out that by virtue of growing numbers alone the facts of life and death in our day are experienced more abstractly than they used to be, the horrors of the twentieth century scarcely require any special pleading from existentialists or any other group of intellectuals to make themselves directly felt in our midst. Perhaps it is the loss of religion which has helped cut us off from the thrust of the ultimate verities, though one could argue just as plausibly that only as a consequence of this development are we obliged to face them in all their stark terror. Personally, I suspect that the easiness of death or its opposite is today, as always, a highly individualistic matter, which has little to do with the winds blown by a particular *Zeitgeist*.

11. The distinction between the personal and the social is open to the charge of being simplistic. Admittedly, the manner in which a person succeeds or fails in forging his own self is at least in part determined by the environment in which he lives. Conversely, the latter reflects,

if indiscernibly, the presence of each individual interacting with it. But if one grants this truism, there remains the question of priorities: should a man try to clean his own house before undertaking to reform the world? In Stalin's camps, the characteristic location of Solzhenitsyn's fiction, there is little if anything the individual can do about the System. But in this critical setting where the relationship between thought and action is put to an extreme test the individual can, according to Solzhenitsyn, strive for the development of that internalized fortitude which makes his survival as a human being possible. For Solzhenitsyn, the preservation of human dignity, quite distinct, incidentally, from stoic imperturbability by virtue of being infinitely passionate rather than indifferent to suffering, is an inegalitarian virtue whose presence or absence is found in every class of society. Just as Lenin was an elitist of the class struggle, Solzhenitsyn is an elitist of the will. For him, as for Pascal, Kierkegaard, Nietzsche, and Ortega, only those save themselves whose character predisposes them to resist the Crowd.

12. Kant postulated freedom as a regulative principle of Practical Reason, in contrast to the constitutive principles of Pure Reason, according to which the world (Nature) is wholly determined. Kant argues that without freedom or self-determination, however incompatible these may appear with the Newtonian view of the universe he accepted in theory, the very concept of a moral agent would prove untenable. This is not to say that Kant, any more than Tolstoy, solves the problem of free will, but his position is far closer to the ways in which we judge ourselves and others in everyday life.

13. I am grateful to Professor Pavel Kovaly of Northeastern University for letting me consult his then unpublished essay on Solzhenitsyn ("Problems of Anti-Humanism and Humanism in the Life and Work of Alexander Solzhenitsyn," *Studies in Soviet Thought* 11 [1971], pp. 1–18). Therein he has drawn my attention to an extended passage, which underscored my interpretations of the Russian writer as a philosophical novelist in the existentialist tradition. This passage, in chapter 60 of *The First Circle*, comprises Solzhenitsyn's critique of the three laws of *dialectic*. These laws first formulated by Hegel, and subsequently elaborated and commented on by such classical exponents of historical materialism as Engels, Lenin, and Stalin, consist of the following assertions: the negation of the negation, the movement from quantity to quality, and the unity and contrast of opposites. Solzhenitsyn repudiates these laws, taking the Kierkegaardian point of view that at best they delineate processes of thought rather than actualities of life. At worst, especially in the dogmatic Marxist mode of Hegel's subtler meaning, they support the substitution of tendentious falsehoods for the "weird" truths of the human condition as lived and experienced.

14. *The Cancer Ward*, p. 552.

15. *The First Circle*, p. 240.

16. *The First Circle*, p. 344.

17. See note 10, p. 199.

18. The representativeness of the atypical is an epistemological paradox which offends against traditional modes of apprehending reality. Shakespeare's Hamlet obviously is not Everyman, yet in this fictitious char-

acter universal traits of being human are presented to us as expressions of an idiosyncratic personality. At one and the same time, like other chosen individuals in life or literature, Hamlet is unique as well as mankind writ small. For Solzhenitsyn life under normal conditions is unrepresentative of bringing out man's potential for despair or integrity. Only apart from the commonplaces of his ordinary environment, with the dethronement of callousness and the emergence of self-awareness, can his true being be properly scrutinized.

In *The Varieties of Religious Experience* (New York: Modern Library, p. 23) William James states memorably the existential point of view on this issue: "Insane conditions have this advantage, that they isolate special factors of the mental life, and enable us to inspect them unmasked by their more usual surroundings. They play in the anatomy of the body. To understand a thing rightly we need to see it both out of its environment and in it, and to have acquaintance with the whole range of its variations."

On this point, I believe, Solzhenitsyn's position has much more in common with that of the existentialists than with any brand of Marxism or sociological reductionism.

19. Note the connection between ceasing to be surprised by anything and becoming preoccupied with so-called atypical conduct. Party bosses intuitively reject the exception in favor of the rule. In this sense they may properly be regarded as the predatory enemies of classical Russian fiction, a thought beautifully expressed in Solzhenitsyn's much-quoted observation to the effect that a great writer almost inevitably proves a hostile government within the confines of the government in power.

20. The *sharashka* is a sort of elitist prison whose inmates possess special talents which the state wants to utilize. In return for their services they receive privileged treatment. Especially in the tradition of the Russian intelligentsia, nothing could be more inauthentic than a professional physicist cast in the role of a prisoner whose knowledge helps to strengthen a tyrannical regime. Here once again one must credit Stalin with a stroke of genius for "transvaluating values" beyond Nietzsche's fondest dreams.

21. The voice-print project involves the development of a system for the identification of Soviet citizens through an acoustical analysis of their speech patterns.

22. *The First Circle*, p. 228.

23. *One Day*, pp. 21, 53 [Full title: *One Day in the Life of Ivan Denisovich.*]

24. *One Day*, p. 38.

25. *The First Circle*, pp. 236–7.

26. *The First Circle*, pp. 88–9.

27. *The Love-Girl and the Innocent*, trans. Nicholas Bethell and David Burg (New York, 1971), p. 118.

28. According to Sir Isaiah Berlin there exists a sharp cleavage between the freedom to act in the absence of external constraint, characteristic of the Anglo-Saxon philosophical tradition, and the freedom *from* enslavement to a false inner self, predominant in the thought of Kant, Hegel, and the German Idealistic tradition in general. It should be noted here that Tolstoy's profound influence on Solzhenitsyn is in no small measure the consequence of the former's espousal of the primacy

of conscience, coupled with his rejection of all legal and social orders as rooted in hypocrisy. The political anarchism of Bakunin, as well as the Christian anarchism of Tolstoy, was prophetically as hostile to the latent authoritarian tendencies in Marxism as to their chief target, the Russian autocracy. Thus it is no mere accident of personal antipathy which accounts for the mutual break between Marx and Bakunin. Analogously, for all his hatred of the tsarist regime and his excommunication from the Church, the Russian Marxists remained signally unsuccessful in luring Tolstoy into their fold. A significant link between Bakunin, Tolstoy, and Solzhenitsyn is their refusal to substitute the state for God as man's "ultimate concern."

29. It might well be argued that in *The Love-Girl and the Innocent* Solzhenitsyn dramatizes the dire necessity for the pragmatic attitude if a prisoner is to have any prospect of survival in the camps. Yet the burden of the evidence in his novels, including his personal experience, supports the contrary view to the effect that only idealists can save themselves from self-destruction. This need not be a contradiction, provided one takes the trouble to distinguish the possibility of physical extinction from the threat of spiritual or moral suicide.

30. For what is perhaps still the best dialectical discussion of freedom, see the volume of Camus's professor of philosophy, Jean Grenier, *Conversations on the Good Uses of Freedom,* trans. Alexander Coleman (Cambridge, Massachusetts, 1967).

31. *The First Circle,* p. 562.

32. For detailed discussion of Schopenhauer's influence on Tolstoy, see Sigrid McLaughlin, "Some Aspects of Tolstoy's Intellectual Development: Tolstoy and Schopenhauer," *California Slavic Studies* 5 (1970), pp. 187–245. While Mrs. McLaughlin is quite correct in her attribution of Schopenhauer's recurring hold on the mind of the Russian novelist her reference to Tolstoy as an "optimistic Christian" is too *simpliste* to pass muster. Certainly no less than the German thinker and his philosophy Tolstoy's life and thought were suffused by unresolved paradoxes and ambiguities.

33. *Hadji Murad,* in *The Short Novels of Tolstoy,* trans. Aylmer Maude (New York, 1949), pp. 664–5.

34. *The First Circle,* p. 93.

35. On another level Solzhenitsyn draws a similar contrast between two reactions to hoarfrost on a wintry Moscow morning. While the flourishing official finds the dawn of another day an embarrassment of emptiness and unrelieved gloom, the helpless *zek* at Mavrino, apparently condemned to life-long imprisonment, relishes the fullness of the life from within his paradoxically agonizing and humiliating environment.

CHAPTER 6. THE BROKEN ICON

1. For some notes toward the clarification of existential thought as a distinctive philosophical movement, see the appendices.

2. See Martin Malia, "What Is the Intelligentsia?" *Daedalus* (Summer 1960), pp. 441–58.

3. Gogol, "The Diary of a Madman," 1835; Turgenev, *The Diary of a Superfluous Man,* 1850; Ostrovsky, *Diary of a Scoundrel,* 1868; Dos-

toevsky, "The Dream of a Ridiculous Man," 1876; Tolstoy, *The Memoirs of a Madman*, 1884; Chekhov, *A Dreary Story: from the Notebook of an Old Man*, 1889; Chekhov, *Ward No. 6*, 1892; and Valeriy Tarsis, *Ward 7*, 1965. Cf. also Chaadaev's *Apology of a Madman*, 1837, which he wrote because of government persecution for publishing his "First Philosophical Letter" (1836)—an incident which sadly set a precedent, as any student of Russian and Soviet affairs can testify.

4. While one does not normally associate positive ideas with Russian nihilism, there is a curious parallel between the famous epigram of Nietzsche that "man prefers the meaning of the void to a void of meaning" and the situation of these nihilists. Their fervid negativism only partly concealed an equally passionate desire to find a new faith—in the peasant, in socialism, or in nihilism itself.

5. On this point see William F. Woehrlin's recent biography, *Chernyshevskii* (Cambridge, Massachusetts, 1971), especially chapter V.

6. Stalin once told Milovan Djilas that Dostoevsky was a great writer who, however, had a way of corrupting youth. Djilas, *Conversations with Stalin*, trans. Michael B. Petrovich (New York, 1962), p. 157.

APPENDICES

1. Descartes and Pascal

1. Existentialists as a family have been spontaneous anti-utilitarians. From Pascal's devastating destruction of Jesuit casuistry through Dostoevsky's dismemberment of the Crystal Palace, one of their central preoccupations has been with the skeptic rather than with skepticism *per se*, with the thinker behind the System rather than with the System divorced from him, and with dispositions and motives rather than with results. It is scarcely surprising that the existential doubts raised by these disjunctions have never been set to rest, though we live at a time when the abstractions of Descartes in one sense would seem to have triumphed beyond belief.

2. In his Wager, Pascal argues that the attainment of infinite bliss by having masses said in Paris is worth the chance of losing some finite happiness. A sinner in the eyes of God should take such a gamble, if only to escape the everlasting torments of hell. It cannot be emphasized enough that this pragmatic argument for the viability of theistic faith was aimed by Pascal solely at those of his contemporaries who insisted on having a rationale for all their convictions. The author of the "Memorial" clearly did not approach the question of God in this manner.

2. Hegel and the First Generation of the Russian Intelligentsia

1. Martin Malia, *Alexander Herzen and the Birth of Russian Socialism* (Cambridge: Harvard University Press, 1961).

2. It is still customary to accentuate the differences between Slavophiles

and Westerners instead of dwelling on their family resemblances, not the least of which was a shared attraction for the philosophies of Schelling and Hegel. As Marc Raeff has shrewdly observed in his *Russian Intellectual History*, the critical attitude of the Russian intelligentsia in the first half of the nineteenth century, in other words, their intuitive existentialism, grew out of their adherence to an organic view of life and thought which classical German philosophy had so powerfully argued and expressed in conscious opposition to the mainstream of the French Enlightenment. However one may assess today the Slavophile emphasis on *sobornost'* and the *obshchina*, given the reiterated loneliness of contemporary Western man, deprived of virtually all effective religious and communal ties, the fear of the tyranny of the mechanical in modern life expressed as intensely in the writings of Herzen as in those of Khomiakov, cuts very close to our disturbed psyche. The horrors deplored by Herzen from the Other Shore, frequently overlapped with those excoriated by his Slavophile adversaries at home. Seen in this context, the quarrel between the two factions over continued adherence to traditional articles of the Christian faith is comparable to the division between Christian and atheistic existentialists in the twentieth century. In both cases, irrespective of their positive commitment either to some form of theism or a variety of secularism, the two sides are in substantial agreement in their discernment of modern life as dangerously solitary, mechanical, and empty.

3. For a thorough discussion of Hegelian philosophy in nineteenth-century Russian thought, see D. Tschizhevskij, "Hegel in Russland," in *Hegel Bei Den Slaven*, ed. D. Tschizhevskij (Herman Gentner Verlag, 1961).

3. Alienation

1. Nietzsche sees man as subject to two irreconcilable tyrannies: that of *laissez-aller* and that of severe self-discipline. While the latter is indispensable to the flowering of civilization, the former exhibits our unspoiled spontaneity. On the one hand, Nietzsche observes, it is *natural* for us to give childlike, uninhibited expression to our wishes, but, on the other, it is just as *natural* for man to construct theories, compose symphonies, and create other artifacts which require the highest concentration of mental effort and self-restraint.

4. On the Existential Import of Two Philosophical Distinctions

1. Throughout this study, with one notable exception, I have referred to Rousseau as an eighteenth-century precursor of existentialist thought in opposition to Voltaire and the Encyclopedists. The exception is Dostoevsky's self-characterization as the "Voltaire" of his age, by which he meant, presumably, his castigation of its vices and metaphysical conceits as in *Candide*. While Existentialism and Positivism share a common contempt for traditional metaphysics, it would be clearly mistaken to infer from this resemblance that the two philosophical movements are mutually congenial. Similarly, Voltaire's So-

cratic mission, which Dostoevsky may well have admired for himself, should not deceive us into thinking that they saw eye to eye on fundamentals. On the contrary, the reverse conclusion is closer to the truth. My view of this matter has recently been borne out by Judith N. Shklar in her study of Rousseau entitled *Men and Citizens* (Cambridge: Cambridge University Press, 1969). There she argues that unlike Voltaire and his circle, Rousseau was basically pessimistic about any possibility of man's earthly salvation, rejecting both the Idea of Progress as well as the consolations of orthodox Christianity. According to Shklar, both the Spartan ideal of civic duty as set forth in the *Social Contract* and the ideal of family life portrayed in *Emile* constitute a kind of Kierkegaardian "Either/Or" neither of which, Rousseau believed, would ever enable humanity to extricate itself from its natural unnaturalness, each man being divided against himself or in conflict with others. In other words, Rousseau constructed Utopian models in the light of which he judged the perennial imperfections of our condition without proposing any program of action that might once and for all lead to our liberation. If Shklar's interpretation be plausible, as I believe it to be, Rousseau was quintessentially existential, not only by virtue of his unique experiment in self-absorption, as dramatized in the *Confessions* and in his *Reflections of a Solitary Wanderer*, but also by virtue of his unresolved dialectic between two Golden Ages lost to us forever and intrinsically irreconcilable on account of respectively objectifying virtues which cannot coexist in harmony, though each set makes an absolute claim on our nature. In support of Rousseau's prescience, Shklar observes that, since his death, men have conspicuously fled again and again into blind devotion to some impersonal cause or into a privileged enclave of private happiness. Since each position is untenable, it can only serve as a warning against embracing uncritically or totally its antithesis. I might add that Rousseau's intuitive existentialism also emerges from his Nietzsche-like indifference to formal argument in stating his ideas as well as from his Kierkegaardian affinity for looking at things ahistorically, which is to say, as in a state of constant flux without reaching ripeness in time.

2. Even Vladimir Nabokov, who often seems to take special pride in dissociating his fiction from this tradition, repeatedly introduces historical characters into his novels. For a striking case in point, see his sarcastic biography of Chernyshevski interpolated in *The Gift* (trans. Michael Scammell, New York: Capricorn Books, 1970). Similarly, the first forty pages of his recent novel *Ada* (New York and Toronto: McGraw-Hill, 1969) prove unintelligible unless the reader grasps Nabokov's allusions to nineteenth-century Russian history and literary controversies.

Suggestions for Further Reading

The following represent a few highlights from an inexhaustible literature. With very few exceptions, only works in English are listed here. Works cited in footnotes are generally not included.

For those who want to familiarize themselves more with the Russian historical scene, Nicholas Riasanovsky's one-volume *A History of Russia* (2nd ed., New York, 1969) is excellent. A more detailed study has recently come out in English: P. Miliukov, Ch. Seignobos, and L. Eisemann, *A History of Russia*, trans. C. L. Markmann (3 vols., New York, 1968–69). Thomas G. Masaryk's *The Spirit of Russia*, trans. E. and C. Paul (2 vols., New York, 1955) retains its value as an interpretation of philosophical and intellectual developments. An indispensable work for the student of the Russian populist and socialist movements is Franco Venturi's *Roots of Revolution*, trans. F. Haskell (New York, 1960). An excellent collection of source material can be found in Marc Raeff, *Russian Intellectual History: An Anthology* (New York, 1966). See also Sidney Harcave, ed., *Readings in Russian History* (2 vols., New York, 1962); Thomas Riha, *Readings in Russian Civilization* (3 vols., Chicago, 1969).

Standard histories of Russian philosophy are: V. V. Zenkovsky, *A History of Russian Philosophy*, trans. George L. Kline (2 vols., New York, 1953) and N. O. Lossky, *History of Russian Philosophy* (New York, 1951). The three-volume anthology *Russian Philosophy*, ed. James M. Edie, James P. Scanlan, and Mary-Barbara Zeldin, with George L. Kline (Chicago, 1965) is also valuable. *The Russian Idea* by Nicolas Berdyaev, trans. R. M. French (Boston, 1962), gives an excellent survey of major currents in Russian thought.

For a basic history of Russian literature see D. S. Mirsky's *A History of Russian Literature*, ed. Francis J. Whitfield (New York, 1961). A

220 · *Suggestions for Further Reading*

perceptive treatment of some Russian writers and their view of the self is provided by Renato Poggioli's *The Phoenix and the Spider* (Cambridge, Massachusetts, 1957). An illuminating study showing the connections between Western European and Russian nineteenth-century fiction is *Dostoevsky and Romantic Realism* (Chicago, 1967) by Donald Fanger. A notable work dealing with a tradition in Russian literature diametrically opposed to the theme of the present book is Rufus Matthewson's *The Positive Hero in Russian Literature* (New York, 1958). The most recent comprehensive study of Russian writers in English is Helen Muchnic's *Russian Writers: Notes and Essays* (New York, 1971). Unsurpassed as a first-hand account of the Russian intellectual scene in the first half of the nineteenth century are Alexander Herzen's memoirs *My Past and Thought*, trans. Constance Garnett and Humphrey Higgens (4 vols., New York, 1968).

Chapter 1: For a detailed discussion of Gogol's life and works, see V. Setchkarev's *Gogol: His Life and Works*, trans. R. Kramer (New York, 1965). A one-sided, though quite provocative, work is V. Nabokov's *Nikolai Gogol* (Norfolk, Connecticut, 1944). The most recent study is V. Erlich's *Gogol* (New Haven, 1969).

For the most interesting portrait of Gogol as a lecturer in history at the University of St. Petersburg, see the memoirs and early letters of Turgenev. From these sources, we learn that Gogol's first lecture was a triumph, doubtless due to the fact that he poured all his knowledge of medieval history into its presentation. But, for the rest of the semester, he had nothing left to say, and his students became quite restless and bored. At one point he passed around daguerreotypes from current history books before dismissing his class. Subsequently, as his desperation grew ever greater, he put a large handkerchief around his face with the result that his students could barely hear his mutterings. Finally, following his resignation, he put his whole academic experience in a nutshell, writing to his mother: "Unrecognized, I ascended the podium, unrecognized, I stepped down from it."

For classical discussion of the problem of the Absurd in modern thought see Hume's *Dialogues Concerning Natural Religion* (especially the last two chapters), the discussion of the antinomies of Pure Reason in Kant's *Critique of Pure Reason*, Kierkegaard's retelling of the Abraham story in *Fear and Trembling*, and Camus's *The Myth of Sisyphus*. Also worth mentioning is Hans Vaihinger's *Philosophy As If* (1911), which was inspired by Kant's postulates of Practical Reason (the regulative principles) and Nietzsche's espousal of illusion and fantasy as essential elements in a meaningful life.

Chapter 2: Of the multitude of biographical and critical studies on Dostoevsky, K. Mochulsky's *Dostoevsky* (Princeton, 1967) is the most authoritative, though slanted toward a religious interpretation. Among the more interesting recent studies is R. Lord's *Dostoevsky, Essays and Perspectives* (London, 1970). My interpretation of Dostoevsky as the Devil's Advocate is confirmed by Philip Rahv, "The Other Dostoevsky," *New York Review of Books* (April 20, 1972), pp. 30–38.

On the theme of intellectuals in modern life the following works strike me as seminal: Julien Benda, *The Betrayal of the Intellectuals*, trans. R. Aldington (Boston, 1959), and Thomas Mann's *Betrachtungen eines Unpolitischen*. A diversified collection of essays on this subject is *On Intellectuals*, ed. Philip Rieff (New York, 1969). A key essay on the divided consciousness of the modern intellectual is Turgenev's "Hamlet and Don Quixote: The Two Eternal Human Types."

For a new look at the history of Russian intellectuals and the Russian intelligentsia, see Michael Confino's brilliant essay "On Intellectuals and Intellectual Traditions in Eighteenth- and Nineteenth-Century Russia" in the Spring 1972 issue of *Daedalus*, pp. 117–49. Among the numerous arresting points made by Professor Confino, two strike me as being especially insightful, first, that under the progressive Tsar, Peter the Great, Russian intellectuals, far from being the avowed enemies of absolute monarchy, supported the regime in its support of radical Westernization and related advanced ideas. In short, the Russian intelligentsia does not necessarily have to be and has not always been in fact the advocate of an antiestablishment ideology. Second, and even more subtly, Professor Confino argues that, strictly speaking, there may have been no more than one generation of the Russian intelligentsia, namely that of the 1860s and '70s. According to his analysis, Herzen and his contemporaries of the 1830s and '40s constituted a loosely connected network of three circles of isolated individuals without any substantial impact on Russian society at large, while the radical intellectuals of the 1890s had, for the most part, already given up the intelligentsia's devotion to freedom of thought and the liberation of mankind. Without denying a continuity of attitude and concern on the part of the *intelligenti* over two centuries of Russian history, Professor Confino's observations force us to reexamine and revise hackneyed generalizations about his subject.

Chapter 3: The amount of critical material on Goncharov is decidedly limited. There is no comprehensive work on him in English, and thus A. Mazon's *Un Maître du roman russe: Ivan Goncharov, 1812–1891* (Paris, 1914) is the only serious non-Russian study available. Janko Lavrin's *Goncharov* (Cambridge, 1954) is a short, though useful, biography. The problem of boredom in Goncharov's fiction is treated in great detail in Walther Rehm's "Gontscharow und die Langeweile" in *Experimentum Medietatis* (Munich, 1947). The problem of boredom in modern philosophy is taken up by Kierkegaard in the "Diapsalmata" of *Either/Or*, in many of Nietzsche's aphorisms, and by Heidegger in *Sein und Zeit*. "Ivan Goncharov, A literary Quarrel: Turgenev as 'Plagiarist,' " *Encounter* (June 1971), pp. 24–32, was the first appearance in English of Goncharov's somewhat "psychopathic" account of this famous controversy.

Chapter 4: The plethora of secondary literature on Tolstoy is as great as that on Dostoevsky. Unfortunately, Boris Eikhenbaum's classic studies are not available in English. Henri Troyat's *Tolstoy*, trans. Nancy Amphoux (New York, 1967) is especially valuable for its use of Tolstoy's diaries. For an illuminating discussion of Tolstoy's religious ideas, see chapter 2 in Richard Niebuhr's *Christ and Culture* (New York, 1951). A suggestive exploration of Tolstoy's philosophy of history is to be found in Sir Isaiah Berlin's *The Hedgehog and the Fox*. An interpretation of Tolstoy's works along existential lines which had considerable influence on my views is Mark Aldanov's *Zagadka Tolstogo* (Providence, 1969).

Considerable light on the general problem of authenticity in modern literature and life was shed by Lionel Trilling in his Norton Lectures at Harvard University during the fall term of 1969–70. A further worthwhile discussion of this problem can be found in *The Politics of Authenticity* (New York, 1970) by Marshall Berman.

Chapter 5: While critical literature on Solzhenitsyn has been growing at a rapid pace, nothing published thus far can be called outstanding. A newly translated study is Georg Lukács' *Solzhenitsyn*, trans. William David Graf (Cambridge, Massachusetts, 1971). For a detailed, and sometimes amusing, account of Solzhenitsyn's relationship to the Soviet state, see *Encounter* (January 1971), pp. 35–38.

Chapter 6: On the relationship between the world of the Russians and the world of the existentialists, one should look at:

Lev Shestov. *Kierkegaard and the Existential Philosophy*, trans. Elinor Hewitt (Athens, Ohio, 1969).

Nicholas Berdyaev. *Dream and Reality*, trans. Katherine Lampert (New York, 1951). *The Destiny of Man*, trans. Nathalie Duddington (New York, 1960).

S. L. Frank. *Reality and Man,* trans. Nathalie Duddington (London, 1965).

On the survival and revival of existential realism since the October Revolution, the following memoirs, written by victims of ideological persecution, are of special interest.

Nadezhda Mandelstam. *Hope Against Hope,* trans. Max Hayward (New York, 1970).

Eugenia Ginzburg, *Journey into the Whirlwind,* trans. Paul Stevenson and Max Hayward (New York, 1967).

Andrei Amalrik. *Involuntary Journey to Siberia,* trans. Manya Harari and Max Hayward (New York, 1970).

A. Anatoli (Kuznetsov). *Babi Yar,* trans. David Floyd (New York, 1970).

Zhores A. Medvedev. *The Medvedev Papers,* trans. Vera Rich (London, 1971).

Appendix 1:

For the keenest existential critique of the Cartesian *cogito* see Kierkegaard's discussion in the *Concluding Unscientific Postscript.* One of the most provocative recent interpretations of Pascal's thought in relation to the main Western philosophical tradition is to be found in Lucien Goldmann, *The Hidden God,* translated by Phillip Thody (New York, 1964).

Appendix 2:

An outstanding inquiry into the impact of Hegel's system on nineteenth-century thought in general, and on Tolstoy's epilogue to *War and Peace* in particular, is Nicola Chiaromonte, *The Paradox of History* (London, 1971). Chiaromonte's focus on the idea of fate as a central problem of modernity sheds a great deal of light on the diverse efforts of the Russian intelligentsia to come to terms with the dialectic of Absolute *Geist* or with Marxist epiphenomenalism.

Appendix 3:

Of many recent studies of alienation one of the more philosophical is: Richard Schacht, *Alienation* (Garden City, New York, 1971).

Index

Index

Absurd, 1–29, 101, 142, 151; dramas of the, 3, 72, 75, 166; theater of the, 70
Absurdity, 1–29, 63; Age of, 1; bureaucratic, 13–17; formal, 2, 4, 17–29; situational, 2, 4, 6–17
Action Française, 31
Aeschylus, 31
Aesthetic Education, 45
Age of Absurdity, 1
Akakievich, Akakiy, 11–12, 15, 16, 26
Alcibiades, 101
Alexander I, 126, 136
Alexander II, 40, 165
Alyosha *see* Karamazov, Alexei (Alyosha)
Amalrik, Andrei, 85
Anatoli (Kuznetsov), A., 167
Andrey, Prince, 107
Anhedonia, 75–79
Anna Karenina, 22, 39, 102
Anti-Christ, 100
Aristotle, 40, 101
Arkady *see* Kirsanov, Arkady
Atheismus im Christentum, 49
Attack upon Christendom, 100
Augustine, Saint, 106, 107
Auschwitz, 140
Austen, Jane, 120
Ayer, Sir Alfred J., 161

Babbitt, George F., 75
Babi Yar, 167
Bach, Johann Sebastian, 88, 124, 148
Bakunin, Mikhail, 53, 159, 160, 165, 168–69
Barth, Karl, *deus absconditus* of, 1, 24
Bashmachkin, 26–27
Baudelaire, Charles, 41, 75
Bazarov, Evgeny, 35, 53, 163, 165–66
Beauvoir, Simone de, 74, 161
Beckett, Samuel, 69, 74, 132, 146
Beethoven, Ludwig van, 38, 122, 123
Belinsky, Vissarion Grigoryevich, 37, 104
Bentham, Jeremy, 165
Berg, Alban, 158
Bergson, Henri, 31
Berlin, Isaiah, 147
Berlin, University of, 161
Bloch, Ernst, 49
Blok, Alexander, 29
Bolshevik Revolution, 47, 137, 155, 167, 169
Bonhoeffer, Dietrich, 114
Boredom, 63–85; anhedonia, 75–79; elementary notions of, 66–71; literary-historical expressions of, 73–75; lived experience of, 71–73; Oblomovitis, 79–85

Bouvard et Pécuchet, 4
Bovary, Charles, 3
Brothers Karamazov, The, 37, 49, 52
Buddenbrooks, 74
Burckhardt, Jacob, 59, 100, 164
Byron, George Gordon, Lord, 74, 99

Calvin, John, 79
Calvinists, 66
Camus, Albert, 74
Cancer Ward, The, 123, 130, 131, 133, 134, 135, 136, 152, 158, 163
Carlyle, Thomas, 74, 79, 81, 145
Categorical imperative, 5
Catherine the Great, 34
Chaadaev, Pyotr Yakovlevich, 164
Chaplin, Charlie, 71
Charron, Pierre, 155
Chekhov, Anton Pavlovich, 68, 132
Chernyshevsky, Nikolai Gavrilovich, 48, 66, 168
Chichikov, Pavel Ivanovich, 8–10, 13, 16, 17, 24, 26, 27, 142, 146, 163
Churchill, Sir Winston, 27
"Civilization, uneasiness of," 90
Claggart, John, 96
Clapham Sect, 74
Coleridge, Samuel Taylor, 157
Concluding Unscientific Postscript, 71
Confession, 104–105
Così fan tutte, 15
Courage to Be, The, 4
Cox, Professor Harvey, 169
Crime and Punishment, 30, 40, 43, 156
Crystal Palace, 144

Darwin, Charles Robert, 99
Dead Souls, 4, 5, 7, 8–10, 13, 24, 45, 132, 146, 162
"Death of Ivan Ilyich, The," 18, 107, 115, 116, 118
Decembrists, 129
Demea, 49

Descartes, René, 71, 144, 160–61
Deus absconditus, 1, 24
Devils, The, 38, 45, 46, 52, 54–62, 76, 151, 157, 168, 169
Dewey, John, 161
Dialogues Concerning Natural Religion, 4, 49
Diary of a Lunatic, The, 105
"Diary of a Madman, The," 12, 20, 28
Diary of a Writer, 38
Dickens, Charles, 40
Dobrolyubov. Nikolai Alexandrovich, 83–84
Don Giovanni, 45, 119
Dontsova, 133
Dostoevsky, Fyodor Mikhailovich, 14, 30, 33, 34, 35–62, 68, 75, 76, 78, 82, 99, 104, 105, 114, 116, 118, 122, 124, 126, 127, 131, 132, 138, 139, 144, 146, 149, 151, 157, 158, 159, 160, 162, 163, 166, 167–69, 170; as devil's advocate, 35–40
Double, The, 158
"Dream of a Ridiculous Man, The," 49
Dynamo Stadium, 143

Eichmann, Adolf, 4, 140
1812 Overture, 124
Either/Or, 122
Eliot, T. S., 71
Emancipation, paradox of, 64–65
Endgame, 84
"*Engagement*," 74
Engels, Friedrich, 169
Enlightenment, 70, 161
Epimenides the Cretan, 2
Eternal Return, 18
Être et le néant, L', 86, 114
Existentialism, 20, 22–24, 25, 35, 89, 99, 157, 159, 160–61, 163–64, 166–67; in Solzhenitsyn, 133–39

Father Sergius, 90, 121, 126
Fathers and Sons, 164
Faust, 81–82, 83

Faustus, Dr., 45
Fichte, Johann Gottlieb, 99
Fiodorovich, Ammos, 26
First Circle, The, 123, 130, 131, 137, 141, 145, 146, 151, 152
Flaubert, Gustave, 3, 4
Form of the Good, 136
Fourier, François M. C., 165
Frank, Joseph, 44
Franklin, Benjamin, 105
French Revolution, 33, 99, 158, 160
Freud, Sigmund, 19, 20, 87, 90, 92, 103, 159
From the Other Shore, 61
Fyodorovna, Praskovya, 110–11, 115

Gatsby, Jay, 93, 96
Gerasim, 116
Gide, André, 164
Ginzburg, Eugenia, 129
Goethe, Johann Wolfgang von, 20, 81
Gogol, Nikolai Vasilievich, 1, 5–29, 45, 48, 99, 104, 106, 132, 137, 139, 141, 144, 145, 146, 151, 154, 158, 159, 162, 166, 167, 168; *Lebenswelt* of, 7; sexlessness of, 162
Goncharov, Ivan Aleksandrovich, 63, 82, 84, 151, 159, 162–63, 166
Good, Form of the, 136
Gorky, Maxim, 103, 149
"Gospel of work," 74
Goya y Lucientes, Francisco José de, 33
Grand Inquisitor, 51–52, 160, 169
Grotesque, 142, 144, 145
Grotesqueries, 139–46
Growing Up Absurd, 17

Hadji Murad, 102, 152
Hamlet, 31, 34, 35, 96, 168
"Hamlet and Don Quixote," 35
Hecuba, 96
Hegel, Georg Wilhelm Friedrich, 3, 6–7, 13, 19, 58, 59, 99, 125, 161

Hegelian System, 3, 6–7
Heidegger, Martin, 28, 60, 73, 74, 75, 86, 87, 98, 100, 101, 102, 107, 109
Herzen, Alexander, 1, 53, 61, 160, 169
Hitler, Adolf, 1, 19, 29, 61, 97, 116, 128, 137, 140, 141, 164; Final Solution of, 1
Hobbes, Thomas, 65
Hölderlin, Johan C. F., 98, 101
Homais, Monsieur, 74
Hope Against Hope, 29
Hume, David, 4, 12, 49, 70, 79, 99

Iago, 93, 96, 98
Idiot, The, 162
Ilyich, Ivan, 15, 18, 107–10, 111, 112–17, 118, 135
Inauthentic, 86, 89; and the Existential Tradition, 98–101; and Tolstoy, 102–17
Inauthenticity, 86, 87–88, 92–127; deception and self-deception, 96–98, 124–25; deviousness, 95; duplicity, 95–96; instability, 93–94; pretense, 94–95
Indispensable Man, 92
Industrial Revolution, 67, 98
Inquisition (the), 50–52
Inspector General, The, 4, 10–11, 16, 17, 24, 25
Intellectual (the): as connoisseur, 45–49; as revolutionary, 52–62; as unbeliever, 49–52; as voyeur, 40–44
Intellectuals, 30–35, 39–62, 63–64
Involuntary Journey to Siberia, 85
Iskra, 168
Ivanovich, Ivan, 27–28
Ivanovich, Peter, 109–11, 113

James, Henry, 162
James, William, 24, 31, 33, 65, 91, 161, 162
Job, 41, 50, 52
Johnson, Dr. Samuel, 71

K., Joseph, 137
Kafka, Franz, 17, 137, 162
Kant, Immanuel, 5, 21, 48, 88, 98, 117, 130, 136, 160
Karamazov, Alexei (Alyosha), 40, 49, 50, 51, 52
Karamazov, Dimitri, 52
Karamazov, Ivan, 39, 49–52, 61, 163, 166
Karataev, Platon, 131, 155
Karenin, 90–91, 121
Karenina, Anna, 90, 93, 96, 120, 121
Kehre, 102
K.G.B., 147
Khlestakov, 10–11, 12, 16, 17, 24
Kierkegaard, Sören Aabye, 6, 7, 15, 22, 30, 31, 35, 36, 38, 39, 43, 45, 46, 48, 49, 51, 58, 63, 69, 71, 74, 79, 81, 82, 89, 93, 95, 98, 99, 100, 101, 102, 106, 122, 130, 134, 159, 161, 162, 163, 165
Kirilov, 39, 54, 59–61
Kirsanov, Arkady, 165
Kleinmalerei, school of, 5
Koestler, Arthur, 164
Kondrashev-Ivanov, 136
Kostoglotov, 132, 134, 136
Kostya, 134
Kovalev, Major, 5, 12
Kremlin, 152
"Kreutzer Sonata, The," 106, 117–18, 119, 120, 121

Landowska, Wanda, 106
Lawrence, D. H., 75
Lebenswelt, 67
"Legend of the Grand Inquisitor, The," 49, 50, 52
Leibnitz, Baron Gottfried Wilhelm von, 112
Lenin, Nikolai, 32–33, 140, 151, 159, 167, 168, 169
Letters and Papers from Prison, 114
Levin, Konstantin, 104, 154
Lewis, Professor C. I., 5
Libération, 143
Litvinov, 130

Liza, 43, 44
Locke, John, 95
Look Back in Anger, 74
Lord, Robert, 38
Love-Girl and the Innocent, The, 134, 145, 146, 151
"Lucerne," 103
Lysenko affair, 143

Machiavelli, Niccolò, 96, 160
Madame Bovary, 3, 74
Madman (the), 106
Malia, Martin, 48, 158
Mandelstam, Nadezhda, 29
Mandelstam, Osip, 29
Manilov, 27
Mann, Thomas, 128
Marx, Karl, 19, 31, 41, 53, 64, 85, 98, 135, 141, 148, 151, 159, 160, 164, 169
Marxism-Leninism, 140
Matryoshka, 76–77
Mauvaise foi, concept of, 86–87, 98, 110
Mavrino Institute, 136, 141–42
"Meaning of the Russian Revolution, The," 103
Mephistopheles, 83
Merleau-Ponty, 142
Mill, John Stuart, 44, 46, 122, 157
Modern Times, 71
Monas, Sidney, 14
Montaigne, Michel Eyquem de, 155
"Moral equivalent of war," 65
Mozart, Wolfgang Amadeus, 15
Myshkin, Prince, 8, 39
Myth of Sisyphus, 2, 74

Nabokov, Vladimir Vladimirovich, 20
Napoleon, 10, 13, 17, 18, 24, 126, 131, 136, 152
Natasha, 107
National Socialism, 164
Nechaev Affair, 151
Nekhlyudov, 103
Nero, 67

Nerzhin, 132, 136, 137, 148, 149, 156
New Testament, 169
Newman, John Henry Cardinal, 162
Nicholas I, 14, 29, 139, 152
Nicholas II, 151, 154
Niebuhr, Reinhold, 15
Nietzsche, Friedrich Wilhelm, 18, 21, 30, 31, 36, 38, 39, 59, 62, 65, 70, 88, 89, 98, 99–100, 102, 119, 123, 126, 138, 159, 161, 164, 165
Nihilism, 164–65
"Nihilism and *Notes from Underground,*" 44
1984, 66
"Nose, The," 12–13, 17
Notes from the House of the Dead, 49, 131, 146
Notes from Underground, 41, 114, 131
Noumenal, 21
Nozdrev, 24
Nozze di Figaro, Le, 15
Number One, 152

Oblomov, 159
Oblomov, 79–85, 154
Oblomovitis, 79–85
Occam's Razor, 112
October Revolution, 146, 159, 166
Odintseva, Madame, 166
Oedipus Rex, 40
Old Testament, 50
One Day in the Life of Ivan Denisovich, 131, 141, 142, 151
Onegin, Eugene, 74, 79, 84
Ortega y Gasset, José, 98
Orwell, George, 66
"Overcoat, The," 5, 11–12, 26, 48
Overman, myth of the, 39
Owen, David, 3

Panopticon, 165
Papageno, 45
Paradox of emancipation, 64–65
Parkinson's Law, 17
Parmenides, 98

Parsifal, 88
Pascal, Blaise, 3, 4, 36, 37, 38, 68, 70, 73, 82, 102, 106, 117, 144, 159, 161
Pechorin, Grigori Alexandrovich, 79, 84, 163
Pensées, 68
Peter Principle, 17
Peter the Great, 14
Petrashevsky circle, 37, 62
Petrovna, Varvara, 46
Phaedo, 115
Phenomenal, 21
Philo, 49
Philosophes, 14, 33, 34, 88, 89, 157
Pico della Mirandola, Giovanni, Count, 23
Pisarev, Dmitri Ivanovich, 165
Plato, 7, 40, 51, 95, 98, 101, 115, 116, 136
Plekhanov, Georgi Valentinovich, 144, 151, 163
Poems in Prose, 130
Politics, inconsequence of, 128, 129–30, 150–56
Poor Folk, 37
Pope, Alexander, 103
Poprischin, 28
Porter, Jimmy, 74
Poseidon, 101
Potemkin, Grigori Aleksandrovich, 131
Pozdnyshev, 117, 118–19, 120, 121–22, 123, 124–25
Pushkin, Aleksander Sergeevich, 167–68
Pythagoras, 95

Quixote, Don, 168

Ranke, Leopold von, 13
Raphael, 38
Raskolnikov, 8, 39, 52
Raw Youth, 82
Reason, 2, 3, 61, 70
Reductio ad absurdum, 4–5
Reign of Terror, 33

Reminiscences, 103
Repression, 87
Republic, The, 51
Resurrection, 102
Robbers, The, 48
Roosevelt, Eleanor, 131
Rostov, Pierre, 104, 120
Rostova, Natasha, 120
Rousseau, Jean Jacques, 21, 70, 83, 86, 89–90, 91, 92, 101, 110, 151, 159, 161
Rudin, Dmitri Nikolaevich, 79, 84
Rusanov, Pavel Nikolaevich, 134–35, 138
Russian literature: Golden Age of, 167; Silver Age of, 167

St. Petersburg University, 16
Samsa, Gregor, 75
Sartre, Jean-Paul, 22, 69, 74, 79, 86, 87, 98, 114, 135, 136, 161
Schelling, Friedrich W. J. von, 99
Schiller, Johann C. F. von, 45, 48, 49, 99
Schopenhauer, Arthur, 22, 59, 68, 103, 105, 122, 130, 151
Schubert, Franz Peter, 158
Scott, Sir Walter, 164
Season in Hell, 75
Seducer (the), 82
Sein und Zeit, 60, 75, 86, 107
Selected Passages from Correspondence with Friends, 21
Shakespeare, William, 47, 48, 93, 103, 122
Sharashka, 131–32, 136, 141, 142, 146, 147, 149
Shatov, 39, 54, 55, 58–59, 168
Shestov, Lev, 37, 38, 39, 40, 52
Shikin, Major, 149
Sickness unto Death, The, 43
Sisyphus, myth of, 2, 74
Smoke, 130
Snow, C. P., 91, 164
Sobakevich, 9

Socrates, 21, 30, 31, 32, 33, 40, 82, 101, 122, 132
Solzhenitsyn, Alexander, 14, 123, 128–56, 158, 159, 160, 163, 166; and existentialism, 130, 132–33, 133–39; *Gogolesque* conception of, 131
"Song of Igor's Campaign," 146
Sophocles, 31, 40
"Sorge," 74
Soviet Writers, Union of, 145
Spinoza, Baruch, 70
Spiridon, 131, 132, 152, 155–56
Sportsman's Sketches, 130
Stalin, Josef, 29, 57, 58, 61, 116, 128–29, 131, 132, 136, 137, 139, 140, 141, 142, 143, 144, 145, 147, 148, 149, 151, 152, 154, 155, 159, 167, 169
Stalin Prize, 131
Stavrogin, Professor Nicholas, 39, 45, 47, 52, 54–58, 59, 75, 76–79, 131, 154, 168, 169, 170
Stendhal, 132
Stolz, Andrei, 83
Stranger (the), 74
Subject to Fits, 162
Superfluous Men, 79, 80, 81, 83, 84, 92
Suvorin, Alexander, 40
Swift, Jonathan, 71
Symposium, 117

Tchaikovsky, Peter Ilich, 124
Thales, 101
Tikhon, 76, 77–78
Tillich, Paul, 4, 8
Tolstoy, Alexey, 131, 134
Tolstoy, Count Lev Nikolayevich, 15, 17, 18, 36, 38, 39, 64, 86, 89, 90–92, 93, 99, 102–27, 131, 132, 134, 135, 136, 137–38, 143, 144, 149, 150, 151, 152, 158, 159, 160, 163, 166; and sexuality, 106, 117–27
Trial, The, 137
Trollope, Anthony, 164

Trotsky, Leon, 168, 169
Trukhachevsky, 120, 123
Turgenev, Ivan Sergeevich, 35, 44, 53, 104, 130, 131, 132, 151, 162, 164, 165, 166, 168
"Two Concepts of Liberty," 147

Uncaused Cause, 5
Underground Man, 37, 39, 40–44, 49, 52, 118, 127, 154, 158, 163, 170
"Uneasiness of civilization," 90
Union of Soviet Writers, 145
Urchristentum see Ur-Christianity
Ur-Christianity, 98
Use and Abuse of History, 102

Verkhovensky, Peter, 45, 47, 54, 55, 56–58, 59, 60, 75, 103, 168, 169, 170
Verkhovensky, Stepan, 45–48, 49
Virgin Soil, 130
Voltaire, 33, 50, 66, 88, 161
Vronsky, Alexei, 121

Wagner, Richard, 88
Waiting for Godot, 1, 63, 69
Walden Two, 66, 138
War and Peace, 17, 102, 126, 131, 135–36, 152
Weltschmerz, 73
Werther, 73
What Is Art?, 102, 106
What Is to Be Done?, 66
Wittgenstein, Ludwig, 67, 70, 86
Women's Liberation, 119
Wordsworth, William, 102
World War I, 65, 116
World War II, 97, 129, 141, 146, 154, 155
Wozzeck, 158

Yasnaya Polyana, 102, 103, 106
Yeats, William Butler, 128
Yesenin, Sergei, 149, 156
Youth, 90

Zakhar, 79, 83
Zarathustra, 39, 100
Zeitgeist, 33, 58, 162
Zosima, Father, 40, 49

DATE DUE

DEMCO 38-297